# Celebrating Women

**Pitt Series in Russian and East European Studies**

Jonathan Harris, Editor

Choi Chatterjee

# Celebrating WOMEN

Gender, Festival Culture, and Bolshevik Ideology, 1910–1939

University of Pittsburgh Press

Published by the University of Pittsburgh Press, Pittsburgh, Pa., 15260

Copyright © 2002, University of Pittsburgh Press

All rights reserved

Manufactured in the United States of America

Printed on acid-free paper

10  9  8  7  6  5  4  3  2  1

LIBRARY OF CONGRESS CATALOGING-IN-PUBLICATION DATA

Chatterjee, Choi.
  Celebrating women : gender, festival culture, and Bolshevik ideology, 1910–1939 / Choi Chatterjee.
    p. cm. – (Pitt series in Russian and East European studies)
  "A version of chapter 6 was previously published in 'Soviet Heroines and Public Identity, 1930–1939,' The Carl Beck Papers in Russian and East European Studies no. 1402 (Pittsburgh, October 1999)."
  Includes bibliographical references and index.
  ISBN 10: 0-8229-6110-5 (cloth : alk. paper)
  ISBN 13: 978-0-8229-6110-9 (cloth : alk. paper)
  1. Women–Soviet Union–Social conditions. 2. Women and communism–Soviet Union–History. 3. International Women's Day–Soviet Union. 4. Women–Soviet Union–History. I. Title. II. Series in Russian and East European studies.
HQ1662 .C465 2002
305.42'0947–dc21

2001006538

To Didibhai, who urged me to abandon the godless communists and study British history.

# Contents

Acknowledgments ix

Introduction: Holidays and History 1

1. International Women's Day: Rituals of Revolution 10

2. The Two Stories of the February Revolution 37

3. Why Do We Need a Women's Holiday? The Contest for Definition 59

4. Popular Theater and Women Onstage 83

5. The Language of Liberation 105

6. The Public Identity of Soviet Women 135

Epilogue 159

Notes 163
Selected Bibliography 203
Index 215

# Acknowledgments

I discovered the joy of Russian studies in Hari Vasudevan's challenging seminars at Calcutta University, and I thank him for his intellectual support. I would like to thank Alex and Janet Rabinowitch at Indiana University, Bloomington, for their generosity and friendship over the years. For better or for worse, Alex is directly responsible for bringing me to this country and promoting my academic career. As a foreign student, since I was ineligible for both the IREX and ACTR grants, Alex made it possible for me to spend a year in Moscow by creating an exchange fellowship with the Russian Humanitarian State University, Moscow. David Ransel was a great source of encouragement in the early days when I questioned the value of cultural history. He also convinced me that rather than survey Soviet festivity in its entirety, the history of International Women's Day was a worthwhile project. I am also indebted to Ben Eklof, Hiroaki Kuromiya, Phyllis Martin, James Riley, Jeff Wasserstrom, and William Cohen for their advice and encouragement. Stanley Burstein at California State University, Los Angeles, has been a model mentor and I have learned from him that it is possible to combine scholarship with a heavy teaching load, and preserve your sense of humor at the same time. Phillip Goff, Ping Yao, Kate McGinn, Lynn Hudson, and Jane Rose have contributed in more ways than they know to the completion of the manuscript. I also want to thank my students and colleagues at the History Department for creating a congenial and stimulating atmosphere.

Over the years several colleagues have read parts of the manuscript and I am very grateful to them for their advice and suggestions. I especially want to thank David Spaeder, Mary Cunningham, Karen Petrone, Barbara Walker, and James von Geldern, for their insightful comments and friendship. I am also indebted to Richard Stites, Sheila Fitzpatrick, Lynn Mally, Eve Levin, Elise Kimmerling Wirtschafter, Laura Phillips, Shoshanna Keller, Robin Bisha, Roshanna Sylvester, and Douglas Northrop for reading parts of the manuscript and giving me excellent criticism. Mary Zirin has been especially generous with her time and advice, and her passionate commitment to Russian literature has been a great source of inspiration. I also want to thank Viktoria Ivanova for adopting me into her family and making my visits to Russia that much more memorable. Sergei Kerpenko, Zoia Khotkina, Irina Tverdokhleba, Irina Tarakanova, and various archivists in Moscow helped me locate materials and answered my numerous questions about Soviet history with intelligence and patience.

I am grateful to the History Department, the Russian and East European Institute, and the Center for Global Change and World Peace at Indiana University, Bloomington, for funding help in the initial stages of this work. Assistance from the Kennan Institute helped me complete the first round of revisions. The California State University, Los Angeles, provided funds, research grants, and release time that enabled me to travel to Russia to finish my archival research and writing. Jonathan Harris and Niels Aaboe of the University of Pittsburgh Press not only believed in the project, but also guided me through the final phase of preparing the manuscript for publication. The comments of the anonymous reviews greatly enriched my work, and I am grateful to Kathy Meyer for her excellent editing.

I also want to take this opportunity to thank a few members of my family, especially my parents, Nonda and Deb Kumar, and my aunt, Manjari, for the unquestioning love and support that they have extended over the years. They instilled in me the belief that intellectual pursuit is the highest calling, and that ideas do have the power to change people's lives. My husband Omer's scientific positivism cut through my cloudy political beliefs and forced me to examine Soviet propaganda for what it was rather than what it should be. I have enjoyed our stimulating conversations and arguments about Marxism, feminism, evolution, and the philosophy of history. If there is any originality to this manuscript, he deserves much of the credit for it. Finally I want to thank Shaheen and Damini for their continual impatience with "Mama's work." But for their harassment this work would never have been completed.

# Celebrating Women

# Introduction

## Holidays and History

In spring 1992 I was invited to attend a private celebration of International Women's Day in Moscow. The winter had been a particularly onerous one even by Russian standards and I marveled that my hosts, given their antipathy to the vanishing Soviet Union, intoned the greetings of Women's Day and handed me the obligatory bouquet of mimosa. The intended irony was not lost on me. As a historian I had had long disputations with Russians both about Soviet history and my political beliefs. And as a self-proclaimed *feministka*, it was no doubt fitting that I sat at a table demurely consuming a meal prepared by women while the men raised their glasses in archaic toasts to "extraordinary women, beautiful women, and how impossible it is to live with them!"

I was attracted to this project primarily because of the incongruous pairing of women and celebrations in Soviet discourse. Why did the Soviets celebrate women? Why were women held up, if only temporarily, as examples, honored in verse and song on that one day? Which women were deemed worthy of celebration and which ones were damned by the silences that interspersed the praise? Finally, how had International Women's Day changed over time from the initial celebration in the prerevolutionary past to the onset of the Second World War?

In this book I address three major issues: the development of Soviet holiday rituals, the strategies of narration and emplotment used in Soviet propaganda for women, and the evolution of the problematic morphology of the New Soviet Woman. On a more specific level, in an attempt to integrate the above themes, I trace the development of International Women's Day in Russia and the Soviet Union from 1910 to 1939. Analyzing the multiple discourses inherent in the rituals, images, and stories produced during this holiday, I outline the changing content of Bolshevik ideology as it pertains to the construction of the public identity of Soviet women and their history.

In prerevolutionary Russia, the term *woman* carried a heavy burden of meaning, derived from the various misogynist pronouncements of the Orthodox Church and peasant folk belief. In the nineteenth century, the notion of woman as seductress and harbinger of doom was overladen with romantic ideas of woman as the incarnation of virtues, the poetic muse, and the wronged victim. Eager reformers marked women as sites for inscription of modernity, as modern mothers, companionate wives, and independent wage earners. Women, through their own activities, whether as *dames de salon*, feminists, or terrorists, contributed prodigiously to the complicated gender mythology. Finally, male intellectuals and professionals compared the weakness of the nascent Russian civil society and their emasculation under autocracy to the subordination of women under patriarchy. By the early twentieth century, the category "woman" had become an overdetermined concept, freighted with contradictory ascriptions from both high and low culture.[1]

Social Democratic writings on the "woman question" were similarly complex and contained a curious compound of radical individualism and communitarian utopianism. True to the pronouncements of scientific and utopian socialism, they believed that women were doubly oppressed under capitalism, first as purveyors of sex and labor in the capitalist market and the family, and second as victims of bourgeois morality and legal structures that perpetuated their subordination to men and limited their right to engage freely in the public domain. Social Democrats unthinkingly reiterated the socialist-utopian belief that only the abolition of private property would lead to the true liberation of women.[2] Viewing women's association with domesticity as the key to the particularity of "women" as opposed to the universality of the category "man," they advocated that women be freed from household responsibilities. They hoped that the establishment of institutions such as child-care centers, dining halls, and laundries would enable women to participate in the state-sponsored production process. Finally, Social Democrats wanted to educate Russian women, reconstruct their daily lives along perceived modern/urban lines, and ensure their participation in the affairs of the community and the state.

Despite being heirs to one of most the ambitious programs for women's liberation in history, in reality Bolsheviks invested little time and effort in attracting women to their revolutionary circles.[3] The most important Bolshevik initiative in the prerevolutionary years was the International Women's Day celebrations of 1913 and 1914. In 1910 at the women's conference of the Second International held in Copenhagen, the delegates decided to annually commemorate International Women's Day to further the cause of women's emancipation. Although the holiday was celebrated in Germany and Sweden by Social Democrats thereafter, it was not until 1913 that the Bolsheviks decided to use Women's Day to popularize their political program among factory women in Russia. The holiday was celebrated sporadically in the next few years, but after the revolution in 1917, Women's Day joined May Day and the anniversary of the October Revolution as one of the more important events on the Soviet calendar.

In the modern era, beginning with the French Revolution, revolutionary festivals and holidays have played an important role in legitimizing new states that succeeded the *ancien regimes*.[4] Since participation in festive rituals creates a sense of belonging in the newly imagined community, revolutionaries used mass rituals to inculcate new values and beliefs among the populace.[5] Although women's needs occupied a subordinate position and were routinely ignored by the Communist Party, during the month of March, especially around Women's Day, issues relating to women took on a spurious urgency in the press, party circles, trade unions, women's departments in various ministries, workers clubs, and schools. As organizers assumed that women would be bored at purely political meetings, it was hoped that the ludic elements of the holiday, theatrical shows, community dances, children's performances, and free meals would attract women to public festivities where they would be exposed to party ideas and programs.

But Soviet ritual was more than just an effective tool for cultural management. Holidays served to temporarily empower the participants by drawing them into the network of Soviet existence. On Women's Day, women sang revolutionary songs, acted in plays, wrote articles for wall newspapers, and retold their lives at public venues. At mass meetings and demonstrations the achievements of exemplary women were held up to public acclaim. Newspapers and journals carried lengthy articles about the status of women in the Soviet Union and abroad. Both the rituals and ideological content of Women's Day changed over time but the celebration itself and the rhetoric associated with it served as the chief locus for the articulation of state discourses for and about women. As a result, each year International Women's Day generated a considerable body of propaganda in the shape of speeches, policy pronouncements, reports, and various genres of fiction such as plays, poems, cartoons, short stories, and biographical sketches of notable women. While the Marxist program for women's liberation marked the outer parameters of this field of propaganda, the policies of the regime violated the ideological integrity of these principles. At the same time, the proliferation of celebration discourses multiplied the points and means of dissemination, further stretching the boundaries of orthodox Marxism. Often during International Women's Day the party and the Zhenotdel (Women's Section of the Communist Party) published slogans that were directly inimical to each other. What remained constant in the propaganda, however, were the motifs of change, transformation, and the female ability to survive, improvise, and prevail above all odds.

Public literature converted Soviet women from object to subject, stripped them of an ahistorical passivity, and endowed them with a formidable capacity for action. Women's lives were narrated synchronically and encoded the transformation of both domestic and public space. While the development of the female character through revolutionary time and space constituted the main organizing principle, men were often represented as a hindrance that disrupted the social intercourse of the state and politically conscious women. Women's stories from the 1920s and 1930s were replete with the symbolic erasure of men and the arbitrary silencing of their voices. While Soviet heroines grew stronger, husbands and fathers displayed a distressing capacity for moral and ideological degeneration. The symbolic demise of the consanguinal male was often paralleled by the growing veneration of male political leaders.

Celebration propaganda inserted women at the critical junctures of the Soviet past such as the February Revolution and the first Five-Year Plan, even though their contributions were often represented ambiguously. In Soviet propaganda women could no longer exist at the forgotten margins of history, as various literary devices forced them to confront the challenge of new opportunities. Simultaneously, narratives about women domesticated the grand drama of violent change and rapid transformation that lay at the center of Soviet history. In public discourse as the New Soviet Woman improvised and even triumphed through the dislocations of war, civil war, and collectivization, cataclysmic state policies were rendered mundane and endurable. At the same time the existence of these extraordinary heroines in these tumultuous times validated the Soviet system in comparison to the staid bourgeois order. Finally, in various forms of propaganda the Russian woman was transformed from a feudal symbol of Russia's backwardness and oppression into a cultural marker that broadcast the progressiveness and modernity of the Soviet Union to the world.

But the celebratory discourse did not preclude a persistent harping on the negative qualities of Russian women. There was a widespread consensus in Bolshevik circles that women were the most backward section of the proletariat and therefore innately counter-revolutionary.[6] The subtext of Russian female backwardness was omnipresent in Women's Day propaganda but it would be facile to dismiss it as a mere reflection of Bolshevik misogyny. Rather, it served as a counterpoint to illustrate the achievements of Soviet women. In fact, the epithet of backwardness was essential if only to prove the magnitude of the Soviet achievement and the progressive nature of the October Revolution. Just as tsarist feudalism served as a convenient counterfoil to Soviet narratives of modernization, the backwardness of Russian women valorized the Soviet women and served as a temporal reminder of the impressive speed with which the Soviet Union had been able to achieve its goals.

The yearly production of material for Women's Day, intended primarily for female consumption, constituted a distinctively Soviet practice that was innovative in the context of early twentieth-century politics. Thus, rather than counterpose the "real" to the "ideological" or try to situate Bolshevik ideology in the quotidian, I view these holiday discourses as an integral aspect of Soviet politics that deserves investigation as a historical phenomenon. Women's Day celebrations were not merely symbolic—camouflage for the exercise of power—but were a strategic form of cultural practice that marked the distinctiveness of Soviet civilization, legitimized the Soviet mission for women, and articulated the Soviet construction of gender.[7]

In a recent monograph, Nancy Ries has claimed that while some cultures locate value in distinctive consumerism, or ritual participation, Russians privilege language above all other things and see it as one of their most valuable resources.[8] Western historians have blamed the Soviets for failing to solve the "woman question" and criticized the misogyny and patriarchal attitudes that lay beneath the revolutionary rhetoric about gender equality.[9] But the precise noncorrespondence of ideology and reality constituted an important element of the Soviet experience. Propaganda for women was characterized by a literary style that was marked by excess, distortion, and outright falsification. Our liberal orientation may lead us to denounce a style of political narration that lacks material accountability, but one should not discount the importance of changes at the ideological and linguistic level. The capacity to articulate scenarios of radical change in women's lives was not merely a substitute for concrete action, but was in itself a form of political practice. Soviet women, unlike the vast majority of their counterparts in the Third World, were given the opportunity to imagine alternative lives and rethink their relationships to family, community, and state. Not all the new visions were progressive or even desirable, but Soviet women were forced to confront change at an unprecedented rate and negotiate public identities accordingly.

The word *public* constitutes the keynote of this book, and there is little here that deals with the popular, the private, and the authentic. I am primarily interested in the published languages that the state used in its correspondence with the imaginary Soviet woman and the way she was constructed and reconstructed by competing public discourses. While Marxist theorists predicted that the liberal distinction between the public realm and private would collapse with the advent of socialism, a new public sphere emerged in the Soviet Union[10] that was markedly distinct from the public realm of liberal imagination. This new public sphere was the creation of the state rather than an arena for critical-rational discourse of an informed citizenry.[11]

The price of admission to this space was the exposure to a body of hyperbolic and extravagant ideas known as propaganda that was loosely based on certain themes of Marxist ideology. Although propaganda presented itself as a series of rational constructs, it relied heavily on symbolic forms of expression such as narratives, rituals, and images. Participation in Soviet holidays, demonstrations, and public parades; reading newspapers and journals, watching plays and sport displays, listening to the radio, all entailed an engagement in the public sphere for both the representatives of the state and the citizens. In the interplay of languages and discursive practices, new identities were created. Some historians have argued that people resisted the totalitarian dictates of Stalinism; others have claimed that private individuals either learned to "speak Bolshevik" or used elements from the vocabulary of official pronouncements to fashion their identity.[12] While the question of how people perceived and reacted to the discourses of the state is a very important one, it presupposes that we know what the state was actually saying. This, I believe, is far from the case, and I will read the artifacts of Soviet propaganda to understand the various messages being communicated to women and to analyze how the narrative strategies and literary forms of propaganda influenced the content.[13]

Chapter 1 begins with an analysis of selected themes from Marxist writings on the "woman question" which formed the staple of Bolshevik propaganda from prerevolutionary days to the 1930s. The public identity of Soviet women was constructed around certain key issues such as citizenship, the welfare state, women's labor and reproductive obligations, and the relationship between the sexes. I explore the concept of Women's Day and the reasons for its centrality to Soviet women's history.

The second chapter treats Women's Day in 1917 when women in Petrograd chose to protest against widespread food shortages. Although women played a key role in the February Revolution and helped to define the agenda and the strategies of revolt, their militant participation has been minimized in Soviet accounts. At the same time, by dating the February Revolution from International Women's Day, the Bolsheviks claimed authorship of an event in which they played a very limited role. Analyzing the ambiguous representation of women's actions during that critical period, I present a re-reading of the February Revolution.

During the 1920s, the subject of chapter three, the effects of the civil war forced the Bolshevik Party to institute a policy of half-hearted cooperation with market forces. Similarly, propaganda for women was redesigned to fit the new circumstances. In the early years of NEP, the Zhenotdel engaged in a prolonged battle with the party to define the agenda for a woman's movement. Women's Day propaganda often reflected the disagreements between the party discourse and the Zhenotdel pronouncements. During this period certain Bolsheviks questioned the very existence of International Women's Day. In this chapter, I look at the various sources of popular opposition to and popular support for Women's Day.

Massive female unemployment during the 1920s created what often seemed an unbridgeable distance between the state agencies and women. Often, Women's Day celebrations functioned as the sole points of contact between them. Given this context, the Zhenotdel and the Agitprop section of the Party disseminated propaganda on women's issues on a wide scale. My analysis of the propaganda literature of this period focuses on two outstanding themes—namely, the juxtaposition of the Lenin cult and the "woman question," and the construction of the international significance of Women's Day.

Chapter 4 analyzes the texts of Women's Day theater from the 1920s to look at the new popular discourse created around the key concepts of masculinity/femininity, state/community, centralization/voluntarism, and revolution/power. In this chapter I also examine the various personae that the New Soviet Woman assumed in theatrical propaganda as Bolsheviks made an effort to ground their ideas in the popular idiom.

Chapter 5 takes up the first Five-Year Plan beginning in 1928, which once again necessitated a reworking of the concept of women's emancipation. During this period, as an offshoot of the cultural revolution, the Zhenotdel used International Women's Day to launch a campaign called the *kul'turno-bytovoi pokhod* (campaign for the reconstruction of daily life) in 1929. This was superseded by the new "Campaign to Introduce Women into Production" in 1930. In this chapter I examine the different gender representations used in the two campaigns and argue that the Five-Year

Plan marked the beginning of the use of a particularly Stalinist discourse for women.

The 1930s, the subject of chapter 6, witnessed the unprecedented elevation and celebration of selected Soviet heroines in the public sphere. The state needed examples of heroic and modern Soviet women for propaganda purposes, and the discourse on Soviet heroines was manipulated to justify Stalinist policies of industrialization and collectivization. Between 1934 and 1939, Women's Day, a hitherto insignificant holiday, was transformed into a national holiday. At state-sponsored receptions throughout the country, eminent women from various professions were publicly commended by party officials for their services to the state and were asked to recount their life histories. These accounts reveal a depth of information on the construction of a modern female identity in the 1930s. Using these transcripts in conjunction with "official" biographies of women, I analyze the creation of a female public identity in the 1930s in relation to concepts of family, community, state, and patriarchy, and show how the revolutionary chronology was reordered in public memory.

**o n e**

# International Women's Day

## Rituals of Revolution

> Comrades, our holiday has arrived
> Women workers, our sisters dear!
> Our holiday that binds with a firm thread
> Our dreams, our sacred tears.
>
> Forward, forward! —The mighty call thunders
> Growing from the golden distance afar
> In the crowded ranks, ever louder resounds,
> Our tumultuous song of labor.
>
> Today our holiday of labor, today our holiday of need,
> Step forward. Widen the path!
> Together with our husbands, brothers, sisters and fathers,
> All those who thirst and long for freedom.
>
> Sisters, mothers, wives, slaves of labor,
> Of hapless, anguished lives!
> Forward boldly with us. A bright future
> We'll forge amidst our bleak lot.
> —S. Dal'niaia, "Nash prazdnik," in *Rabotnitsa*,
> no. 1–2 (February 23, 1914): 3.

### Bolsheviks and the Woman Question

The Bolshevik political project was perhaps the single most ambitious one in the twentieth century and in this was burdened by the memory of the French Revolution. In ambition and scope the Bolshevik revolution resembled the French prototype, but an important distinction lay in the attention that Bolsheviks paid to the gender hierarchy. When the French revolutionaries established the political rights and privileges of the universal citizen, the citizen was male. The creation of the female political subject was not sought and the exclusion of women from the public sphere was both an overt objective and a concomitant realization.[1] The Bolsheviks, however, based their vision of the postrevolutionary state on the inclusion of minority groups, particularly women, excluded from the liberal order.

Although the Bolshevik ideology for women aspired to create a set of enduring myths about the New Soviet Woman, the exigencies of the revolutionary situation destabilized gendered identities. As a result, the public selfhood of Soviet women was constantly mediated by competing definitions of class, occupation, sex, family, community, citizenship, party, and state. Female identity in the Soviet Union was constructed as a continuum, composed of various building blocks or ideograms, which were deeply symbolic and functioned as convenient shorthand to more complex philosophical assumptions.[2] Ideograms were rearranged to suit the demands of the current political situation or could be reinforced by importing new ones. At the linguistic level, ideological innovations could be rendered mundane while continuity could be represented as revolutionary. Therefore, the very elasticity of gender ideology could accommodate both continuity and change.

Although Bolshevik thinking about the "woman question" was grounded in classical Marxism, public propaganda used this philosophical bedrock selectively and creatively. Friedrich Engels, in *Origin of the Family, Private Property and the State*, perhaps the most influential Marxist text on women's issues, asserted that in any society the status of women was determined primarily by the prevailing mode of production and its attendant property relations. Borrowing heavily from the works of anthropologists, Engels argued that the origin of patriarchy was rooted in the creation of private property. To ensure the transmission of property to their own kin, men had to establish the paternity of children by enforcing monogamy on women. Despite the dubious merits of this argument, by historicizing the family Engels brought into question the validity of the "innate" and "natural" functions of women that patriarchal discourse ascribed to them.[3]

Marxism also implicated capitalism and patriarchy in the oppression of women; thus, according to its tenets, the "woman question" could only exist in a capitalist society. If capitalism, by the laws of historical materialism, was doomed to extinction, so too was its cultural superstructure, which perpetuated the subordination of women.[4] In postcapitalist society, women would be important primarily as units of labor. The Bolsheviks had few reservations about using women in factory production, and they took very literally the second part of the Marxist dicta about the contribution of each according to his or her abilities. The 1918 constitution mandated labor as the primary duty of all citizen. And as Stalin said very succinctly, "it is not property status, not national origin, not sex, nor office, but personal ability and personal labor that determines the position of every citizen in society."[5]

Regarding reproduction and domestic labor, the question arose whether the act of biological reproduction was socially useful labor. Aleksandra Kollontai argued that reproduction ultimately guaranteed the existence of the labor republic, so the state should facilitate motherhood by providing ideal conditions for it. This argument received great prominence in the 1930s when biological reproduction was valorized as socially useful and necessary. On the issue of domestic labor, Marxists were unanimous in their condemnation of women's exclusive engagement in household tasks. August Bebel painted a romantic picture of a postsocialist society in which human beings engaged in productive work without compulsion or fear, untrammeled by social prejudices and bans. He argued that with the dawn of socialism, the bourgeois nuclear family would be redefined. Domestic duties that tied women ineluctably to hearth and home would be socialized. Communal organizations would take on the tasks of cooking, cleaning, and washing; crèches, kindergartens, and schools would care for children in a scientific and hygienic manner, providing both physical and intellectual nourishment.[6]

This was the essential contradiction of Marxism: On the one hand it envisaged the disappearance of the bourgeois state; on the other, it foretold an enormous increase in the functions of the socialist state. Who would organize mechanized laundries, dining halls, and child-care facilities? Until the dawn of true communism, Bolsheviks believed that the state should protect the rights of women and children, ensure that women had access to education, relieve women from the onus of domesticity, and promote them to positions of power and authority. The modern vision of the welfare state, therefore, originated both from Marxist thinking and Soviet practice.[7]

Where did men fit into this scenario of the patriarchal state and women? If one reads the Marxist texts about conscious women one is struck by the progressive displacement of the male. Analyzing Engel's *Origin of the Family*, Alfred Meyer comments, "throughout the book, Engels conveys the impression that matriarchy was preferable to male domination and that it corresponded to a nobler and more humane way of life. Matriarchy reigned in a communistic, property-less community blessed with equality, sexual freedom, general self-respect, and respect for others." While Bolsheviks never endorsed matriarchy as a political principle, in propaganda and fiction men were often represented as disrupting the social intercourse of the state and politically conscious women. Kollontai's fiction is replete with the symbolic diminution of men. As her stories progress, her heroines grow stronger, while men seem doomed to betray their principles and ideological beliefs.[8]

While literary critics have focused their attention on Kollontai's heroines such as Vasilisa Malygina, her male characters serve an equally important function for the purposes of historical analysis.[9] In *Vasilisa Malygina*, Vladimir, the antihero, exemplifies in bold relief the moral hazards inherent in ideological compromise.[10] Although he starts as a revolutionary, Vladimir lacks the discipline to pursue his political goals with the courage and tenacity that Vasilisa exhibits. The period of the New Economic Policy (NEP) provides the ideal mise-en-scène for his weak character and lax adherence to the principles of Communism. As the director of a factory he revels in his mansion, servants, and bourgeois lifestyle, which includes a mistress. Vladimir inevitably betrays Vasilisa both physically and spiritually. As readers, we are aware from the beginning that Vasilisa's love for him is misplaced, and we wait impatiently for her to regain her clarity of vision and psychological equilibrium. Eventually, ideological integrity triumphs over sentimental dependence on Vladimir; Vasilisa's recovery of self is far more important than the trite ending, where she decides to return to the textile factory and raise her child in a commune. Kollontai appears less interested in providing a solution to the pitfalls of heterosexual relationships than in showing us that women can be self-reliant and find meaning in their creative activities.

Kollontai's *Autobiography of a Sexually Emancipated Communist Woman* shows the struggle in her personal life to harmonize her unstinting attachment to work (labor?) and a desire for emotional fulfillment. Like her heroines, Kollontai claimed that sentimental love is "an expenditure of precious time and energy, fruitless, and in the final analysis, utterly worthless." On a less radical note, Nadezhda Krupskaia, who made the obligatory references to the identical aims of proletarian men and women, observed that as soon as women gained monetary independence they stopped being subservient to their husbands. The 1918 Code of Laws upheld the equality of legitimate and illegitimate children and assigned to the mother the right to identify the father in a conscious attempt to reduce the power of patriarchy. Even during the years of Stalinist conservatism it was common to find the symbolic dismemberment of male supremacy in stories about Stalinist heroines.[11]

But it is important to remember that Bolshevik ire was reserved for the local, the consanguinal male. The Bolsheviks made no attempt to dismantle patriarchy per se, but they tried to replace the authority of the local male, of fathers, brothers, and husbands, with that of the absent, omnipotent male of socialist patriarchy. This trend started with the veneration of the dead Lenin and other Communist leaders and found its apotheosis in the cult of Stalin. Often in Soviet fiction, the heroine was aided in her pursuit of modern goals such as completing her education or increasing her labor productivity by the inspiration provided by Lenin or Stalin. More immediately, a wise Communist mentor afforded guidance and wisdom to faltering heroines when they were held back by backward husbands and fathers.

Other essential criteria that made up the female self in Bolshevik representations were the motif of backwardness and the situational identity of women. Social Democratic canonical writings on women contain several imaginative denunciations of unreconstructed Russian women and, by extension, their femininity. Krupskaia, following in Engels's footsteps, castigates working women as unfit and positively dangerous mothers. Clara Zetkin, in her notoriously forthright manner, declares, "We must not conduct special women's propaganda, but socialist agitation among women. The petty, momentary interests of the female world must not be allowed to take up the stage." Kollontai's comment that "at a time of unrest and strike action . . . the self-centered, narrow minded and politically backward 'female' becomes an equal, a fighter and a comrade," is a pithy version of Russian socialists' attitudes toward the apolitical Russian woman.[12]

Backwardness, conservatism, and disinclination to action were not considered innately feminine characteristics but byproducts of a woman's tragic past. For a party that claimed to be the vanguard of the future, the Bolsheviks were obsessed with history, and women's history was invariably narrated in the tragic vein familiar to those steeped in the literary traditions of Pushkin, Turgenev, and Nekrasov. In the Bolshevik version, however, suffering was neither ennobling nor an inevitable mark of gender. Rather, suffering stemmed from a lack of understanding about the true reasons for their misfortune. As a result women privileged family over class, the domestic space over the social realm, and passivity over revolution.

"Natasha's Dreams," a short story in *Rabotnitsa* commemorating International Women's Day in 1914 features a young, unemployed protagonist, Natasha, who has three dreams.[13] The first three segments of the story represent the loss of self, the failure of family, and the absence of community. Natasha's arbitrary dismissal from her place of work symbolizes the alienation of labor under capitalism and the disintegration of community. In her first dream she sees a vision of herself luxuriously attired and mistress to a rich man. But she rejects his advances because she finds the sale of sex even more distasteful than the sale of labor. In her second dream Natasha is a poor working woman whose son dies of neglect and lack of medical attention as her husband stands by helplessly. (The inability of the male to take decisive action is noticeable in both instances.) Finally, in the last dream, Natasha is confronted by the transformational powers of true community, of a harmonious working collective of male and female workers who are made strong and wise through political knowledge and class consciousness.

If women were to be partners in the revolution, they would have to shed the guise of Russian femininity and take on the personae of Bolshevik women, which included *tverdost'* (steadfastness), dedication to revolution, and an immense capacity for personal heroism and self-sacrifice.[14] But Bolshevik ideology, unlike liberalism, never used arguments from nature to reify women's biological incapacity to act as competent citizens in the public sphere. Instead the core tenet of Bolshevism rested on the assumption that the cultural reconstruction of women was possible as long as women made the choice to internalize the prescriptive mores and values inherent in Bolshevik propaganda. Bolshevism, therefore, was both a call to arms and a prescription for self-regeneration.[15]

Thus, the notion of the female comrade as articulated in Bolshevik propaganda was not the unencumbered self of liberal theory or the bearer of inviolable and individual rights, but the situated self or the communitarian self, whose identity was located at the intersection of the obligations to the commonweal and the party. A woman's identity was imagined in terms of her relationship to the family, children, community, and the state, and not necessarily in that order. Even Kollontai, who upheld her right to a private life over the interests of the party, nonetheless advocated motherhood as a social obligation.[16] We see other Social Democratic women exhibiting similar opinions and, according to Karen Honeycut, "in Zetkin's view the totality had priority over the particular, 'the interests of the species' over that of the female sex, and the welfare of humanity over the rights of the individual."[17]

The Bolsheviks also used the status of women under Soviet rule as a way to prove their modernity and their vanguard position among European nations.[18] Lenin claimed that the Soviets had achieved more freedom for women in the few years of its existence than the collective legislation of bourgeois democracies. In 1919, he said, "The position of women furnishes a particularly graphic elucidation of the difference between bourgeois and socialist democracy . . . in no bourgeois republic . . . nowhere in the world, not even in the most advanced country, have women gained a position of complete equality."[19] The veracity of this statement was far less important than the emergence of a particular style of discourse in which women functioned as a marker or an index of progressiveness.

Finally, the central organizing principle that gave Soviet writings on women an unmistakable character was the notion of transformation, the telescoped progression of cataclysmic events, and the rapid acceleration of the historical process. Revolution implied that the quotidian would be drastically changed beyond recognition, and Bolshevik propaganda from its very inception refused to offer the benign liberal anodyne of improving the present. Women instead were socialized through Bolshevik discourse to accept swift change as necessary, desirable, and inevitable. History for better or for worse was to be writ large on women's bodies and domesticated by the narration of women's lives through the sequence of revolutionary events.

**From Word to Deed**

While in the realm of Marxist theory women's liberation was dependent on changes in the material context, Social Democrats advocated few practical solutions to achieve this goal. Similarly, in Soviet propaganda the hyperbolic and emancipatory potential of the Marxist discourse occluded the adoption of concrete steps toward its realization. This was not a Soviet invention but had historical precedence in the prerevolutionary years. Thus when the Bolsheviks decided to work among the proletarian women in St. Petersburg, they chose to use International Women's Day to gain entry into their ranks rather than pursue more traditional means of politicization. Similarly, in most Soviet historical accounts, as well as in propagandistic pieces on the Bolshevik women's movement, it became customary to include a description of the International Women's Day celebrations of 1913 and 1914 as the most important political initiatives of the prerevolutionary years. The selection of this particular artifice, both organizational and literary, is more than coincidental. The vocabulary of festive ritual allowed for the succinct juxtaposition of two central themes: the uniquely Bolshevik program for women's liberation and the narratives of female suffering and backwardness. Since it was important for the Bolsheviks to prove that all innovations in Russian politics prior to the revolution were of their making, the sponsorship of Women's Day gave the Bolsheviks a claim of being deeply implicated in the Russian women's movement.

Despite attempts to construct a respectable genealogy for Bolshevik association with the working women of Russia, the party record was a dismal one. While women workers participated in labor strikes, the revolutionary events of 1905, and campaigns for insurance in 1912, party influence on these activities, despite widespread assertions to the contrary, was barely discernible. A few Bolshevik women such as Inessa Armand and Konkordiia Samoilova tried to recruit women workers through the unions and clubs after 1905 when these institutions became legal. Aleksandra Kollontai, technically belonging to the Menshevik wing of the Russian Social Democratic Labor Party, was an ardent advocate of Marxist feminism and an energetic activist for women's causes, but after her disruptive participation in the historic first All-Russian Women's Congress of 1908 she fled the country to escape arrest. Inessa Armand later wrote that it was only in 1913–14 that the working woman began to participate in an organized manner in the socialist struggle and that the International Women's Day celebrations of 1913 marked the first occasion of conscious political activity by proletarian women in Russia. Kollontai emphasized the innate propaganda value of what she called the political awakening of Russian women. According to her, the involvement of proletarian women in the celebrations of 1913 signaled to observers in Europe and America that if the "most backward section of the working class—working women" were raising their voices in protest, then the labor movement in Russia was indeed alive and well.[20] Women's Day etched a public persona, a voice, and a collective consciousness on the hitherto inchoate mass—proletarian women—and recorded their political entry into Bolshevik history. When the events of Women's Day in 1913 and 1914 were later enshrined in history as central episodes of a Bolshevik women's movement in prerevolutionary Russia, it was an occurrence of considerable political magnitude. Propagandists used the celebrations to create a particular narrative, one that emphasized the painful birth, slow maturation, and triumphal coming of age of Soviet women, exemplifying in dramatic detail the depth of Bolshevik commitment to women's liberation.[21]

**International Women's Day**

Clara Zetkin proposed the idea to dedicate a day entirely to women's issues. One of the first theorists and activists to blend socialism and feminism, Zetkin was an ardent supporter of the international suffrage movement. As an orthodox Social Democrat, she did not endorse the movement for suffrage unequivocally, but as a matter of strategy argued that the right to vote could only work to the advantage of proletarian women. At the International Socialist Congress held at Stuttgart in 1907, to strengthen organizational ties between socialist women in different countries, Zetkin roundly criticized Austrian socialists for suppressing the mention of suffrage in their agenda. As Zetkin said, proletarian women may have marched separately from bourgeois women, but they fought together for suffrage because it represented a step in the general democratization of society.[22] Zetkin's motion for universal suffrage was upheld by a vote of 47 to 11 at the meeting and was later reaffirmed at the women's conference of the Second International, held in Copenhagen in 1910.[23]

To ensure that the movement for female suffrage took concrete shape, Zetkin introduced a proposal at Copenhagen that called for the annual commemoration of a socialist women's day. Each year, March 8 was to be celebrated in all countries as International Women's Day and would be organized around the demand for suffrage.[24] The date was chosen in commemoration of demonstrations by women workers in the New York City needle trade on Sunday, March 8, 1908. Hundreds of women had gathered on Rutgers Square in Manhattan's Lower East Side to demand the vote and the unionization of the needle trade workers. The impressive show of female force on that day had caught the attention of European socialists, including Zetkin, who asked that the American women's demonstration be commemorated annually as an International Women's Day dedicated to further the cause of women's emancipation all over the world.[25] The majority of the delegates accepted her proposal, and in 1911 the first Women's Day was celebrated internationally.

Although Women's Day meetings had been organized in the preceding years in other European countries such as Germany and Sweden, the proposal for a Women's Day was ignored by the Russian Social Democratic Labor Party (RSDRP) until 1913. Kollontai had long pleaded with the Russian Social Democrats to organize women workers in urban Russia and had even suggested setting up a bureau for women as an adjunct party organization. Despite her antipathy to feminism and her ambivalence about the value of the suffrage movement, Kollontai believed that Women's Day would be an excellent medium through which to organize women workers and attract them to the Social Democratic ranks. However, her recommendations were ignored and ridiculed as feminist deviation.[26] In 1913, however, the Bolsheviks decided to celebrate International Women's Day in both St. Petersburg and Moscow.

The Bolsheviks' celebrations coincided with the three hundredth anniversary celebrations of the Romanov dynasty, ironic since the end of the dynasty is dated from Women's Day in 1917. There is little unanimity among historians as to why the Bolsheviks suddenly chose to celebrate the holiday in 1913. While some argue that the Bolsheviks were alerted to the revolutionary potential of women workers by their participation in strike movements, others feel that there was little qualitative difference in women's activities during this period.[27] Reading through Soviet sources, however, it is apparent that, far from being impressed by the revolutionary consciousness of the Russian women, Bolsheviks were roused to action by what they perceived as the extreme backwardness, ignorance, and complete disinclination for political action on the part of proletarian women. According to P. F. Kudelli, the Bolsheviks pushed for a Women's Day celebration in order to recruit women workers, who were backward and tended to participate in strikes in a desultory manner, and then only around narrow family concerns and economic interests.[28] The prominent tactical question was how to involve women in the general proletarian struggle on a sustained basis. As a first step, the Central Committee of the Bolshevik Party decided to organize International Women's Day in 1913 in the hope that the event would energize apathetic women workers in Russia. Thus, from its very inception in Russia, Women's Day, unlike celebrations in other European states, was used not to promote the cause of female suffrage but as a legitimate means of recruiting working women into the ranks of the Bolshevik Party.[29]

Apathy in certain cases could be interpreted as a profoundly counterrevolutionary activity, and Samoilova voiced a general Bolshevik conviction when she wrote that "the backwardness of women, their thoughtless examinations on questions of political life makes them a blind instrument in the hands of the enemies of the working class, who exploit their backwardness to conduct reactionary agitation against worker peasant power and against the party of the working class."[30]

While it was sufficient to awaken the sound proletarian instincts of male workers through exposure to socialist propaganda, women in the Bolshevik worldview were pictured as areas of darkness and therefore suitable sites for cultural inscription. Women workers, unlike male factory workers, were not even capable of developing "trade union consciousness."[31] The close association of women with the domestic sphere made them a suspicious ally, and the degree of attachment to the nuclear family became a litmus test for revolutionary aptitude or ineptitude.

### Women's Day in 1913: Political Alliances and Tensions

According to most Bolshevik sources, Kudelli and Samoilova were the moving spirits behind the event. In early 1913, the St. Petersburg committee of the RSDRP organized an International Women's Day holiday commission led by Samoilova and Kudelli, including two factory workers, Alekseeva and Nikiferova. Members of the holiday commission had long discussions and arguments on how best to organize Women's Day. Finally, they decided to start by publishing simple articles in *Pravda* about the significance of International Women's Day.[32] The newspaper published several articles in January 1913, explaining to their readers what Women's Day entailed and why the Bolsheviks had decided to celebrate it. To commemorate the event, the holiday committee decided to hold meetings with members of various trade unions in St. Petersburg, to arrange discussions on the status of the woman worker in industry, and to collect data on the condition of women in industry.[33]

Women's Day actually presented a moral dilemma to the Bolsheviks. As archenemies of the feminist movement, they were loath to engage in any activity that involved only women. Therefore they compromised by reiterating that Women's Day did not represent a feminist deviation by party members and that the sole reason for organizing Women's Day was to politicize the primitive consciousness of women workers. An article in *Pravda* declared, "Our women for the first time today will enter the general family of the proletarian movement, and for the first time, will feel the strong ties that bind her, not only to the women workers of different countries, but to the working class in general."[34]

The dialectic of inclusion, however, presupposed the "other," and in this case there was no absence of threats to the integrity of the proletarian community. To the extreme horror of the Bolsheviks, a few professional societies also decided to organize lectures on "women's issues" at the People's University in St. Petersburg to mark the holiday. No denunciatory resolutions were taken, but such a close association with bourgeois groups was felt to be extremely undesirable.[35] The tsarist government, as well, represented another menace to the existence of an exclusively socialist women's movement. In the interest of security, the holiday committee published a false date (February 10, 1913) to deceive the police, when all along they had planned to hold the meeting on February 17. The St. Petersburg chief of police granted them permission to hold a "Scientific Morning" to debate the *zhenskii vopros,* or woman question, at the Kalashnikov Bourse. To further the illusion, tickets were printed up for five kopeks (although the function was actually free). Kudelli writes that they invited the wife of a judge to perpetuate the fiction that Women's Day was actually a bourgeois and/or feminist affair.[36]

The evidence suggests that although there were deep differences of opinion between the feminists and the Bolsheviks, their strategies and efforts to raise recruits for their causes often overlapped and there was considerable dialogue, however acrimonious, between the groups. In this case, the feminists, far from being merely a smoke screen, joined in the preparations for Women's Day in both St. Petersburg and Moscow, and at the actual event spectators were exposed to both the feminist and Marxist explanations for the oppression of women.

The temporary alliance, though a tactical one, was anything but peaceful. Even before the time came to take stock and evaluate the results of the first Women's Day celebration, there was a full-scale war for the vote of the woman worker. In their arguments, both the feminists and the socialists represented themselves as the authentic voice of proletarian women. The feminists fired the first salvo. Maria Pokrovskaia, the editor of *Zhenskii vestnik,* wrote a scathing attack on the limited nature of the Bolshevik program for women's liberation and leveled some significant and telling criticisms.[37] She reminded the Bolsheviks that their interest in celebrating Women's Day had been stimulated by the popular meetings and lectures that the feminists had been organizing among working women.[38] Citing as proof a letter printed in *Pravda* by a woman worker, Pokrovskaia argued that economic oppression was not the only handicap under which the working woman labored; she was discriminated against both within the family and by society. Pokrovskaia went on to say that the influence and control of men was very apparent in the preparations for Women's Day, as little attention was being paid to the oppression of women within the family.[39]

Pokrovskaia's argument was unassailable on most points, and Samoilova in reply held the traditional Social Democratic line. She argued that while feminists wanted to use Women's Day to advance the fight for electoral rights, working women realized that the holiday had a deeper significance. They wanted to effect, in concert with male comrades, a wide-ranging transformation of the social, economic, and legal structures (the phrase was a euphemism for revolution). Samoilova also claimed that the Bolsheviks, not the feminists, were the initial sponsors of Women's Day.[40]

In their efforts to propagandize women workers, female Bolsheviks were walking a tightrope. On the one hand, there was a growing realization among Social Democrats, caused by the increasing participation of women in strikes, that as a tactical measure it would be prudent to organize woman workers.[41] But on the other hand, the innate misogyny within the party, which manifested itself in deep suspicion of everything perceived as feminist deviation, made the recruitment of women very difficult for the organizers. Female Bolsheviks were well aware of the patronizing and combative attitude of male workers to women workers. Samoilova had roundly criticized the actions of male workers who refused to support strike actions by female colleagues and the attitudes of reactionary husbands who refused to let wives join trade unions. But rather than attribute these actions to the unequal status of men and women in society, she sought to persuade the workers that it was in their interest to allow and encourage women to join the labor movement, just as it was in the interest of women to ignore feminist propaganda and join the proletariat cause.[42]

Two competing conceptions of politics were at work here. On the one hand, Bolsheviks employed strictly utilitarian arguments to convince women that proletarian revolution, and not feminism, was the only guaranteed path to liberation. On the other hand, there was an explicit denial of female agency in the political language intended for the consumption of women workers. This spirit of colonization was very apparent in the special commemorative issue of *Pravda* published on Women's Day, February 17, 1913. A lead article claimed that "Women's Day has set itself the goal to awake the working woman to social life and raise her to the standards of an all class movement and unite her together with the male worker." The metaphors are those of a sleeping beauty resuscitated with the socialist kiss of life and admitted to the bosom of her proletarian family. Kollontai, in her piece on Women's Day in the same issue, criticized the under-representation of women in workers' organizations. She wondered if this political apathy was due to women's oppression as sellers on the marketplace, or their duties as mothers, or simply a characteristic of their sex. Kollontai also mentioned the immense problems women's committees in socialist parties faced in trying to awaken the woman worker to consciousness and attract her to political organization.[43] The articles all agreed that without raising women's political awareness it would be impossible to attract them to sustained political work.

Thus, Women's Day, unlike Mother's Day, was not a celebration of women and female cultural norms, but was used in a purely instrumental capacity, as a social goad on the unformed conscience of the female proletariat. This tutelary attitude and conviction of moral superiority were increased when Bolsheviks actually met female members of the proletariat. Sometimes women workers were openly hostile to members of the party, but more often they were extremely disinclined to act in any "public" capacity.[44]

The holiday commission had decided to let a peasant woman and a working woman speak at the Women's Day meeting and describe their life experiences. But it was very difficult to get working-class female orators since they were afraid to speak in public and much tact and persuasion was required to overcome their "indecisiveness and fear." Finally, they found two "brave" souls, Shura Alekseeva, a textile worker, and Kartacheva, a clerk. The first was groomed to give a lecture on the life of a woman worker in a factory, and the second was persuaded to give a lecture on the life of peasant women. Alekseeva later recalled that she distributed tickets for the Women's Day meeting among women in factories.[45]

The celebration was held at the Great Hall of the Kalashnikov Exchange on Kharkhov Street. On the morning of February 17, 1913, the streets were lined with colorfully dressed working women with red flowers pinned to their blouses. Others sold bouquets of red carnations to raise money for prisoners and those going into exile. However innocuous the label "Scientific Morning" sounded, the city police were taking no chances, especially as it was a mere four days before the celebrations of the three-hundredth anniversary of the Romanov dynasty. Correspondence between the city police and the Okhrana, a police agency in charge of suppressing revolutionary activities, reveals that, despite Bolshevik attempts to deflect suspicion, the authorities were fully aware that the event was sponsored by the Social Democrats. They were apprehensive that the Social Democrats were going to celebrate Women's Day on a large scale, perhaps hold meetings and lectures and possibly even sponsor a street demonstration. Accordingly, police sergeants were instructed to keep a strict eye on the public on streets, boulevards, theaters, and other public areas in the cities. Even before the meeting started, charges were laid against the St. Petersburg committee in charge of the Menshevik publication *Luch* and its editor for bringing out a special number dedicated to the proletarian women of Russia.[46]

Both mounted police and policemen on foot manned the entrance to the Kalashnikov Hall. Inside the hall, policemen occupied the first two rows and loudly admonished speakers whose speeches drifted dangerously close to revolutionary rhetoric. At exactly one o'clock, the doors of the hall were closed and many people with tickets were turned away. Because of the large number of people milling around the entrance, the speakers had to squeeze into the premises with great difficulty.[47] Despite these restrictions, more than one thousand people managed to pack the hall to hear the speakers.

In her memoirs, Shura Alekseeva writes that she spent a long time preparing her speech on the conditions of women's labor in industry. She sought out Anna Ulianova (Lenin's sister) and Samoilova for help and rehearsed the summary of the paper over and over again:

> Never before had I spoken in front of such a large audience, and naturally, like any novice orator, was confused. The policemen in the front row were directly in front of me. They moved, scraped their chairs, talked and laughed,

and I suddenly realized that I could not remember a single word or idea from the précis. Looking at the notebook, the letters seemed to swim and I could not understand or remember a single thing. I stood there. And then literally, someone pushed me. I laid aside the notebook and began to speak of the life of the female textile worker.[48]

As a textile worker, Alekseeva had plenty of first-hand experience and spoke fluently and movingly of the terrible conditions of labor in the factories. Women workers from the audience murmured approvingly, moved about, and even rose from their seats agitatedly when Alekseeva described the lot of working women in spinning factories. Although the law mandated an eleven-hour working day, many women worked for eighteen hours for a payment of ten to twelve rubles a month. In the central industrial region, especially in the Tver province, women in textile factories made as little as two to four rubles a month. As a result, women had no time to spare for their own intellectual development or to attend to the needs of their family. Alekseeva continued: If women's strikes had been unsuccessful hitherto, it was due to their disorganization. She called for all women to join the proletarian family and march hand in hand for a brighter future.[49]

Alekseeva also spoke about prostitution and scolded the "bourgeois dames" who felt that working women were drawn to its ranks through foolishness. It was dire need that drove women to that shameful trade, not frivolity. She complained that within the factories foremen oppressed women and forced them to sleep with them.[50] She appealed to trade unions to guard women workers and defend them against administrators. Alekseeva saw little contradiction in the logic of women being raped sexually and economically by the male factory administrators and then turning to their male co-workers for protection. In spite of themselves, socialist women were transferring gender relations of a capitalist society to the future proletarian community.

The speech was loudly applauded, but Alekseeva was so convinced that she had ruined her presentation that as soon she walked off the stage she burst into tears. Samoilova was very amused by her reaction and tried to comfort her by praising her performance. Tears may have been a relief for her overwrought nerves, but probably Alekseeva had already realized the revolutionary import of her speech. Certainly the watching gendarmes had since she was arrested that same night.

The rest of the session was less dramatic. While the feminist Margarita Nikolaevna Margulies-Aitova spoke about the need for women workers to join other women in their quest for suffrage, other Social Democrats stressed that the development of capitalism in Russia was creating new cohorts of proletarian revolutionaries. Praskov'ia Kudelli presented a historical sketch of the development of the consciousness of Russian women. She started with a description of the "slave woman" typified in the *Domostroi* and contrasted her with the woman of the nineteenth century, who rejected the old morality and bravely fought for the realization of her utopian socialist principles. The introduction of capitalism in Russia, however, changed the picture and the woman worker entered the historical stage with interests and goals identical to that of male workers.[51] Kudelli's speech encapsulated the two polar images of women that were to figure prominently in the Soviet morality play—as oppressed counterrevolutionary denizen of the domestic sphere and as selfless and revolutionary comrade-in-arms.

Kudelli could not resist a dig at the feminists and at their attempts to deflect women workers from their "natural" class affiliations. While she admitted that it was necessary for women to achieve full political rights and status, she nevertheless cautioned that the most important demands of proletarian women were economic in nature and that members of other classes did not share these interests. Because of this, the liberation of the woman worker could not be in the interests of other classes and could be achieved only by the "will of the members of the proletariat, irrespective of gender."

Kudelli tried to analyze the consequences of the 1905 revolution, but at this point the gendarmes interrupted. The hall was plunged into a deathly silence and everyone was afraid that the meeting would be closed. But Kudelli changed the subject and was allowed to finish to a stormy ovation.[52] When the audience tried to sing revolutionary songs the police again interfered. As the police circular had stated, all signs of public disturbance were to be contained, and a thousand people singing militant songs might easily provoke a riot, especially among the people standing outside the hall. In ineluctable degrees, Women's Day changed from a benign gathering of women to an event that challenged the validity of both the patriarchal and political principles that lay under the tsarist order.

Apart from the Bolsheviks, several other organizations, such as workers' clubs and some of the women's courses for higher education, took it upon themselves to celebrate Women's Day in St. Petersburg. The city police carefully monitored most of the gatherings, and where speakers raised sensitive issues such as a shorter working day or maternity leave, the meetings were arbitrarily closed down.[53] In Moscow, surprisingly, the police did not censor or control the International Women's Day meeting organized by the members of the Third Women's Club.[54] As in St. Petersburg, the Bolsheviks managed with great difficulty to persuade a nervous young woman worker, Masha Platonova, to speak at the large function. And like their comrades in St. Petersburg, Moscow Bolsheviks entered into a temporary alliance with the liberals. Ekaterina Kuskova, a former Marxist and then a Kadet feminist, explained to a crowded audience the revolutionary significance of Women's Day and the role of the working woman in the proletarian movement. The holiday was also celebrated in Samara, Tiflis, and other industrial centers of Russia. In Kiev, working women met in small groups in various parts of the city. The meetings were lively and unconstrained, and nearly 150 women workers participated in them. However, the meetings caught the eye of city authorities and the next year Women's Day celebrations were banned in Kiev.[55] As Women's Day resonated across the country, greetings poured into *Pravda* headquarters from various institutions and organizations such as the Social Democratic faction in the Duma, groups of political prisoners, women in exile, workers from the Putilov factory, a group of dressmakers from Ekaterinoslav, and women workers from Krasnoiarsk.[56]

While the Bolsheviks were keen to differentiate their political position on the "woman question" and resolutely avoid all comparisons with feminists, others failed to recognize their uniquely radical stance. Conservative and liberal newspapers downplayed the revolutionary significance of the incident.[57] Furthermore, Okhrana reports did not identify Women's Day celebrations exclusively with the Bolsheviks as did later Soviet writings. The feminists were more gratifyingly perceptive, and an editorial in the *Zhenskii vestnik* complained that there was little discussion about the legal disabilities that perpetuated women's subordination to men and infringed upon their personal freedom.[58]

The socialists, however, were satisfied with the results of the first

Women's Day celebration. Anna Elizarova writes that from the first Wom-en's Day, female enrollment in unions, clubs, and illegal organizations grew tremendously. The St. Petersburg Okhrana concurred: "It was not celebrated very widely, but it served towards awakening the solidarity of women workers, and their interest in political party work. . . . Women have been elected as members of the committees of various cultural-educational organizations and professional unions."[59] The Bolsheviks were sufficiently pleased with the results of their efforts in 1913 to start planning an even bigger production for the next year.

**Celebration to Revolution**

In 1914, as in the previous year, there was little unanimity about the holiday. Some Mensheviks thought that the day should be spent in advancing such demands as passage of the maternity insurance bill, women's political rights, and wage increases commensurate with inflation. And Kudelli was keen to work with Kollontai and organize Women's Day together with the Mensheviks. But this idea was firmly vetoed by Samoilova and Elizarova, and the Bolsheviks decided to use the day as before, to enroll women in the ranks of the worker's movement against capitalism and autocracy.[60]

Preparations for Women's Day in 1914 began nearly two months in advance. Several women workers were coached to present reports, and it was decided that meetings would be held in every working-class suburb of St. Petersburg at the Kalashnikov Exchange, the People's House of Panin and Nobel on the Vyborg side, at Nash Teatr on the Obvodnyi canal, and on the Bolshoi Grebetskoi. While it was undeniable that the women workers evinced a greater interest in the holiday preparations in 1914, the Bolsheviks still continued to harp on the backwardness of women workers as a theme. An article in *Put' Pravdy* on February 4, 1914, complained bitterly that although the newspaper had requested information on the condition of women workers in various industries, very few organizations had bothered to reply. The revolutionary consciousness was slow to develop, and Bolsheviks hoped that the publication of *Rabotnitsa*, the first socialist women's journal on Women's Day would accelerate the process.

Little is known about the birth of this journal; according to Soviet historians, Lenin was the inspiration behind the venture. But Krupskaia, in her autobiography, recollects that when Inessa Armand came to visit them in Cracow in 1913, she proposed publication of a special magazine intended especially for the woman worker. Lenin approved of the idea and wrote to his sister Anna Elizarova in December 1913 to ask her to start organizing an editorial board for *Rabotnitsa*. In a letter to Samoilova, dated December 12, 1914, Krupskaia outlined a plan for the journal, and suggested that it include several sections such as the state of the workers' movement, the participation of women workers in insurance campaigns and trade unions, women's work conditions in domestic and industrial service, international labor news, current events, and a section on women and family life.[61]

Thus, far from functioning as an autonomous sphere for the women workers to express their thoughts and feelings, the discussion in *Rabotnitsa* was formulated according to a preexisting script. Everyday experiences of women workers, on the shop floor and in the home, were to be classified according to Bolshevik categories. The journal was to create a certain worldview among its readership through the very selection of topics. This was not a crude attempt at censorship, but through the medium of the press the Bolsheviks sought to create a certain ideal type of woman reader and inculcate in her a Bolshevik understanding of the world.[62]

While change was always represented as desirable in the articles, the present was shown in the most ahistorical manner possible. Ignoring the rural background of most women workers, articles in *Rabotnitsa* presented women workers' lives as successive stages of exploitation set in the factory environment exclusively. While the language tended to be melodramatic, the life cycles of women were narrated in a repetitive and mechanical manner, robbing the events of their actual tragedy. As a child laborer, a young girl was not allowed to play or even attend the deathbed of her mother. A young girl's dreams of a happy romance are shattered when a factory overseer rapes her. A mother barely earns enough to feed her children while the grueling factory routine drains her of vitality and strength.[63] Proletarian female destiny encompassed loss and degradation as in the conditions of capitalism the woman worker was robbed of her youth, family, self-respect, and dignity. Suffering and dispossession was omnipresent in the Bolshevik construction of womanhood, both before and after the revolution. But prior to 1917 there was little awareness of how the situation could be ameliorated. Indeed, since the present was always shown to be static and unchanging, women were rarely offered solutions to improve their status apart from the ubiquitous panacea, a socialist revolution. But after 1917 the journal became far more dynamic, and every issue contained the central message that it was possible for women to completely transform their personal lives and immediate surroundings.

Two editorial boards were established, one in St. Petersburg, and one in Paris. But the birth of the journal was fraught with a series of problems. Not only were there money shortages but disagreements between the editorial staff and their physical separation further aggravated the situation. Bolsheviks campaigned among workers to raise funds, and sometimes groups of workers, both male and female, collected money to help defray publication costs. Once they received permission from the authorities to publish the journal, the editors decided to publish *Rabotnitsa* twice a month and date the arrival of the first issue with Women's Day so as to garner free advertisement for the journal. In a strangely transgendered metaphor, *Rabotnitsa* was dubbed "the youngest brother of the proletarian press."[64]

In 1914 the Bolsheviks decided to obtain official sanction for all Women's Day meetings from the city police.[65] But the police realized the revolutionary import of Women's Day and refused to grant permission for more than one meeting to be held at the Fedorov Hall on the Peterburgskii side of the city. The city authorities closely monitored the event. The editorial board of *Rabotnitsa* worked feverishly in order to publish the first issue on International Women's Day and had gathered for a last-minute meeting at Kudelli's tiny apartment on Nevskii Prospect on February 18, 1914. Everyone was in an unusually cheerful frame of mind and they joked about the irony of publishing a truly "legal" journal in tsarist Russia and that, too, on International Women's Day. Suddenly, the door flew open and several policemen burst in with a search warrant and arrested the editorial board of *Rabotnitsa*—Kudelli, Samoilova, Rozimirovich, and Drabkina. The next night thirteen other members of the holiday commission were arrested. The police seized incriminating correspondence, proclamations, brochures, photographs, identity cards, and money.[66]

Liudmilla Menzhinskaia, while on the way to the apartment, had a feeling that she was being followed.[67] After she had managed to shake off her shadow, she decided to wait at the apartment of Rozimirovich, secretary for the Social Democratic Faction in the Duma. While waiting there, she heard the police enter the building, at which point she managed to escape via the back stairs, losing a pair of galoshes in the process.[68] Menzhinskaia was arrested a couple of days later. The women were housed temporarily at a prison on the Vyborg side where they met other Bolshevik sympathizers, who were arrested for advertising Women's Day among factory workers. In all, thirty women were arrested. As Samoilova wrote later,

> What perverse irony of fate. We all dreamed of International Women's Day February 23, the one day when drawing apart the bars of our prison, tsarist Russia, we felt ourselves to be free citizens of the world; instead we, along with thirty others fell into the tsarist prison, in an iron cell, and we were divided from each other with iron walls and grilles with padlocks.[69]

But the Bolsheviks were not docile prisoners, especially since some, like Kudelli, had former prison experience. When the guards refused permission to open the small ventilators in the damp, dark cells, they banged on the doors and screamed and shouted until their demands were met.[70] Because Samoilova had left her infant son behind, her sister was allowed to visit her. Through this intermediary, the women prisoners heard of the Women's Day meeting and the publication of *Rabotnitsa*. The news flew around the prison and the women sang revolutionary songs.[71] This act of defiance was their way of commemorating the holiday in prison. The Bolsheviks were freed in a couple of weeks but banned from the Petersburg province and exiled to Novgorod for three years during which they were subject to police surveillance.

Although the police had confiscated the proofs of *Rabotnitsa* and arrested the editorial board, they could not prevent twelve thousand copies from hitting the streets on Women's Day.[72] Elizarova, who was late for the meeting on the night of February 18, had escaped arrest and subsequently played a crucial role in editing and distributing the journal. She was helped in her effort by other women, notably Emilia Solin-Alekseeva.[73] Although Elizarova did not mention names, she pointedly spoke of the enormous difficulties she faced in getting the journal published, including money shortages and refusal by printers to work with her. However,

Elizarova, with the help of women workers, managed to put out seven issues of the journal before the authorities banned it later that year.[74]

Through a policy of coercion and repression the authorities managed to turn a relatively peaceful event into one fraught with revolutionary portent. They refused permission to a number of Women's Day meetings planned by trade unions and cultural organizations. They also took preventive measures to forestall the appearance of contingents of women on the streets and increased surveillance in all parts of St. Petersburg. Agents of the police tracked and reported the circulation of proclamations advertising Women's Day, but defying the police ban, women workers met in dispersed groups across the city to celebrate their holiday. Wherever *Rabotnitsa* was sold, crowds huddled to read it aloud on the streets. Early in the morning of February 23, a group of women workers arrived at the People's House of Nobel. They read the notice canceling the meeting and despite the presence of mounted police, stood around excitedly discussing the ban. There was a similar impromptu gathering of protesting and disappointed women at the gates of Hall of the Kalashnikov Exchange. Various trade unions held meetings on the outskirts of the city. In factories where women predominated, women workers absented themselves and warned their bosses in advance that they were going to take Sunday off to celebrate Women's Day.[75]

At seven o'clock in the evening, about 450 workers arrived at the Fedorov Hall on the Malaia Grebetskaia, the only place where the police had originally given the Bolsheviks permission to hold a meeting. But as most of the Bolshevik speakers were in jail, only V. P. Menzhinskaia spoke, calling for the expansion of the struggle for voting rights, the eight-hour working day, and protection of female and child labor. Panova, a shop assistant, spoke of the conditions of trade clerks. As the police refused to let substitute speakers talk, the meeting closed early at nine o'clock. But the angry and restless crowd wanted to hear more and jeered at the police. Conservative police records estimated that a crowd of 150 walked toward Kamennyi Island Avenue singing revolutionary songs such as "Awake, Arise Workers," but were soon dispersed.[76]

But both the liberal and the socialist press reported that instead of a paltry 150, there were several thousand people that night walking toward

Kamennyi Island Avenue waving red flags and singing the *Marseillaise*.[77] Unlike the previous year, when it was mostly a women's affair, this year Bolsheviks' hopes of turning Women's Day into an all-proletariat holiday was fulfilled and working-class men turned out in large numbers to commemorate Women's Day. They stopped trams and buses, and soon a large number of policemen arrived to put an end to the demonstration. Under the sting of the whip this unruly group soon dispersed and some workers were arrested. But later that night, a group of three hundred workers headed over the Troitskii Bridge shouting "We greet Women's Day," and "Away with despotism." The police dispersed the demonstrators and a couple of workers were arrested.

After 1917 the events of Women's Day in 1914 passed into the annals of the legendary exploits of Bolshevik women.[78] But at the time, Bolsheviks were anything but pleased with the subdued celebrations. A woman worker from the factory Novyi Aibaz wrote to say that she imagined that Women's Day was celebrated in Western Europe amid much pomp and circumstance, with citywide meetings and demonstrations. Why, then, were Russian women deprived of their holiday? She replied, "Comrades, we ourselves are guilty! Our 'celebration' should persuade us workers, that only cohesion, organization and initiative from us is our answer." She lamented that out of the huge number of workers living in St. Petersburg, only seven hundred people appeared at the Fedorov Hall.[79]

Festivities in Moscow were even more moderate owing to the repressive measures adopted by the police. There were a few small meetings of women in factories and one organized by domestic workers. The largest meeting in Moscow was organized by a group of textile workers on the outskirts of the city in the forests protesting the banning of the Women's Day celebrations. As *Pravda* claimed quite accurately, the class bias of the tsarist society was very apparent. Although workers were forbidden from celebrating Women's Day, the Moscow branch of the League of Equal Righters was allowed to hold a meeting. Later, the feminists claimed that they were subject to detailed police scrutiny; however, they did not feel it incumbent to invite women workers, even though all their meetings had been banned.[80] And when a group of women weavers did show up at the League of Equal Righters' meeting uninvited, they were not given an opportunity to participate in the debate. Possibly, the experience of the previous year had soured the feminists and they had realized that, given the implacable hostility of the Bolsheviks, there was little political mileage to be gained in associating with them.[81]

From the police reports it is evident that the celebrations of Women's Day in various parts of the empire were strictly supervised, and consequently the day proceeded without incident in most Russian cities. In Samara, where the Social Democrats had organized a public lecture on the theme of the "Proletarian women and their participation in co-operatives," the police closed down the meeting when a spirited discussion broke out. In Kiev, where all meetings were banned, the Social Democrats distributed proclamations throughout the city on the night of February 23. In Rostov on the Don, the police noted great enthusiasm for the holiday among the proletarian and intelligentsia circles. And proclamations advertising Women's Day were distributed in Kronstadt.[82]

Due to the increased repression during the war years and the exile of Bolshevik organizers like Samoilova and Kudelli, there were no Women's Day celebrations in 1915 or 1916. A few Bolshevik women, enrolled in the Bestuzhev Courses in St. Petersburg, tried to bring out hectographed copies of a booklet commemorating Women's Day, but sweeping arrests at the women's university forestalled such plans.[83] Instead, the Bolsheviks in the city brought out proclamations that blamed war deaths, conscription, and rising inflation on the machinations of international capital. The leaflets exhorted women workers to step forward in defense of their hungry children and unemployed husbands and brothers, to build up their organizations and to call for an end to war. Once again, while the exploiters were presented as alien figures, the relationship of women to working-class politics was configured through familial relationships.[84]

Despite the relatively limited nature of Women's Day festivities in pre-revolutionary Russia, it is featured as one of the founding moments in subsequent histories of Soviet women. The elements of the story could be arranged to fit the general pattern of the Bolshevik master myth—the backward but receptive working women of St. Petersburg, the brave and selfless Bolsheviks, the pusillanimous Russian bourgeoisie and their feminist ideology, and the repressive tsarist state. The working woman's lack of political acumen and her inability to organize was underlined in order to justify the overwhelming necessity of Bolshevik leadership. Moreover, the Bolsheviks were credited with more than providing political guidance to a disorganized cohort; they actually induced in women the consciousness that they were being exploited by the capitalist order. Before the proletariat could act, they had to be aware of the historical role that they were destined to play as the "universal class." Also, proletariats had to know their enemies, not as immoral individuals, but as a class whose exploitative position was derived from their relationship to the means of production.

Two other peculiarly Bolshevik lessons can be derived from these accounts. While Bolshevik women displayed considerable initiative and ability in organizing Women's Day, the holiday did not represent a feminist deviation within the party. In fact, sponsorship of Women's Day offered Bolshevik women an important medium through which to distinguish their brand of socialist feminism from that of bourgeois feminists. Even *Rabotnitsa* was intended to act as a cultural bridge to working women, another means by which they could be persuaded to join the Bolshevik movement. Finally, by suppressing Women's Day celebrations the tsarist state proved its reputation as an intransigent and nonliberal order within which workers' demands could never have been met.

It is significant that the female workers in Petrograd started the February Revolution in 1917 on International Women's Day. They realized the symbolism of raising the standard of revolt on a proletarian holiday. On the other hand, the widespread strikes in factories on February 23 were in flagrant violation of Bolshevik orders. The women demanded bread despite Bolshevik attempts to turn them toward "political" questions. Thus it would seem that while both Bolsheviks and working women accepted the importance of Women's Day, they had opposing notions of its meaning and significance. The contest for meaning would be a protracted one.

two

# The Two Stories of the February Revolution

Turning to the narratives of the February Revolution, we find that women as agents or victims were strangely absent. If women appear at all, their actions have little or no significance for the larger understanding of the revolution. Spectators, principal actors, and historians both Marxist and liberal all agree that women were an important element in the chaotic events of February. But after acknowledging the historical role played by women in starting the revolution, the historian gets down to the "serious" history of the activities of the Duma, the ineptitude of tsarist ministers, the armed forces revolt, and the roles played by the various socialist parties. Women rarely leave a record of their activities, and what little there is happens to be the testimony of a few women participants in the revolution who were loath to emphasize their activities or to even credit them with any particular significance. Unfortunately, women's silences have all too often been interpreted as lack of participation by posterity.[1]

Perhaps the first historian to accord women's involvement a measure of analysis was Leon Trotsky, who in his *History of the Revolution* wrote that the "February Revolution was begun from below, overcoming the resistance of its own revolutionary organizations, the initiative being taken of their own accord by the most oppressed and downtrodden part of the proletariat—the women textile workers, among them no doubt many of them soldiers' wives."[2]

Apart from the representation of women as the catalytic element of the February Revolution, Trotsky went on to acknowledge that women played a very important role in winning the soldiers over to the cause of the revolution.[3] Subsequently, women have figured in two roles—leading the spontaneous bread riots on day one of the revolution, mediating between male workers and soldiers, and helping in the creation of a critical alliance against the forces of autocracy. But for the rest of the historical narrative, women seem to suffer from a curious visible invisibility.

In the historical literature available the Bolsheviks had the most to say about women. Unlike other political parties in Russia, the Bolsheviks had a clearly defined agenda for women. Since they controlled the means of historical production in the Soviet Union, their sources would be logically the most informative, but here too gender reared its ugly head. The representations of women's roles in Bolshevik narratives seemed both equivocal and problematic. While assessing the role that women played in ensuring the success of the February Revolution, I will also analyze in this chapter the chronology of the events, including why the February Revolution is historically dated from February 23. Although it seems just as logical to date the beginning of the revolution from the Putilov strike on February 18, most Soviet and Western scholars agree that the revolution started on Women's Day, February 23.[4] I will reconstruct the possible reasons for adopting this particular chronology. I will also investigate the Bolshevik historiography of the February Revolution in order to elucidate the motives behind their ambiguous representations of this event.

The revolutions of February and October were cast in deeply gendered terms, as the feminine and the masculine revolutions, respectively. This can be further decoded as the revolutionary exemplar and its failed antithesis. If February is an example of how not to have a socialist revolution, the reason is due partly to the unruly participation of women which destabilized the Bolshevik political categories, and which called into question the organizing principles of a socialist revolution.[5] This can be further verified when we turn to the Bolshevik accounts of women's participation in the October Revolution. Since this revolution, in contrast to its hapless predecessor, was presented as a product of Bolshevik planning and forethought, historians have little trouble crediting women activists with exemplary revolutionary demeanor.[6] In October, under party guidance, women workers were formed into medical units to support the Red Guards. They helped maintain order on the streets, sustained communications between institutions in various districts, and served on revolutionary troikas. A few women even figured among the troops that "stormed" the Winter Palace. February, in contrast, was rendered doubly problematic, not just due to the "nonpolitical" nature of women's conduct during the event, but due to Bolshevik failure to orchestrate or even predict the revolution.

**Women's Day and the Chronology of Revolution**

It was difficult for the Bolsheviks to arrive at a historically accurate appraisal of the February Revolution since they played a negligible role in guiding the events. Following the successful conclusion of the revolution, the Bolsheviks were barely represented in the Workers Soviets, the loci of revolutionary power. The February Revolution deviated from the accepted model of revolution, as it originated, not in the conscious strike action of the proletariat, but in the spontaneous and uncontrolled riots of a "dark," backward, and—in the Bolshevik lexicon—decidedly counter-revolutionary cohort of women workers. Urban women workers had traditionally displayed a notorious indifference to Bolshevik propaganda, and rather than attributing this to the failure of their political strategies, the Bolsheviks decoded this apathy as evidence of women's apoliticism and lack of intellectual development. The February Revolution, therefore, seemed a direct refutation of Leninist theory and, subsequently, Soviet scholars alternated between castigating the "spontaneous" actions of the female proletariat of Petrograd in February and, at the same time, trying to prove that the events of February 23 were part of a larger Bolshevik plan. In the second version of the story, the disturbances on the first day of the revolution were represented as a female response to Bolshevik agitation conducted on February 22 and 23 in honor of International Women's Day.

The very first attempt to settle the chronological boundaries of the February Revolution were articles composed by A. I. Elizarova and M. I. Ulianova published in *Pravda* on March 5 (18) and 8 (21), 1917. The articles, entitled the "Chronicle of Events," gave prominence to the role of Petrograd women in starting the strike movement on February 23. On March 7, a Bolshevik poster printed in the first page of *Pravda* proclaimed openly that the "first day of the revolution was Women's Day—day of the International Working Women," and went on to say that Women's Day was a call to revolution, and in truth the revolution started from this day. Then again on March 10, 1917, an article in *Pravda* highlighted the factory women's role in starting the revolution and said rather coyly, "We were happy comrades that our so to speak delicate hands started everything."[7]

Despite this bid for glory by association with a socialist holiday, there were no overt claims that the Women's Day demonstrations were caused by Bolshevik propaganda and agitation.[8] Aleksandr Shliapnikov was the first to claim that the strikes and demonstrations of women workers on Women's Day were a result of meetings organized by Bolsheviks. He also mentions that female Bolsheviks demanded that the Vyborg District Committee hold a series of meetings on February 23 to commemorate Women's Day. Designated party orators were instructed to speak about "War, inflation, and the position of the woman worker" at these meetings. Shliapnikov offered little direct evidence that the St. Petersburg Bolshevik committee had originally planned to use Women's Day to call for a general strike in Petrograd, but he reported that the Women's Day meetings in factories were very successful, and working women from the factories in the Vyborg quarter were the first to respond to the Bolshevik call for "To the Nevskii." In response to the Bolshevik propaganda, women workers poured onto the streets calling for bread, and an end to war, and persuaded workers from other factories to lay down their tools and join their demonstrations.[9]

This account was flatly contradicted by V. N. Kaiurov and I. D. Chugurin, both veteran Bolsheviks, who were present during the events of February in Petrograd. They offered a very different account of Bolshevik preparations for Women's Day. Kaiurov writes that during a meeting at the Lesnyi district of Petrograd on the eve of Women's Day, he warned the women workers to maintain discipline, to follow the party directives, and refrain from any independent action.[10] Chugurin confirmed this lack of preparation on the part of Bolsheviks for general strike action on Women's Day and added that since the Bolsheviks had planned to call a citywide strike on May 1, they did not want any premature labor disruptions in the city.[11]

According to David Longley, both Chugurin and Kaiurov's articles were written in 1923–24 at the instigation of Stalin in order to discredit Shliapnikov, his role in the February Revolution, and by extension the

Workers Opposition.[12] This would explain the discrepancy in the accounts. But with the progress of time, Shliapnikov's view of the Bolsheviks arranging the Women's Day meetings and fomenting the strikes among women workers was accepted by Bolshevik historians. By the 1930s and thereafter, history books were asserting with complete authority that the February Revolution started on International Women's Day when the women of Petrograd responded to the Bolshevik call to arms by erupting onto the streets with cries of "down with autocracy."[13]

The Bolsheviks were not the only political organization to celebrate Women's Day in Russia. The bourgeois feminists adopted it in the prewar years, and they celebrated the event quite lavishly in 1914. In 1917 the Mezhraiontsy and the Left Mensheviks were as active in making preparations for Women's Day as the Bolsheviks.[14] The Mezhraiontsy started planning the Women's Day celebrations as early as December 1916 and created a commission composed of women representatives from the Mensheviks, Bolsheviks, and the Mezhraiontsy. However, the members of the different political parties could not agree on slogans, and the committee soon fell apart. But the female members of the Mezhraiontsy continued with their efforts to unveil a propaganda campaign on Women's Day, and achieved a certain degree of success.[15]

The leaflet issued by the Mezhraiontsy on Women's Day in 1917 outlined in graphic detail the hideous costs of the First World War. The poster cited eloquent images of loss, both physical and emotional. The casualties of war included dead sons and fathers, inflation and hunger, orphaned children, and young girls forced to walk the streets. The leaflet was intended as a militant battle cry to raise the standard of revolt against the tsarist government and the Russian capitalists.[16] It explained that nothing short of the overthrow of autocracy and its replacement by a revolutionary government would bring the war and its attendant horrors to an end. All this was standard Social Democrat fare, but what was decidedly Bolshevik in this was the statement, "But women joined the workers family late, often they are afraid and do not know what to ask for or how to press their demands. Their backwardness and slavishness has been exploited and continues to be exploited by the capitalists."[17] It seems that the Mezhraiontsy shared the Bolsheviks' ambivalence about the revolutionary potential of proletarian women and despaired of sustained political activism from them. Nonetheless, the leaflet was issued in order to stir women to action and to help them identify their real enemy, the capitalists and the government, rather than expend their energy on attacking bakeries and grocery stores.[18]

Due to this low estimation of female political consciousness by the Social Democrats, nobody took Women's Day seriously and certainly nobody believed that women would act as the catalyst in the revolution. Sukhanov, the chronicler of the revolution, commented that few observers believed that the events of February 22 and 23 presaged the beginning of the revolution. In fact, on February 21, he overheard a couple of female typists talking about the food supply crisis, the lines at the stores, the unrest among women, and their attempts to attack storehouses. One of the typists commented that this was the start of the revolution. Sukhanov's immediate reaction was that these "philistine" girls knew nothing about revolutions.[19]

Subsequently, Western historians, probably in response to Bolshevik claims of leadership in the revolution, took pains to demonstrate that Bolsheviks did little or nothing to celebrate Women's Day in 1917.[20] However, the celebration of Women's Day in prerevolutionary Russia never was undertaken by the party in general but was a small-scale affair that was run exclusively by low-ranking female members with limited resources. In 1917, none of the members of this active group of Bolshevik women were present in Petrograd. Krupskaia, Armand, and Kollontai were abroad, Samoilova was hiding in Moscow, Anna Elizarova was in jail, and Rozimirovich was in exile in Siberia. Moreover, the authorities had suppressed *Rabotnitsa*. During the war years socialists were savagely repressed and the tsarist police arrested them at the slightest provocation. According to one count, in 1917 in Petrograd alone, there were 889 women prisoners imprisoned for committing political crimes.[21]

In 1917, however, Women's Day ceased to be an exclusively women's affair and the Vyborg Bolshevik committee made some effort to celebrate the holiday. During the war years the Bolsheviks brought out leaflets commemorating the event and drawing attention to the plight of women workers suffering under wartime conditions of inflation and spiraling costs of living. In 1917, the decision to hold Women's Day meetings at a series of factories and have male Bolsheviks address them constituted a deviation from standard Bolshevik policy and showed increased awareness of the party to the needs of women workers.[22] But despite this increased involvement of male colleagues, during Women's Day most of the speakers in factories on that occasion were women.[23]

It was one thing to organize a Women's Day meeting, however, and quite another to persuade the women workers to go on strike. Most Bolshevik accounts draw a straight line of causality between Women's Day meetings and the start of the February Revolution. But the evidence shows no such cause and effect. Rather than responding to the call to revolution by socialists, women of Petrograd used the holiday to press for their demands for bread. At the most it can be claimed that Women's Day meetings exacerbated the existing anger and dissatisfaction among the urban population and precipitated mob action in some places.[24] Moreover, it appears that at several factories women workers held meetings to celebrate Women's Day independent of any socialist activity. From all accounts, the decision to go on strike was entirely spontaneous, and as early as February 21 there were rumors circulating in the city of an impending strike that was to commence on Women's Day. It is hard to trace the origin of rumors, but all sources point to the textile workers as the main source of unrest. The textile workers went on strike on the 22nd, and by February 23 had persuaded enough people to join them that the authorities were talking about serious disorder in the city. The Bolsheviks, of their own admission, had little or no influence over textile workers, especially the new female recruits to the industry.[25]

**Food Riot or Revolution?**

As already demonstrated by historians, the First World War imposed dreadful privations on the Russian people. Initially, the war and the draft resulted in rising employment opportunities for women. By January 1917, there were 129,800 women working in the factories of Petrograd, constituting 33.3 percent of the Petrograd labor force. Most of these women were concentrated in the textile industry and tended to be young and single. Women were also employed in low-paying unskilled jobs in metal, food, tobacco, leather, and chemical industries. The work conditions were quite appalling and in some cases life-threatening. The management expended little effort to maintain workplace safety, and as a result accidents were a common occurrence. When the restrictions on the length of the workday were lifted in 1915, the workday could last as long as 13 hours in some cases. Pay was miserably low, and wartime inflation tended to eat up wage raises. According to one calculation, women's wages actually fell during this period and some sections of women workers—for example, those in the printing trade, were on the brink of starvation in 1917.[26]

Food prices had been rising in the city since the beginning of the war, and by 1916 the shortage of food was serious enough to affect even the wealthier people. The price of bread rose from 3 kopeks in 1913 to 7 kopeks in 1917. Meat, ham, and sausages disappeared from the stores, as well as essential goods such as boots, soap, and medicine. When Rittikh was appointed the new minister of agriculture, he tried to levy a forced grain tax on the countryside, but this policy was a dismal failure and the food supply shortages to the city continued to grow.[27]

Food pogroms had been fairly common in Russia during the war years, starting as early as 1915. In Petrograd on April 6, 1915, a crowd of women looted a large meat market where the sale of meat had been suspended. Later in August of the same year, in the working class district of Petrograd, rampaging crowds smashed windows and ransacked 103 shops. In the ensuing chaos, a number of policemen were hurt.[28] Socialists believed that these food riots—attacks on bakeries, butchers, and food warehouses—were mainly the work of women and adolescents. The socialists dismissed them as *bab'i bunty* (women's uprisings), or as peculiarly women's affairs, headed primarily by the *soldatka* (soldier's wife), often a synonym for a prostitute. In their estimation, these violent, disorganized, and spontaneous actions were devoid of any edifying political character. Pogroms could not be classed as an economic strike, and it was widely believed that members of the conscious proletariat strata were rarely involved in the screaming melee of housewives and soldiers' wives. Lenin warned against the attacks on food stores, and advised the Bolsheviks to concentrate on organizing serious demonstrations against the forces of autocracy.[29] Socialists across the left-wing spectrum agreed that the workers' instinctive class hatred should be focused on government institutions, and the dissipation of revolutionary energy in unplanned urban riots should be avoided.

Bolsheviks, in proclamations to the workers, condemned spontaneous and violent raids on stores and called for organized protest against inflation. The notion that food pogroms were the work of women was deeply ingrained among them. Bolshevik posters for Women's Day during the war years stressed repeatedly that the high prices of bread, meat, coal, matches, and other necessities of life were caused by the evil machinations of capitalists who, protected by the tsarist government, were waging a world war and oppressing the women worker for the sake of commercial profit. The International Women's Day poster, issued by the Mezhraiontsy in 1917, highlighted the same point. It outlined the terrible calamities brought on by war and asked, "Women comrades are we going to bear this in silence any longer, venting our rage only now and then on small shop owners?" The socialists tried to explain to the working women that attacking individual stores would have little impact on improving the material conditions of the working class; it could only be achieved by sustained working-class action, impelled by a larger political vision and guided by the socialists.[30]

The misreading of the revolutionary potential of food riots was partly due to the widespread, though erroneous belief that women instigated them. According to recent evidence, food riots occurred throughout the Russian Empire during the war years, and in most cases attracted the support of both male and female workers, including the elite metal workers in Petrograd and workers in the oil, railway, chemical, textile, and tobacco industries.[31] The Bolsheviks made an error of drawing a sharp distinction between the political and the economic, not realizing that the two in the popular mind were deeply intertwined. They also underrated the cohesiveness of the working class. Although the Bolsheviks directed a considerable part of their propaganda exhorting women workers to join the family of the international proletariat, they did not realize that women workers were not isolated by sex. Rather, they were closely linked through family and marital ties with the proletariat and the soldiers in the army. This was aptly demonstrated during the course of the food riots, when the soldiers, while confronted by women asking for bread, often refused to fire on "our wives."

Surprisingly enough, the tsarist secret police were aware of the insubstantiality of the line dividing large-scale food riots and political demonstrations against the tsarist state. A police report from October 1916 warned that serious disorders were imminent, due not to revolutionary propaganda, but to the crisis in food supply to the cities. At the same time, the report cautioned that the revolutionaries would be quick to establish their control over urban food riots.[32] This warning was repeated in a report dated February 23, 1917. In it, the informer wrote that strong dissatisfaction was brewing among the working class and that riots could erupt at any moment, which the social democrats were hoping to control and convert into revolutionary demonstrations.[33]

## The Tactics of Revolution

Actually, when the revolution started, it took a while for the socialist parties to get their act together—that is, if they ever did. The February Revolution combined all the elements of the food pogroms in that Women's Day was inaugurated with the looting and plundering of bread stores. At the same time, women workers in factories decided that the only way to make a meaningful protest against the lack of food and necessities of life was not to demonstrate in isolation, but to persuade and, if necessary, force their male comrades to join them in their march to the center of the city.

From all accounts, the revolution began in the Vyborg region among the textile workers.[34] Some of the largest textile factories in this worker district—for example, Nevka cotton factory, as well as Nikolskaia, Sampsonievskaia, and Vyborg each employed more than a hundred women workers. The first factory to erupt on the streets was the Sampsonievskaia Manufactory. Already on February 22, though the factory was still operational, groups of women burst onto the shop floor and tried to stop the machines. They also gathered in clusters on the street and shouted for bread. The morning of the 23rd, women workers decided to bring in workers from other factories to join this general call for bread.[35] The textile workers from Sampsonievskaia went to Eriksson, Novyi Lessner, and Baranovski, three large metal factories in the Vyborg suburb which employed thousands of workers. Obviously, if workers from these factories turned out in force, it would give muscle to the women's movement. This tactic of *sniatie* (forcing workers to put down their tools), was a part of the Russian labor tradition of protest that women used with consummate skill, turning a localized strike into a citywide revolution. One can only guess at the motivation of the women in involving other factories, but the tactic snowballed into a mass movement that eventually paralyzed the city.

On the morning of the 23rd, large crowds of women filled the streets on the Vyborg side of the city. On their way to the Nevskii Prospekt, the city's main thoroughfare, the women persuaded workers of the factories that lay in their path to join them in their march for bread. Women used a wide range of strategies, ranging from moral suasion to the administration of intense pressure in order to co-opt male co-workers into their ranks. For example, women workers from the Nevka cotton factory sent delegates to the Eriksson factory to ask if the workers would support their strike. This precipitated a great controversy among the socialist leaders about whether they should join the demonstration or not. But it soon became apparent that the majority of the 4,500 workers of the factory were ready to set down their tools and join the women. This willingness to follow the women's lead led the Bolsheviks to suspect that, unbeknownst to them, the workers had been planning a general strike.[36]

However, women on this day were often militant and did not hesitate to scream and shout until the menfolk acceded to their demands. Crowds of women textile workers approached the road before the metal factory, Novyi Lessner, in a combative mood, shouting for bread and an end to war. They waved their hands at the workers and called to them to put down their tools and come out to the streets. The women started throwing a barrage of snowballs and metal bits at the windows of the factory. Initially, some of the workers were hesitant, but the younger workers were very enthusiastic about the strike, and soon the 7,500 factory workers poured onto the streets. When the women saw them coming, they set up wild cheers and, holding the workers by the hand, dragged them toward the Bolshoi Sampsonievski Prospekt.[37]

At times women workers were obviously irritated by the long-winded deliberations of their male colleagues about the viability of joining the general strike. A worker at the metal factory later recalled that on the 23rd, during a meeting held in the courtyard of his factory, a group of women burst in from the neighboring cigarette factory, Gavaner, and mounted the rostrum. One of them, sporting a red band on her chest, announced in a loud voice, "Comrades enough discussion!!! Come into the streets and we will ask for bread and freedom." After such imperious summons the workers marched resolutely to the street and joined the crowd.[38]

Often, when the women were barred from approaching workers at a factory, they turned violent and vented their frustrations in a purely physical manner. Thus, on the morning of February 24, a crowd of roughly five thousand women and teenagers approached the gates of the Petrograd military horseshoe factory with shouts of "stop work." They tried to break into the factory compound but were soon halted by a contingent of policemen. The angry crowd hurled snowballs in response, then backed off and attacked a small store, breaking the windows and scattering loaves of bread on the street. They also tried, albeit unsuccessfully, to overturn a tram car. Finally their violent tactics paid off, and at twelve o'clock the workers from the Petrograd military horseshoe factory rushed out to the streets with cries of "bread."[39] A similar event happened at the Obukhovskii steel foundry, where despite low turnout, the workers hadn't yet joined the general strike. The morning of the 24th nobody started work, as a group of hungry and enraged women attacked nearby stores and broke windows. As the women defended themselves against the city police, the workers of the factory joined in the scuffle. After this encounter, a decision was taken to join the February uprising.[40]

In other places, women workers, often through their steadfast resolution to go on strike, inspired their male co-workers to support them. Thus at the telephone factory Lorenz, activist Marfa Vasilieva almost single-handedly called a successful strike. Already that morning, in celebration of Women's Day, women workers had presented red bows to the men. The administration was aghast at this symbolic declaration of war but unsure of what steps to take. Then Marfa Vasilieva, a milling machine operator, stopped work and declared an impromptu strike. The workers on the floor were ready to support her. The foreman approached, hoping to convince her to continue working, and asked why she had ceased work. She replied that she and her family were hungry and that there was no bread in the stores. The foreman informed the management and sent her a loaf of bread. She took the bread but refused to go back to work. The administrator asked her again why she refused to work, and she replied, "I cannot be the only one who is satiated when others are hungry." Women workers from other sections of the factory gathered around Marfa in support and gradually all the other women ceased working. Soon the men downed their tools as well, and the entire crowd rushed onto the street. A similar phenomenon occurred at the factory Aibaz, where, despite the administration's promise to supply bread to the workers, the women workers refused to return to work.[41]

Women's actions unfolded in various ways, and the disruption of transport facilities was a common tactic during this period. As a means of paralyzing the city and creating chaos, it was a superb strategy. Although contemporary observers saw it as an expression of the spirit of aimless destruction and violence, the halting of tram cars perhaps had the effect of directly transmitting to the authorities the depth of public anger and outrage about the conditions in Russia. Like the tactic of *sniatie*, disruption of traffic proceeded in various ways. The distinction between the representation of activities of Petrograd women workers and those of Bolshevik women is interesting. Observers report that roving bands of women on the street tried to stop the tram cars and forced passengers to dismount, and women and teenagers broke the cars' windows. Often they failed to stop tram cars due to the intervention of the police, but they established a certain tactic of revolution that the Bolsheviks soon adopted.[42]

In her memoirs, N. F. Agadzhanova, a low-level party activist in Petrograd, wrote that during the revolution all Bolsheviks were instructed to help disrupt the Petrograd transport system. Agadzhanova, acting under party orders, stood between the rails of a tram car and forced herself to keep her place, although it showed no signs of slowing down. But the tram did come to a halt right in front of her. She felt terrible for a few moments, but soon recovered her nerve and, climbing into the cab, angrily demanded that the driver hand over his keys. When he refused to comply, she flung herself on the driver and wrested the key away from him forcefully. Luckily, such gallantry was not always called for, as during the war years, in the absence of men, women conductors manned the city tram cars. These women were quick to join the general strike and soon all transport ceased in Petrograd.[43] Agadzhanova's heroic account was a perfect example of Bolshevik revolutionary behavior. Acting under party instructions, it was permissible for individual members to display exemplary courage. But her bravery was tempered by discipline and as such served as an idealized contrast in Bolshevik mythology to the sporadic and disjointed efforts of the milling crowds of women.

As the striking workers from the Vyborg side began their march to the center of the city, they were joined by thousands of housewives who had been standing for hours in bread lines in front of bakeries.[44] When these women learned that there was no bread at the stores, they joined in the march to the Petrograd municipal Duma to demand bread. The masses of women workers, angry housewives, and wives of soldiers helped swell the militant ranks of revolutionaries. Women participated in huge numbers in the street demonstration and helped sustain the momentum of the revolution up until the resignation of the tsar. Several observers, both right-wing and socialist, report that women walked the streets of Petrograd often with infants in their arms or leading small children by the hand. They write of roving bands of women singing revolutionary songs. Metal worker Taras Kondratiev described the excitement in the worker slums and likened the women and children who poured out on the streets to swarming bees.[45] Others spoke of the terrible expressions of indignation and rebellion on the faces of the women.[46] The seething crowds, the teeming streets, the excitement of revolution was pervasive, affecting both the participants and observers. Rodionova, a tram car employee, describes her feelings as she marched with the crowds: "I felt as if my customary existence was crumbling, but I rejoiced in its ruin."[47] Maria Golubeva, a Bolshevik, writes in her memoirs about how she longed to be on the streets: "I was drawn to the streets, to the crowds, to the masses, where it was necessary to understand and explain what was happening."[48] The didactic function of a Bolshevik was never to be forgotten, and it was important to impress contemporary events with a peculiarly Bolshevik significance.

### Symbolic Dimensions of the Revolution

The February Revolution was a polyvalent phenomenon and the battle for power was fought at different levels. In the tumultuous events that ensued, everyone understood the significance of symbols. There was an overt contest for meaning at various levels, for example, the socialists worked to transform the "food riots" into a political struggle against the tsarist government. Orators at street corners harangued the crowds about the political implications of their demonstrations and tried to substitute the demands for "bread" with demands for the "abdication of the tsar." Often, the struggle between the old order and the emergent one was waged not in words, but through the symbolic use of cloth and color. Among socialists, making the banners was considered "woman's work." Maria Pavlova, whose apartment on Sverdlovsk Street in Petrograd was used during the war years for the Central Committee meetings of the party, recalled making several red cotton banners with revolutionary symbols.[49] During these days, while working women on the streets sported scarlet bows or ribbons on their blouses, some bourgeois women opened their balconies and waved white handkerchiefs to show their antipathy to the revolutionary events unfolding before their eyes.[50]

Class conflict naturally surmounted gender ties, and in the February Revolution women were pitted against women as each side tried to protect its own and at the same time strove to exact the requisite number of victims from the other. In a chilling account, a woman worker, Sinitskaia, describes her participation in the arrest of a tsarist police officer. When the crowd approached the officer's apartment, his wife at first did not open the door, and then claimed that he was not at home. The crowd refused to believe her and insisted on ransacking the place. But all their searches yielded nothing and they were leaving when Sinitskaia had the happy thought of checking in a chest that stood in the hallway. The wife swore that it was empty and she didn't have the key, but when they forced it open the police officer was found curled up in the interior. It was not surprising that so many policemen found it prudent to dress as women while fleeing the capital. It would seem that women's clothing gave one a measure of physical immunity while at the same time investing one with impeccable revolutionary credentials.[51]

While the summary judicial procedures of a revolutionary moment had a dark side, bands of women not only arrested class enemies but, like their precursors in France, helped in the liberation of prisoners from the notorious tsarist prison, the Petrograd Solitary Prison and the Women's Prison, better known as the Kresty.[52] As the prisoners emerged underclad into the icy February air, Agadzhanova, ever resourceful, along with a group of armed comrades, broke into a nearby clothing store and outfitted themselves with warm clothes. In the retelling of the event, the author comments on the strict revolutionary legality maintained by the Bolsheviks. Agadzhanova wrote out a detailed list of the clothes taken, affixed her signature, and left it with the owner. One wonders if she or he was ever paid back.[53]

Although the revolutionary moment allowed women to eschew traditional social roles, female anxieties of rape and mutilation were omnipresent. During the course of the revolution, politically active women were arrested in large numbers as the weakening autocracy tried desperately to stem the revolt of the masses. Elena Stasova, a Bolshevik, was arrested on February 24 after attending a political meeting of lawyers. She was locked up at a local police station and, during the course of her incarceration, the jail was packed with women political detainees. The prisoners rejoiced in their cell as the sounds of gunfire wafted up from the streets, but on the evening of the 27th an unnatural hush fell over the jail, and the warders quickly disappeared. A little later a group of men burst in and asked the prisoners to step out of their cells. The women panicked as they were convinced that a gang of Black Hundreds had broken into the premises. Clutching blankets and pillows, the women followed the men out into the corridor, hoping that once out on the street they would have a chance to run for freedom. However, it soon transpired that a crowd of people had stormed the police station in order to liberate the political prisoners.[54]

The revolutionary ambience, nonetheless, allowed for remapping gender identities. In the ensuing revolutionary maelstrom, the social and sexual order was turned upside down. Women workers seized the opportunity to reject traditional appellations and articulated a new notion of self. A. I. Kruglova, a worker in the factory Promet, and a longstanding Bolshevik, recalled that both male and female workers from her factory took to the streets on Women's Day. They were armed with banners and called for bread and an end to war. The women were soon stopped by a detachment of soldiers. Noticing Kruglova at the head of the column, the commanding officer asked her, "What are you marching for. Go tend to your own affairs, *baba* [hag]!" The word *baba* in Russian carries derogatory connotations, and Kruglova refused to accept this sexist appellation. The revolutionary moment offered a chance of creating new female identities replete with new political and juridical implications. Kruglova replied, "I am not a *baba*, but a *rabotnitsa* [an independent female factory worker], wife and sister of the soldier." This short interchange signified the transformative potential of revolutionary discourse. Kruglova demanded to be identified as a *rabotnitsa*, or an independent civic subject, but at the same time she used kinship metaphors to represent her affiliation with the soldiers.[55]

**Violence or Negotiation?**

The class and kinship ties between women and soldiers formed a crucial episode in the unfolding revolutionary drama. The fate of the February Revolution was contingent on the reaction of the military regiments stationed in Petrograd, and in the ultimate analysis the revolution was successful because the tsarist government refrained from using force in the initial stages of the revolution. This was also due to the fact that the number of policemen and Cossack detachments available in Petrograd were insufficient to control the situation. When the government finally decided to use military action in suppressing the civil disorders, the Pavlovskii and Voliinskii regiments mutinied and threw their lot in with the striking workers. Although the army had been subject to a great deal of antiwar propaganda by the socialists during the war years, until February 1917 there was no clear indication that the soldiers would support a civil uprising. During the revolution itself, the mood of the Cossacks and other armed units was extremely hard to read. Although the army wasn't called out in force until February 26, armed bands of Cossacks from the Don regiment were out on the streets as early as the 23rd. On Women's Day, a contingent of Cossacks guarded the Liteyni Bridge and prevented the strikers from crossing from the worker suburbs on the outskirts of Petrograd to the city center. As the workers came face to face with the armed soldiers it became apparent that they could either appeal to the soldiers for support or engage in outright warfare. Although the socialists did not adopt a clear tactic vis à vis the armed forces, and there were skirmishes and instances when the army actually resorted to shooting, on the whole the revolution was not a violent one. More often than not, the workers adopted a strategy of cooptation.

Women were an invaluable asset while negotiating with army units and proved particularly adept at persuading soldiers not to fire. This was a tried and true Russian tactic, and in former peasant rebellions in Russia women were often sent in the vanguard by male peasants in the hope that the authorities would refrain from firing on them. Also, women arrested in agrarian rebellions were treated much more leniently than their male counterparts.[56] Whatever the actions undertaken by women during the revolution, the myth that was created around the roles played by them focused exclusively on women workers as a liaison element between male workers and male soldiers. Trotsky wrote that a "great role is played by women workers in the relation between workers and soldiers. They go up to the cordons more boldly than men, take hold of the rifles, beseech almost command: 'put down your bayonets and join us'."[57] Of course, women could and did cajole the soldiers to refrain from firing. A soldier who lowered his rifle at the appeal of a woman did not call his courage into question; he merely proved his humanity. Therefore, women minimized bloodshed, true to the cultural stereotype, while satisfying male honor on both sides and bringing about a rapprochement.

This romanticization of women's relations with the soldiers reached its apotheosis in an autobiographical novel about the February Revolution written by a Bolshevik army officer. It conveys an idea of the metaphors and symbolism used to describe the relationship between the army and the working women:

> A detachment of Cossacks, with an officer at their head, was riding out of the red gates of the Anichkov Palace. They formed into a line, taut as a bowstring, and rode down on the mob . . . the young Cossack officer rose in his stirrups, turned to his men, drew his saber from the sheath, and suddenly the drawn sabers flashed like white lightning, moved upward, and back to rest on the Cossacks' shoulders. The only sound that could be heard was the resonant ring of the approaching hoofs. . . .
> Then a girl walked out from the crowd. She wore a dark padded jacket and huge shoes with galoshes. A simple knitted shawl of the same color as the Cossacks' coats was bound tightly over her head. She crossed over to the Cos-

sacks, walking swiftly and lightly. She was quite close to the Cossack officer. A thousand eyes followed her, and a thousand hearts were numb. Suddenly, she threw away some wrapping paper—and held out a bouquet of fresh red roses to the officer.

The officer was young. His epaulets flashed gaily. His saber, polished like a mirror, was firmly held in a strong hand—but suddenly the blade wavered helplessly and dangled, flashing but harmless, from the supple white-gloved wrist. The officer leaned over and took the nosegay.

A mad riotous shout went up—such a shout as I had never heard and never expect to hear again. It was a wild bellow of uproarious joy.[58]

Not all women workers were as romantic and young, nor were roses easily obtained in the depths of the Russian winter. But the image of the woman workers successfully disarming soldiers was used as a tropic device in memoirs and historical accounts. To a certain extent this was an accurate portrayal. Women stood outside army barracks of the Preobrazhenskii regiment singing revolutionary songs and tried to persuade soldiers to join the revolution. Although initially the doors were closed, the soldiers soon poured out of the barracks to join the workers.[59]

Women textile workers tried the same strategy outside the barracks of the Grenadiers. The textile workers beat on the locked doors and exhorted the soldiers to come to their support. The doors opened and the soldiers not only crossed over to the workers, but even distributed weapons among them.[60] Women held steadfast in face of danger from armed units and persisted in crying, "don't shoot on your mothers and sister," or "we are starving." Often, when an open fight between male workers and soldiers seemed imminent, women workers would intervene and persuade the soldiers to join the revolution, instead of shooting at the workers. Soldiers, while standing firm in front of male workers, were unable to hold their resolve when approached by women.[61] Women tried to influence the soldiers by using the traditional feminine weapons of tears and suckling infants at their breasts.

What is underrepresented in the literature, however, is the fact that many of the women were armed and participated in violent encounters with soldiers when they proved deaf to their entreaties. Sometimes women aggressively initiated hostilities by calling out insulting remarks and choice epithets to the police. Women joined in attacks on loyalist army officers and helped to disarm them. In a classic clash between city police forces and workers on the Vyborg side, women workers were prominently involved when the enraged crowds beat to death the policemeister, Colonel Shalfeev. Similarly, when female factory workers at the tobacco factory Laferm saw a mounted police patrol attack a crowd of demonstrators near their factory, they rushed to the defense of the unprotected marchers. According to one observer, the women looked so fierce and militant that the police patrol turned tail and fled.[62]

Women's violence was not restricted to encounters with the armed forces. They broke into police stations and set documents on fire. Women also helped in the sacking of the apartment of Protopopov, the incompetent and unpopular Minister of the Interior.[63] They attacked bakeries, dairies, and grocery stores. They looted the food reserves, broke windows and mirrors, and scattered furniture onto the street. Perhaps the most common target was the bread store.[64] After all, the revolution was about bread, and although the Bolsheviks made spirited attempts to maintain revolutionary discipline, their entreaties fell on deaf ears. The women clung to their agenda with tenacity and their militancy challenged the repressiveness of the tsarist administration.

**Gendered Representation of the Revolution**

In the Duma, Alexander Kerensky, a socialist deputy, and the future prime minister of Russia, gave an impassioned speech referring to the hunger of the masses. He used the words "hungry and wild women" repeatedly to characterize the originators of the revolution. The entire revolution was cast in deeply gendered terms by both observers and participants, by those who supported the revolution and those who opposed it. The category of woman and the attributes of femininity were used as metaphors by many commentators. But regardless of the political orientation of the person applying the appellation of femininity, it carried negative connotations. The empress of Russia, one of the most hated symbols of tsarism, dismissed the revolution as the naughtiness of young boys and girls while at the same time the insurgent crowds were waving banners that read "Down with the German Woman!" Pitirim Sorokin, a conservative witness to the revolution, lamented the effeminacy of the Russian ruling class and their emasculation, which made the revolution possible. On the other side of the political spectrum, Mstislavsky, a socialist revolutionary, likened the failure of the socialist parties to anticipate the revolution to the foolish virgins in the gospels that were caught napping.[65]

The Bolsheviks had the most trouble drawing up a history of events that would satisfy both veracity and honor. Perhaps if the Bolsheviks had played a more decisive part in the events of February they would have more easily drafted an acceptable historical account, but the fact remains that theirs was a negligible role. Also, further complicating the picture was their ambivalence about the role of women in the revolution. On the one hand, it suited them to date the revolution from Women's Day, it being a Bolshevik holiday, since it gave the Bolsheviks an opportunity to co-opt the February Revolution into party genealogy. Thereafter, the consensus was less clear. The predominant elements of the revolution—a citywide strike for bread, mob violence and random looting of stores, the lack of clearly defined political goals, and finally the unplanned and chaotic actions of the teeming crowds—all pointed to the unsatisfactory character of the revolution and its complete failure to fall into the Leninist schema. I. I. Mints compared the February and October revolutions: "the difference lay in the organization of the masses: in the October revolution, the degree of organization was at an incomparably higher level than that during the February days."[66]

Initially, historians such as Genkina, Pokrovskii, Shelavin, and others were forced to admit that the February Revolution was a *stikhinii* (elemental) event, implying that it was both spontaneous and uncontrolled.[67] At the same time they were unwilling to abandon the chronology of the revolution that dated the beginning to February 23, International Women's Day. Under Stalin, accounts of the February Revolution were reconstructed in completely ahistorical terms. According to this narrative, the Bolsheviks called for Women's Day demonstrations and led the women of Petrograd in calling for an end to war and autocracy. The use of the word *spontaneous* was restricted, and the revolution was presented as a product of Bolshevik forethought and planning.[68] Subsequently, this account continued to be used in Soviet historical and semihistorical literature.[69] But in 1959, when historians like Burdzhalov and Lieberov began to take a closer look at the literature on the February Revolution, they revised the story and asserted that the February Revolution contained elements of both spontaneity and organization. According to these authors, the disorganization and lack of control was prevalent during the first two days of the revolution (when women were predominant in the riots and disturbances), while beginning with the third day one could discern resolute and planned strike action and concrete political goals in the uprisings.[70] In more politically correct accounts, Soviet historians show that Bolsheviks were able to direct the uncontrolled revolutionary activity of women textile workers toward organized ends.[71]

Strangely enough, the first day of the revolution was Women's Day in more than one sense. It was the only day of the revolution during which women dominated the urban space and set the political agenda. Their demands were clear and simple: they called for bread and an end to the war. Although these demands were temporarily submerged in subsequent events, all the elements that made the revolution a success unfolded the first day; the tactic of *sniatie*, the overtures to the Cossacks, and the disruption of the city transport system. A combination of these three tactics made the revolution a success. But, unfortunately, the originators of these revolutionary strategies saw the successful conclusion to a different revolution from the one they had initiated. Not only did the food situation not improve, the war dragged on for another year. And more immediately, the new government failed to accord women the right to vote. The participation of women was damned with faint praise. According to the Bolsheviks, the women of Petrograd acted with great *muzhestvo* (manliness) during the revolution, while at the same time their unruly participation threatened to subvert the accepted definition of revolution.[72]

three

# Why Do We Need a Women's Holiday?

## The Contest for Definition

During the civil war years the embattled Soviet regime, while searching for political legitimacy both real and symbolic, arranged sumptuous public festivals in Moscow and Petrograd to commemorate the new revolutionary holidays—the anniversary of the October Revolution, and May Day. Anatoly Lunacharsky, commissar of enlightenment, provided a simple format for the temporal division of holidays into two acts: first, a mass demonstration around a central point where an elevated symbolic ceremony would take place, and second, a more intimate variety show complete with dramatic sketches, recitation of verses, and choral singing. Despite the protracted wrangling among the literary and artistic intelligentsia about the appropriate forms that festivals should take in a proletarian state, Lunacharsky's organizational plan provided the structural basis for subsequent Soviet festivity.[1]

Celebrations during the civil war consisted of variations on Lunacharsky's original theme. The artistic directors of these public events incorporated street demonstrations, carnivals, circus performances, and massive open-air theatrical enactments of mythologized events of the revolution into the festive repertoire. But from most sources it appears that the representation of female form, feminine values, or women's actions played an almost negligible part in the construction of the new symbolic system. For instance, in subsequent theatrical restagings of the events of the February Revolution, women's roles were completely obliterated. The only concession to the existence of the category of "woman" in the new public

Fig. 1. "Chto dala oktiabr'skaia revoliutsiia rabotnitse i krest'ianke" (What the October Revolution has given to working woman and peasant woman). International Institute for Social History. Designer unknown, 1920. BG 13/212.

sphere was the allegorical representation of virtues in the guise of female figures from the Roman and Greek pantheon.[2] But the popularity of classical female forms was short lived, and it wasn't until the 1920s that the Soviets evolved iconic representations of the New Soviet Woman as the *rabotnitsa* (woman worker) and *krest'ianka* (woman peasant).

Similarly, International Women's Day, although listed among the major calendric events in the Soviet Union, was a contested event.[3] The Bolsheviks were uncomfortable with any organization or event that purported to be exclusively a women's preserve. It was believed that such organizations fostered bourgeois-feminist individualism, and were inadmissible in a party that was dedicated to promoting a collectivist ethos.[4] Speaking at a meeting in 1924 Zinoviev recalled that there was a time when the Bolsheviks regarded all work among women as "feminism." He continued that he was not an adherent of feminism in the limited sense of the word, the type of "feminism that consists itself of opening women's eyes, and instead of raising social issues, babbles nonsense about women being a human being, etc., etc. This was petty-bourgeois vulgarity that needed to be discarded."[5] Therefore, the only work permissible among women was that which raised women's class-consciousness and encouraged them to participate in the communist labor movement.

Even after women's exemplary activism during the February Revolution, female Bolsheviks had a very difficult time persuading the leaders of the party to create an organization that would devote itself exclusively to propaganda work among women. Upper- and lower-echelon party members held a deep-rooted belief that special treatment of women would divide the proletariat on the gender axis, thereby weakening the revolutionary potential of the labor movement. Even female Bolsheviks, who advocated the formation of a special organization devoted to propagandizing women, were openly critical of what they termed "feminist deviation." The resumption of the publication of the journal *Rabotnitsa* was not without controversy. Finally, the Zhenotdel was formally admitted as a women's department of the Central Committee of the party as late as August 1919.[6]

Members of the Zhenotdel were subject to both ridicule and harassment, and the importance of their work was constantly called into question. Given this cultural atmosphere within the party, it was not surprising that International Women's Day was barely celebrated during the civil war period.[7] Although the party could afford to fund massive extravaganzas on the occasions of May Day and the October anniversary, foreign intervention, the civil war, famine, and economic devastation were some of the frequently cited reasons for the annulment of Women's Day festivities. The holiday slogans during these years focused on eliciting female help for national defense and labor in the factories and made little concession to the dire material circumstances that militated against women's wholehearted participation in these efforts.[8] With the conclusion of the civil war the party faced the daunting task of reconstructing the economy and restructuring society on the basis of proletarian dictatorship. The cities were devastated, much of the countryside plunged into ruin, and the transport system stopped functioning. Famine stalked the country and there were peasant uprisings in Saratov, Tambov, and other regions of the Volga against the hated system of forced grain requisitioning. The popular support base for the party among the working class in the cities was seriously eroded.

In 1921, citing this situation of national emergency, the party declared that celebrating International Women's Day, an innately superfluous exercise, was a luxury that the country could ill afford. The Zhenotdel argued to the contrary and presented a spirited defense of Women's Day. Kollontai's response took the form of a rambling and lengthy article that was published in *Kommunistka*, organ of the Zhenotdel.[9] She constructed a rationale for celebrating Women's Day, which was in fact an extended justification for the continued existence of Zhenotdel itself. She declared that Women's Day was not merely a "women's holiday," but a political campaign whose celebration would have a positive impact both at home and abroad. Kollontai argued that International Women's Day could be used as a means not just to further women's agendas, but to garner political capital in support of party goals. The primary tasks facing the nation could be explained to a potentially powerful constituency on Women's Day through the medium of public meetings, street demonstrations, wall newspapers, and slogans, concerts, matinees, and lectures.

The support and involvement of Soviet women in industrial production were crucial for the recovery of the economy, Kollontai wrote. There were seventy-three million women in the Soviet Union, and without their voluntary labor contribution the plans for national reconstruction would be seriously jeopardized. But the participation of women was contingent on the re-creation of daily life on a communal and communistic basis. Almost echoing Lenin's *obiter dicta* on the "woman question," Kollontai argued that women had first to be liberated from the onus of domesticity and child care so they could direct their energies toward national goals. Moreover, as mothers and primary caregivers to the future generation, women deserved special care and protection.[10]

Since the successful refunctioning of the Soviet economy was contingent on women's participation in the country's political and economic tasks, Women's Day celebrations could be used in an instrumental capacity to elicit support among women for the party and the Soviet state. Accordingly, the Zhenotdel exhorted various Soviet institutions such as the Commissariat of Enlightenment (Narkompros), Section for Maternity Protection (Okhrana Materinstva i Mladenchestva), trade unions, local soviets, and party cells to use Women's Day as an occasion to construct laundries, dining rooms, and child-care facilities. Zhenotdel also called for employment and promotion of women in factories and the enforcement of labor legislation designed to protect women workers. This would not only provide Soviet women with a viable alternative to domestic servitude but also free their labor for such important national tasks as fighting famine and restoring economic production in agriculture and industry. Also, sustained agitational work among women would create ranks of dedicated communists who would strengthen the social bases of the Soviet state.[11]

Although it seems that Zhenotdel had won the battle since Women's Day was not eliminated from the Soviet festival calendar, the holiday continued to attract derision and overt hostility, both from the party and the population at large. Unlike May Day or the October Revolution celebrations, Women's Day was not a work holiday. In most enterprises that actually deigned to hold a special meeting commemorating the day, employees worked until two in the afternoon and only thereafter were women free to participate in the festivities. When Elena Stasova proposed that Women's Day should be made a national work holiday at the Thirteenth Party Congress in 1924, there was fierce opposition to the plan. Anastas Mikoian, a close associate of Stalin, declared that the number of nonworking days should not be raised. And since the Congress could not decide on the status of Women's Day, the resolution was sent to the Central Committee for a decision.[12] The Zhenotdel attempts to win support for the holiday by stressing its productionist and political functions had been only marginally successful. Even though party involvement in preparations increased significantly from the middle of the 1920s, local soviets, trade unions, and factory committees ignored the instructions of Zhenotdel and the Central Council of Trade Unions (VTsSPS) on how to celebrate Women's Day with impunity.

### Women's Day in the City and Countryside

In view of this questionable legitimacy of the status of Women's Day, it was not surprising that in the sociological surveys of popular responses to Soviet holidays not a single inquiry was directed into the nature, form, and impact of Women's Day. In the early 1920s, Women's Day was barely celebrated in the countryside. In 1922, in a letter to *Krest'ianka*, a Zhenotdel worker described a Women's Day meeting held in a small village, Koromkov, where the assembled peasant women had no idea why they had been summoned, or what it was that they were celebrating. Similarly, a survey conducted in 1923 into the conditions of life and work of agrarian workers revealed that while most of the respondents were aware of May Day and the anniversary of the October Revolution, not a single person mentioned Women's Day. Part of this ignorance was due to the complete absence of political work conducted in the countryside. Internal Zhenotdel reports frankly admitted that very few attempts were made by local cells to propagandize peasant women until 1923.[13]

Thereafter it seems that Women's Day was celebrated in the provinces more regularly. In 1924, *Krest'ianka* claimed that from a survey of data collected in only twenty-seven provinces in the Soviet Union, over 118,455 peasant women had participated in Women's Day events.[14] Sometimes factories that had adopted a village under the *sheftsvo* (patronage) system would either bring a contingent of peasant women to the city on Women's Day or send a group of female factory workers to the village as carriers of the superior proletarian culture. In the countryside, Women's Day usually coincided with the beginning of the spring sowing campaign, and as such the slogans were predominantly concerned with attracting women to the fields. Later, when the cooperative movement got under way, Women's Day activities focused on the recruitment of women to village cooperatives and communes. According to press reports on Women's Day, local Zhenotdel cells and peasant reading huts opened literacy circles, sewing circles, summer crèches, milk centers, and nursing homes.[15] It is hard to arrive at any precise number of institutions opened on Women's Day, and one gets the impression that these offered more cosmetic help than initiating any deep-seated structural changes in the lives of peasant women.[16]

The rituals and forms of Women's Day celebrations tended to vary depending on the locale. In Moscow the party held Women's Day congresses at the Dom Kolonny or the Bolshoi Theater, while in Leningrad the Marinskii Theater or the Winter Theater served as the official venues. High-ranking party members, prominent female Bolsheviks, visiting foreign dignitaries, and rank-and-file Zhenotdel members were invited to these formal gatherings. Initially, in 1920 and 1921, in the industrial suburbs of Moscow, the city Zhenotdel held huge open-air meetings and noisy demonstrations that attracted crowds of over a thousand people. But these types of celebrations were soon abandoned and factories honored veteran women workers with gifts and accolades at more intimate and sober gatherings. Other institutions, where women predominated in the workforce, opened crèches, printed wall newspapers, and arranged concerts, plays, and parties at workers' clubs, and there were matinee shows for children and book exhibitions that featured women. As the decade progressed, Women's Day celebrations became more elaborate and would often span several evenings. They also became more standardized due to the efforts of the Zhenotdel, the VTsSPS, and the section in charge of agitation and propaganda (Agitprop) of the party. These departments circulated brochures and detailed instruction to national and international organizations almost a month before Women's Day. But these efforts notwithstanding, Women's Day remained a troublesome phenomenon that attracted both derision and support from the Soviet populace.[17]

### Popular Reactions to Women's Day

The antipathy of male Bolsheviks to the holiday was mirrored among sections of the population, especially men. Women's reactions were more difficult to ascertain but it appears that they were enthusiastic participants when they organized and controlled the events. At official Women's Day gatherings, rank-and-file women workers often appeared bored and unresponsive. An American reporter, visiting Moscow in 1920, described two Women's Day meetings in Moscow. The first was held in the Palace of Justice in the Kremlin. Despite the lavish surroundings, the women in the audience were wearied by the monotonous speech of a government official: "Many were half asleep, others staring at the walls and ceilings, still others were trying to quiet their restless babies." Although the audience perked up slightly when Angelica Balabanova, a famous revolutionary, started speaking, at the end of the session the questions asked related to the necessities of daily life rather than to Communist philosophy or national tasks. At the Women's Day meeting held on the same day at a local factory, however, the audience was extremely responsive. And the speakers at the meeting, who were factory women, spoke fluently and well.[18]

A film clip of an official Women's Day function in 1924 also showed a restless audience that talked and whispered while speakers delivered emotional speeches with upraised fists and revolutionary enthusiasm. One woman in the audience was obviously asleep. The party cell of the Trekhgorniaia Manufactory reported that in 1922 their Women's Day function was entirely unsuccessful. The speaker at the meeting was mediocre, and the women workers were very upset to learn that no arrangements had been made for a concert. Often the provision of food at the holiday ceremonies was one of the chief attractions. During the early years of NEP, when food was scarce, Zhenotdel instructed Narpit (Narodnoe Pitanie), a share company that was formed to build a network of public dining facilities in the city, to increase food supplies at communal dining halls for the holiday. Where there were no state-run dining halls, Zhenotdel workers, together with the local women workers and housewives, were asked to prepare and distribute food. In honor of Women's Day in 1921 POMGOL, the organization that oversaw the famine relief efforts in the Soviet Union, assigned a million rubles to be distributed among hungry and unemployed women workers and peasants.[19]

The absence of child-care facilities often prevented women with children from partaking in the holiday ceremonies, and both the Zhenotdel and Narkompros suggested that workers' clubs and peasant reading rooms should provide temporary child-care services during the holiday.[20] Zhenotdel also instructed trade unions and local cells to involve women in the preparations for Women's Day. This would facilitate their entry into the sociopolitical life of the nation and also give them a sense that Women's Day was not an alien Soviet ritual in which they were being forced to participate, but a real holiday.[21] To the state, participation in the new Soviet holidays was a measure of the growing legitimacy of the regime. In pursuit of popular acceptance, the Zhenotdel emphasized that the celebratory and festive elements of the holiday should be dominant and that speeches be cut down to a minimum. Journals and newspapers were instructed that the language of Women's Day publications should be clear, accessible, and that articles should be of immediate relevance to the life of workers and peasants.[22]

Despite widespread party propaganda advertising the day as a proletarian holiday, some men were disgusted by what they perceived as a purely "woman's holiday." Male antipathy tended to be stronger in the countryside than in large cities, where fewer men expressed qualms about joining in Women's Day celebrations. In rural areas, landlords would not allow female laborers to visit the celebrations held at the local *izby* (peasant reading huts).[23] Given the incendiary messages contained in Woman's Day propaganda, the emphasis on women's civic and legal rights, the criticism of clerical abuse and marital subordination of women, and the affirmation of the individuality and self-worth of women as equal citizens, the male response was perhaps not that surprising.

A cartoon published in 1923 captures both the revolutionary import of the holiday and the confusion it created in the minds of its recipients. The cartoon pictures a Zhenotdel worker on the porch of a peasant hut, arms outstretched, haranguing a crowd. On the ground in front of her stands a group of peasant women waving red flags. The cartoon also depicts four male peasants with long beards and homemade shoes looking extremely puzzled. The energetic and active mien of the women in the cartoon is in sharp contrast to the men's stereotypical expressions of peasant passivity.[24]

"Babii den'," a short story published for Women's Day, offers certain reasons for this male hostility. The story contains sketches of irate peasant husbands coming home from the fields, expecting dinner, only to find the stove cold and their wives gone. When the peasants realize their wives have gone to celebrate "their women's holiday," they arm themselves with sticks and spades to bring back their errant partners.[25] This violent reaction to Women's Day was not restricted to the realm of literature. As late as 1927 a secret communiqué from the Information Department of the Central Committee of the Party (Inotdel) reported that Communist Youth League

(Komsomol) cells in Moscow, Pskov, Nizhnii Novgorod, and Uzbekistan refused to take preparatory work for Women's Day seriously and in many cases actually disrupted the proceedings. In Zenin', a village situated in the Moscow district, members of the Komsomol refused to provide an orchestra for what they called derogatively a "babii prazdnik" (woman's holiday), and it was only due to the efforts of the women's organizer that the evening was not entirely ruined.[26] Although the report did not specifically detail the acts the young men employed, one imagines that they were variations of the hooliganism that was endemic in worker's clubs during the 1920s.[27]

In Central Asia Women's Day tended to elicit more emotional and violent reactions than in other republics. Zhenotdel attempts to "free" women were seen as attempts to degrade the local culture and challenge the prevailing religious consensus on the position of women in family and society.[28] Here, Women's Day became truly revolutionary propaganda that challenged the reigning patriarchal and feudal order.[29] Women were encouraged to fight restrictions placed on their individual liberty by the Islamic *Sharia'* laws. They were exhorted to join schools, work artels, women's clubs, soviets, and party organizations. The heavy horsehair veil *(parandja)* that enveloped the Muslim woman from head to toe became a focal point of the power struggle between the Bolsheviks and the native clergy. The Bolsheviks, with their flair for selecting emotive symbols, denoted the lifting of the veil, the most visible symbol of women's seclusion in the private sphere, as synonymous with the liberation of women.

In huge public demonstrations, especially in Tashkent and Samarkand, Zhenotdel workers organized mass rallies on Women's Day at which Muslim women dramatically divested themselves of their veils and threw them into a bonfire.[30] The results were shocking and unexpected: often, women on the way home after these iconoclastic acts were either unceremoniously bundled up in shawls by outraged male relatives or in some cases killed and mutilated for dishonoring the family name.[31] Sometimes women also used the holiday to publicly disavow family relationships and affirm the ties of socialist patriarchy that bound the state and conscious female citizens. In one recorded instance in 1925, a Muslim woman named Gasikhanova, resident of a village in Uzbekistan, publicized the sins of her errant husband at a Women's Day meeting. She suddenly appeared at the holiday ceremony and, taking a sign symbolizing the *smychka* (union of workers and peasants) from one of the bearers on the stage, she began to address the audience. However, she was too upset to speak and broke down completely in front of the assembly. It soon transpired that Gasikhanova was the wife of a party official who had abandoned her when she was sick and pregnant. Seeing him at the Women's Day meeting she wanted to tell him that, despite his vile behavior, Uzbek women like her were fighting for their rights and liberation. Her husband took one look at her and promptly left the building.[32]

By choosing to broadcast her husband's sins at a political gathering, Gasikhanova converted a hitherto private matter into an issue of public concern. That was precisely what Women's Day aimed at—erasing the boundaries that divided civil society from the sacrosanct family structure and facilitating the entry of women into the public sphere. In a similar story, a peasant woman, in her address to a conference of delegates held on Women's Day 1925 in Ivanovo-Voznesensk, reported that her husband was so incensed when she proposed to go to the conference that he began to hit her. But throughout the beating she averted her face so her bruises would not be visible when she attended the meeting.[33] While Soviet sources tended to dramatize Women's Day celebrations as sites of resistance to patriarchy—where the new ideology of female emancipation functioned as a weapon in the hands of the weak—the larger significance of the holiday lay in the discourse, where traumatic change and survival were integral parts of the Soviet female experience. In both stories the protagonists weathered the ordeal of abandonment and assault in order to incorporate their stories, and by extension themselves, into the revolutionary chronology.

The day was replete with layers of significance for those opposing it and for those espousing it. Women's Day was more than an event marking the consolidation of female support for the Soviet regime; for the women themselves, it offered a chance for self-expression and often a brief moment in the limelight. With the passage of time the popularity of the holiday increased, and this was especially true in the countryside where amusements were few and the novelty of plays and music drew crowds from afar. Women in Pskov, Stalingrad, Sverdlovsk, and other provinces walked many miles in cold weather to attend their local Women's Day celebrations.[34] Jessica Smith, an American visitor, described a Women's Day meeting in a small village, Arkhangelskoye:

> On March 8th, Women's Day, they (women) came from all over the *rayon* (district). The meeting was scheduled for noon, but all day long the women kept arriving, some on foot, some with horses, some as far as forty *versts* away. It was six o'clock before the meeting opened, and the women waited patiently all day. At night the hall was jammed, with several hundred women standing in the street outside. Each village had its spokesman to greet the conference, to tell of the work the women in her village had done during the last year: how they had worked in the cooperatives, in the soviets; how many had learned to read and write; what they had planned for next year. Some of them spoke well, in clear, ringing voices; many spoke stumblingly, and had to be prompted, and one broke down before she finished, and rushed weeping from the platform. But it was a miracle to see this happening, to see the eyes of these hundreds of women in the dimly lighted hall, realizing for the first time that life held something for them beyond the dull routine of the past.[35]

According to Soviet observers, from 1927 onwards it was clearly discernible that Women's Day was beginning to find a niche in the popular festive consciousness.[36] Ella Winter, another American traveling in the Soviet Union during the first Five-Year Plan, asked a young Komsomol woman to list the holidays she celebrated. She replied, "the Seventh of November, the First of May, the Eighth of March—Woman's Day—days that have real meaning."[37] State officials believed that the growing male participation in the holiday was a true indication of its increasing acceptance among the people. In fact, in almost all reports on Women's Day, the authors commented approvingly that the number of men present at events seemed to rise with every passing year.[38] By accepting the regime's admittedly strange notions on gender relations, the Soviet populace was signifying acceptance of the regime itself.

During the holiday, women dressed in their best clothes, cleaned their living quarters, and prepared special dinners. As the decade of the twenties progressed, it became more common for factories, trade unions, workers' clubs, and peasant reading huts to arrange parties, dances, choral singing, amateur theatricals or film shows, and family evenings in addition to the obligatory meeting. The age-old rituals associated with traditional Russian holidays were subtly transferred to the new civic ceremonies. In fact, a caption in the Soviet journal *Ogonëk* referred to Women's Day as *maslenitsa po-sovetskim*, or the Soviet Shrovetide. Instead of going home, women workers in Moscow who were freed early that day collected in factory courtyards and danced and sang to the accordion while their male co-workers continued to labor at their machines.[39]

### Propaganda Content of Women's Day

Women's Day was a day of reviewing the ranks of female fighters in the Soviet state, to use a military metaphor that was dear to the Bolsheviks. It was also a day in which the Soviet government advertised to its own population, and to communists abroad, the paternal care that the state lavished on its women. Soviet legislation on women's rights to property, divorce, political participation, and abortion was highlighted in publications, wall newspapers, slogans, and editorials. Ministries, trade unions, factories, and agricultural cooperatives coordinated the opening of day-care centers, dining halls, and laundries with Women's Day.[40] Through these acts, the Soviet state publicly affirmed its obligations to Soviet women while simultaneously garnering free publicity for its self-proclaimed paternalism.

While the party advocated that Women's Day be used as a review of what the state had done for women in the past years, Zhenotdel, through their publications and the journal *Kommunistka*, chose Women's Day to advertise the private concerns, fears, and problems of women's existence. While the party emphasized Women's Day slogans that rallied women around national concerns, Zhenotdel underlined the various ways that party and state organs could improve the lives of Soviet women. Kollontai criticized the fact that many male communists believed that the party's only responsibility toward women was to raise their political consciousness and draw them into party work. However, Kollontai said, women had special needs as mothers and caregivers that the party had the obligation to address. She warned that the depredations of war and the resulting inflation, unemployment, and hunger had exacted such a toll on the female population that they were in urgent need of state help before they became able fighters in the proletarian army.[41]

In Women's Day brochures, compiled especially for agitators, and also in the pages of *Kommunistka*, members of Zhenotdel toed a polemical line. On the one hand they endorsed the achievements of the Soviet state in relation to the "woman question," and, on the other, they repeatedly drew attention to the economic plight of women and the various social handicaps they suffered from, especially single women and widows in the countryside. They highlighted the deficiencies in work among women, the intransigence of state organizations in creating institutions that would liberate women from domesticity, the lack of any real attempts to deal with female unemployment, and the trade unions' indifference to the plight of women workers in the workplace.[42]

However, the party easily won the conflict with Zhenotdel, and the bulk of the slogans adopted on Women's Day in the 1920s focused on the reconstruction of the economy, recruitment of women to Soviet institutions, and fulfillment of party mandates. The obligations of women to the state and society were far more important than their individual rights. Members of Zhenotdel, unlike western feminists, did not contradict the basic political premise that, as citizens, Soviet women's primary duty was to help in the creation of socialism. But they argued that the state should create conditions that would help women to fulfill their civic duties more effectively.

Women's Day propaganda, therefore, became a double-edged sword. While Zhenotdel used the holiday to reaffirm the obligations of the party to Soviet women, the party used it to motivate female activism for state-sponsored goals by attacking the stereotypes of femininity imposed by Russian culture. On this day, the press created and circulated peculiarly Soviet fictions of female destiny. Noted female Bolsheviks such as Krupskaia, Zetkin, Armand, and Samoilova, and other lesser-known Soviet heroines were commemorated and feted in the pages of the Soviet press.[43] Stories, articles, and plays about exemplary Soviet women stressed the virtues of political consciousness, self-sacrifice, and adherence to the party line. These women had abandoned their religious beliefs and shown exemplary capacity for hard work, whether on the farm or in the factory, and possessed the rare ability to solve problems by capitalizing on community initiative rather than government intervention.

In this instance, it was not the possession of political and legal rights that defined the woman as a citizen, but her enthusiastic participation in state-sponsored activities and the need to prove herself superior to the backwardness and weaknesses inherent in the membership of the female sex. This imposed an intolerable set of conditions and burdens for citizenship, and the ideals of Soviet womanhood lay far beyond the reach of ordinary women. But the symbolic fleshing of the New Soviet Woman as an ideal that could be realized by every woman was intimately connected with the mythology of Women's Day as a day of regeneration and new beginnings. This emphasis on political rebirth is exemplified in a letter from a peasant woman in the Caucasus who, having participated for the first time in a Woman's Day celebration in 1925, wrote: "Today for the first time I understand the significance of March 8th for oppressed women and understand why workers fought so long for our liberation."[44] In Soviet propaganda, Women's Day was scripted as the dawn of the awakening political consciousness of women. Political acuity in this instance lay not so much in the mastery of a canon of Marxist ideas or writings, as in the acceptance of the October Revolution as the only possible solution to female oppression and subordination.

Women's Day was used to signify a new beginning and liberation in more than one way. Liberation meant not only lifting the yoke of capitalism, male tyranny, and domestic servitude, but actual physical freedom. Often in a grandiose gesture, groups of women prisoners were ceremoniously freed and their sentences commuted on the holiday.[45] One of these liberation moments, from the Novyi Spasskyi Ispravdom in 1924, was captured on film and shown around the country as one of the highlights of Women's Day. Although the nature of these women's crimes was never explained, the publicity surrounding the liberation strengthened the Soviet regime's claims of being the champion of women's rights. In an almost parallel ceremony, prostitutes were rescued from their ignominious trade, admitted into halfway houses, and given some vocational training that would enable them to engage in "honest labor."[46]

**Lenin and the Woman Question**

The image of women being rescued by the Soviet state found its ultimate expression in the symbolism that surrounded Lenin and his relation to the "woman question." On March 8, 1924, a festive meeting was held at the House of Soviets in Moscow. In the film of the actual event, we see that the audience was large and comprised of blue-collar workers and professionals. Stalin addressed the meeting, as did Krupskaia. After the meeting, a group of women workers carrying flowers and the occasional banner with the inscriptions "we promise to fulfill the precepts of Lenin," marched to the Lenin mausoleum. On that cold March morning, amid piles of freshly fallen snow, the women waited patiently in a long line with their children to enter the tomb.[47] The camera lingers on the juxtaposition of the snow and the slow progression of the women toward the hallowed tomb in order to re-create the traditional image of the fallen warrior surrounded by female mourners.

The imaging of Lenin in relation to women has been mainly ignored in studies on the Lenin cult. The multiple personalities that were associated with the leader soon after his death shifted uneasily between the polarities of unchanging and constant virtue and a dearly beloved man of the people. His virtue lay in the fact that he was always right, always knew the correct path to take, and unhesitatingly adopted the most appropriate policies. This peculiar conflation of rectitude and virtue was symptomatic of Bolshevik propaganda and self-imaging in general and was especially visible in both the Lenin and the Stalin cult. Lenin's choices were always vindicated by posterity. One would think that this power of prediction might co-exist uneasily with the Bolshevik belief in science and induction, but it was precisely Lenin's ability to unerringly divine the workings of scientific socialism that raised him to the status of leader of the party, of the masses, and of labor movements around the world.

Lenin's seeming monopoly on knowledge and his ability to correctly explain the conditions of reality extended to Lenin's interpretation of the "woman question." Alone among all the revolutionaries and all revolutionary parties, Lenin, following Marx, problematized the "woman question" and, having analyzed it, provided the only possible solution. His concern for the backward status of women prompted him to ask Krupskaia, then sharing his exile in Siberia, to draft a brochure on the subject. He provided the inspiration for the first celebrations of Women's Day in tsarist Russia, and his keen sensitivity to gender-specific propaganda resulted in the publication of *Rabotnitsa*. Due mainly to Lenin's unceasing concern for women, that most backward cohort, the Soviet government, passed laws that were the most far-reaching steps toward women's liberation undertaken by any state in the world.[48]

Although in reality Lenin was only marginally interested in women's issues and was one of the more vocal proponents of the view that women and their concerns should be incorporated into the general proletarian movement, Bolshevik women and members of the Zhenotdel were relentless promoters of the myth of Lenin as the champion of women. The Lenin cult was not monolithic and was used differently by the party and Zhenotdel, each promoting its own agenda. As Nina Tumarkin has shown, the Lenin myth was manipulated by the party to garner popular support for the Bolshevik cause among the people of the Soviet Union.[49] Therefore, Lenin's advocacy of women's issues was simply another facet of his benevolent public image that the party sought to disseminate. But it was clear that Zhenotdel had a different purpose in mind when they used the Lenin symbol in conjunction with their agenda for women.

Following Lenin's death in 1924, and until the onset of the first Five-Year Plan, Lenin became a focal point of Women's Day propaganda. Short, dramatized sketches of incidents from Lenin's life were performed at Women's Day meetings, and the women's press was flooded with articles about Lenin.[50] Women's Day brochures circulated by the Zhenotdel to workers' clubs and peasant reading huts contained excerpts of Clara Zetkin's interview with Lenin on the "woman question" and included plays featuring Lenin as the main character and articles on Lenin's goals for the women's movement both within the nation and abroad.[51] Though part of this female-specific material was a response to the propaganda hysteria sweeping the nation following his death, it would appear that the Zhenotdel, by establishing a close connection between their agenda and Lenin's pronouncements on women's issues, was seeking legitimacy for their program in both official and popular eyes. Lenin's saying that every cook must learn to govern the nation was used by Zhenotdel to prove that Lenin advocated not only education of women, but also their active involvement in the affairs of state. Lenin's bitter and savage imprecations against domestic work, which turned women into slavish beings, were linked directly to the Zhenotdel's advocacy of the establishment of state-run establishments to relieve working women of domestic chores. Finally, Lenin's belief that without the participation of women, neither a truly proletarian revolution nor a socialist construction would ever be possible was used covertly as an indictment of the Soviet regime's ruthless disregard of economic and social exploitation of women during the 1920s.

In an article published in the *Kommunistka* in 1925, Rakhil Kovnator, a member of the Zhenotdel, stressed repeatedly that Lenin's public pronouncements on the liberation of women were not merely nice-sounding words but an expression of his genuine commitment to the inclusion of women in the socialist sphere. In another article, S. Smidovich wrote rather pointedly that at the Thirteenth Party Congress there was not a single report on the work among women workers and women peasants. She also pointed to the deplorable state of affairs within the Komsomol organizations and the lack of serious attempts to attract young women to their ranks, noting, "didn't Lenin tell us, 'erasing every single trace of the ignoble laws that perpetuated the inequality of women, we pay very little attention to the practicalities of the real liberation of women'." In the conclusion she affirms, "Active work by the Party for the real liberation of women workers and women peasants—this would be fulfilling one of the tasks entrusted to us by Il'ich."[52]

The manipulation of Lenin's legacy was blatant in both examples. *Kommunistka* articles from the 1920s reveal numerous examples of the use of Lenin's legacy to indict the party's lackadaisical approach to the more pressing concerns of Soviet women. Vera Lebedeva, head of OMM, wrote a short piece in which she stressed the fact that even during the height of the civil war, when the very existence of the Soviet Union was imperiled, Lenin found time to cut through the red tape that was making it difficult for her organization to function effectively. Lenin's purportedly keen interest and active involvement in women's affairs was in sharp contradiction to the constant complaints of the party that the lack of resources made it impossible to fulfill any of the demands of the Zhenotdel.[53] Kollontai publicly asserted that there were very few male comrades who supported work among women, except for Lenin and Sverdlov. The majority of party members cited other important matters in order to downgrade work among women.[54]

At the other end of the spectrum, rank-and-file women workers in the Soviet Union used their attachment to the person and the public memory of Lenin to demonstrate their loyalty to the Bolsheviks. During this period it was common for working women and lower-level female party activists to send letters to the press detailing their chance meetings with Lenin in anecdotal form, or retelling stories of their intellectual and political transformation following their exposure to Lenin's thoughts. A strange mixture of self-promotion and hyperbolic praise of the fallen leader dominates the narrative style of these pieces. The themes of a secular resurrection of Lenin and the redemption of women through their connection with Lenin and his philosophy is also amplified. The following stanza, written by Taisa Ulianova, a female spinner, illustrates this point:

> Nobody will forget you, neither this
> Generation, nor the next.
> Your name will be eulogized in song.
> You have died, but only your body has perished,
> Your soul will live amongst us.
> And the fruits of our labors will proudly prove,
> That you can never die.[55]

At the fourth provincial meeting of delegates in Vladimir in 1924, sixty-one women joined the party and announced, without exhibiting the least trace of self-consciousness about the irony of their declaration, that henceforth they were going to be free of all prejudice, all attachment to religion, and spend the rest of their lives fulfilling the precepts of Lenin.[56] In their efforts to construct the Lenin cult, the Bolsheviks borrowed freely from religious imagery and form. Hence, in the Bolshevik myth of redemption, heightened receptivity to Bolshevik philosophy formed a parallel experience to the intense spiritual awareness of new converts. Women who had read the gospel according to Lenin could never go back to their old existence of ignorance and darkness. Often a physical meeting with Lenin formed the crucial moment of conversion to Bolshevism and, thereafter, women's lives were suffused by a commitment to a vision that transcended the limited frontiers of their daily lives. P. Kosareva, a factory worker from Naro-Fominska, recalled that although during her meeting with Lenin she was unaware of his identity, it had a great spiritual effect on her. Later, when she realized that she had actually met Lenin, she was filled with shame at not being a party member. She joined the party immediately and was an active and conscious worker thereafter.[57]

### Women's Day and Internationalism

The very nomenclature of International Women's Day connoted a global awareness of women's issues and militated against alleged female provincialism and narrow preoccupation with domestic affairs. Journals, newspapers, and brochures commemorating Women's Day carried reports on the conditions of women in different parts of the world. Zhenotdel, in instructions to local organizations, stressed that the international significance of Women's Day should be emphasized and amplified at holiday meetings.[58] True to their version of internationalism, in the 1920s there was an attempt to harness communist women's movements around the world to the Soviet exemplar.[59] As in the Soviet Union, Women's Day abroad was constructed not as a mere festive occasion but as a review of female proletarian activism on the political front. Articles in the Soviet press commented approvingly that each year Women's Day served as a political marker for the growing involvement of women in the labor struggle and charted the course of the movement of women from the ranks of spectators to fighters.[60]

On International Women's Day, the Zhenotdel, the Comintern, and the MZHK sent detailed instructions to the women's sections of the Communist parties of Western Europe on how to use the holiday to attract women.[61] In some sense, by establishing the rules and regulations for the celebrations of International Women's Day, the Soviets were using the holiday to further their control over the international communist movement. The slogans adopted for the holiday by the Comintern emphasized solidarity between the Soviet Union and international communist parties. Soviet publications advertised the Soviet path to women's liberation through government intervention and the creation of social and communal institutions.[62] Despite the fact that organizers, such as Clara Zetkin, Liudmilla Stal', Aleksandra Kollontai, and others had spent considerable periods of time in different regions of Western Europe, there was little attempt to analyze the forms of women's movements in various Western European countries against the backdrop of native conditions and cultures.[63] Since delegate meetings of women workers were popular in the Soviet Union during the 1920s, the same method was tried in Germany despite the objections of German women organizers. Communist parties around the world were instructed to use Soviet propaganda strategies to mobilize women.[64]

As in the Soviet Union, women in Western Europe were portrayed as a politically backward constituency. But there was one crucial difference in the European scenario. As the Bolsheviks were forced to compete for women's allegiance with other socialist parties in Europe, they were quick to point to the alleged indifference of the Social Democrats to the "woman question" and contrast it with the communist care and concern for female members.[65] For those reading the propaganda it was apparent that the Soviets were less interested in elucidating the problems of their female constituency abroad and instead used the pages of the women's press to fight their battles with the Social Democrats. Accordingly, the Social Democrats, not the French police, became caught up in the war hysteria of 1913–14 and banned the celebration of International Women's Day in France, urging all socialists to concentrate on the narrow nationalist struggles against the Germans.[66] Only after the French Communist Party broke with the Social Democrats at the conference in Tours did the former actively start work among women workers.[67] In Germany, too, according to the Soviet press, the Social Democrats proved to be completely indifferent to the plight of working women. Although they posed as a party for the working class, rather than espousing any revolutionary sentiments they merely expected monetary dues and unquestioning obedience from the party rank-and-file. In the opinion of the Soviets, this inculcated in the German proletariat a spirit of passivity that was further magnified among naturally docile women workers.[68] Along with their sentiments of national chauvinism and refusal to take a stand against the First World War, indifference to the "woman question" and failure to address the needs of women workers were listed as cardinal sins of the Social Democrats in other parts of Europe.[69]

The anti–Social Democratic propaganda was for the consumption of the politically literate, those who were aware of the difference between Soviet socialism and social democracy. At home the images of the West formed one of the more enduring strands of Women's Day propaganda in the 1920s. In his article on the Soviet press at that time, Jeffrey Brooks refers to the obsession with America that was omnipresent in the Soviet press and presents a fine analysis of the complex imaging of America in both laudatory and derogatory terms.[70] If Soviet identity was constructed within and against the perceptions of what constituted America, the relationship with Europe was less ambiguous. Unlike the technical and industrial might of the United States, postwar Europe did not invoke the same resentment and awe. First, Russians were more familiar with Europe, and this familiarity bred certain contempt. Second, by anticipating the laws of historical materialism it appeared that the Soviet Union had assuaged its traditional feelings of inferiority vis-à-vis Europe. In the nineteenth century Russia could only vaunt its moral superiority against Western European bourgeois decadence; in the 1920s the Soviets could legitimately point to the October Revolution and the socialist government as models of development for war-torn Europe to follow.[71]

In articles about women in Europe, Zhenotdel propagandists sketched ghastly pictures of oppression and repression. Stories of rampant unemployment, long working hours, unsafe working conditions in factories, prohibitive costs of living, wretched living quarters, and oppressive laws formed the staple of reportage about the West.[72] Seldom acknowledging that many of these conditions were to be found in the Soviet Union itself, the articles instead stressed the benevolent policies that the Soviet government had instituted for its women. Concern for women became a crucial feature of distinguishing the Soviet self and the European other. Whereas the Soviet government had passed humane laws that guaranteed women paid leave for childbirth, health insurance, guaranteed employment, and access to abortions, in the West exercising a malignant control over the proletarian female body seemed one of the chief preoccupations of the bourgeoisie.[73] Restrictive divorce and abortion laws formed the backbone of the bourgeois legal edifice that served to keep women under control in the West.

*Rabotnitsa* carried the story of an Englishwoman, Edith Thompson, who unwittingly became an accessory to murder because of British laws that forbade women from obtaining a divorce. According to the story, Edith Thompson fell in love with Fred Baywaters. Her husband, however, refused to grant her a divorce. When Baywaters came to persuade him, Thompson attacked him with a gun. In the ensuing melee, Thompson was killed. An English jury condemned the pair to death by hanging. The writer concluded the piece thus, "to us, in Soviet Russia, this situation seems extremely strange. In England, it is very understandable to English gentlemen, who uphold the existing state order with all their strength. One of the main planks of this social order is the 'highly-moral' family with the subordinate status of the wife, and all those challenging these foundations, in their opinion, deserve to die."[74]

Conditions were scarcely better across the English Channel. According to Liudmila Stal', pregnant workers in French factories were forced to stand at their machines almost until the moment of giving birth. And despite the fact that they came back almost immediately to work, there was no guarantee that their jobs would be waiting for them. Due to this inhumane treatment of mothers, child mortality was extremely high in France. To offset falling birth rates, the French bourgeoisie, instead of providing pre- and postnatal care, passed stringent laws punishing women who tried to terminate their pregnancies. Stal' concludes: "only a socialist revolution, only communism will give the French women-workers humane conditions of existence."[75]

In Soviet propaganda, the tired body of the unemployed female worker was used to symbolize the helplessness of the Western proletariat while the privileged legal status of Soviet women was used to validate the October Revolution and the Soviet experiment. The 1926 Women's Day issue of *Krest'ianka* carried a stark picture of a woman with a gray, prematurely aged face. Her hair was bundled in a scarf, and she was clad in a drab cloak. She sat in a dark room furnished with shabby remnants of furniture. The empty pots at her feet symbolized her hunger. The inscription under the picture read, "This is how our foreign sisters live."[76]

If Western European women stood in urgent need of help from their Soviet sisters, women in the East, especially in colonized countries, were even more deserving of Soviet tutelage. A circular to the Eastern department of the International Women's Secretariat explained, "that whereas in the West where the traditional spirit of reformism undermined the Soviet attempts to Bolshevize the communist parties, the liberation of women in the east proceeded entirely under the aegis of the October Revolution and Bolshevism."[77] Although the articles on this subject described the inhumane work conditions in factories in India, Japan, Egypt, and China, the authors emphasized the growing activism of Eastern women and their involvement in political struggles.[78] Whether this was supposed to serve as a lesson to Soviet women at home is difficult to ascertain. But although female involvement in anticolonial struggles was praised, Soviet propagandists were quick to point out that the nationalist movements were only the first steps in the path to communism. In comparison to the blanket assessments of the labor movement in the West, however, there was an attempt to explain the cultural and social conditions that prevailed in the colonized world which, together with capitalism, served to perpetuate the subordinate status of women. For example, in articles on India, the authors explained the workings of the caste system that fragmented society and created a permanent underclass of social pariahs. Here, the Communists had not only to fight against English capitalists but against a deeply entrenched feudal social order that incarcerated women in separate quarters.[79]

But for the most part images of foreign women were essentially static and were used in part to represent the entirety of capitalist exploitation and oppression. Even their activism in the labor movement seemed more staged than authentic, and unlike the New Soviet Woman, who was endlessly innovative and resourceful, women abroad appeared trapped in the conditions of their material circumstances. If foreign women appeared time-bound and immediately recognizable through their historical specificity (that is, location in the capitalist mode of production), Soviet women were constantly confronting the specter of altered circumstances. During the 1920s, the public persona of the New Soviet Woman was a mutable image that was fluid enough to accommodate various levels of liberation within its parameters.

The next chapter analyzes a selection of Women's Day plays performed in the 1920s. In these productions, Soviet women were forced to cope with the new and revolutionary ideas about love, marriage, sex, work, and family relationships. While the plays lack artistic and literary merit, they offer a vantage from which we can view the Bolshevik constructions of social reality and the changing situation of Soviet women within it.

four

# Popular Theater and Women Onstage

Due primarily to the economic poverty of the New Economic Policy (NEP) era, women's needs occupied a subordinate position in the list of national priorities.[1] Despite the widespread feminization of poverty and the desperate conditions of most Soviet women in the 1920s, concern for women was manifested primarily by the deployment of visual, dramatic, and oral propaganda. During March, especially the weeks preceding Women's Day, themes that were perceived as women's issues took on an immediacy in the press, party circles, trade unions, Zhenotdel, workers' clubs, and educational institutions. Statistics were published and reports were commissioned on the status of women in society. Questions regarding women's enrollment in schools, representation in political and administrative organizations, participation in the workforce, and the creation of a communal lifestyle were hotly discussed and debated.

Bolshevik leaders published articles to underline their political commitment to women's liberation, and the Zhenotdel cells convened political meetings across the nation to commemorate the contribution of women to the revolution. At the local level, the festive elements of this otherwise serious and edifying holiday were expressed in demonstrations and meetings. Workers' clubs and peasant reading rooms staged theatrical shows and organized matinees for children. Pioneer detachments marched and feted the Soviet mothers in song and verse. Local orchestras organized communal singing and choral presentations, and party workers in the city and countryside were firmly instructed to attract entire families to participate in Women's Day parties and social gatherings.

In a world turned upside down, Women's Day functioned as a referential point, legitimizing the revolution and explaining abstract ideas about the emancipation of women through the use of festive ritual. But while Women's Day sought to rally women to the Bolshevik cause, the redefinition of female roles and the category of gender were innately destabilizing as they challenged the traditional sources of social authority. The messages contained in Women's Day propaganda exhorted Soviet women to exorcise their internalized subjugation and dependence. For a brief moment, women were empowered to challenge the power and authority of men, mothers-in-law, and priests, and question the traditional notions regarding the appropriate social status of women. They were also asked to reexamine their functions within the family and the community.

Propaganda on Women's Day was disseminated in various forms: through public speeches, press articles, graphic arts, commemorative poetry and prose, and the theater. In this chapter, I will present a textual analysis of a number of propaganda plays that I discovered in the Lenin Library in Moscow. The plays were published in Women's Day commemorative brochures and circulated by the Chief Committee for Political Enlightenment (Glavpolitprosvet) and the Zhenotdel during the 1920s.[2] With few exceptions, the authors were relatively unknown in theatrical history, and some of the plays were published without the name of the author. The simple prose and uncomplicated stage directions made enacting these plays simple for amateur drama circles in workers' clubs and peasant reading rooms. The format varies from conventional three-act dramas to *zhivoi gazety* (living newspapers), *intsenirovki* (spot dramatizations), and *agitsudy* (theatrical mock trials). Some of these were actually a part of the Proletkult drama circles' and the *Sinnaia bluza*'s (Blue Blouse) repertoires.[3] The use of colloquial speech, the deliberate attempts at rural humor, and the prevalence of folk drama characters in these texts were part of a larger effort to ground Bolshevik propaganda in popular culture. While theater critics criticized the plays for containing little artistic merit both in terms of plot and dramatic execution, they nonetheless continued to be performed throughout the period.[4]

The 1920s were an exciting chapter in Soviet dramatic history. Under the benign cultural policies of this period, theater as an art form flourished in the cultural centers of Moscow, Leningrad, and other provincial capitals.

But amid the myriad experimentation with form, text, and performance, very few plays feature a woman as protagonist or deal with the experiences of women in any meaningful fashion. The well-known exceptions to this general rule are the plays *Mar'yana* by Aleksandr Serafimovich, *Liubov Yarovaya* by Trenev, and *Vireneya* by Lydia Seifullina.[5] Although criticized after their initial productions, these plays subsequently found their niche in the Soviet canon of politically acceptable drama. *Liubov Yarovaya* was regularly produced during the 1930s, and even Stalin reportedly saw a production of it. *Vireneya* appeared on recommended reading lists published for Women's Day in the 1920s and 1930s and parts of it were often performed at holiday festivities.[6]

These texts from the professional stage were set in the civil war period and featured strong, independent women who recognized the innate rightness of the Bolshevik cause in the titanic struggle between good and evil. In all three plays, the heroine's sense of loyalty to the traditional order is subverted and her sense of self is reconceptualized in terms of her loyalty to the new Bolshevik regime. She realizes that it is impossible to find emotional satisfaction with a class enemy. The spectator is left with the sense of a mythic post–civil war society in which women's political allegiances will automatically determine their status and the parameters of their freedom.

*Liubov Yarovaya* is a particularly good example of how the revolution could invade the innermost sanctum of private thought and imprint a harsh sociological template on desire and longing.[7] In the play, Liubov is a devastated widow who is caught in the middle of a civil war engagement. Despite losing her beloved husband and comrade-in-arms, Mikhail, she continues as a schoolteacher and an energetic though nonparty supporter of the Bolsheviks. She regrets that in the past she lacked the revolutionary ardor of her husband and had entreated him to forsake his activism. But when he reappears as an officer in the White Army, she is aghast at his political choice. Although he tries to win her over to his side by asserting his moral authority as the purveyor of truth, Liubov has matured considerably in his absence. She refuses to accept him in either of his patriarchal roles as husband or intellectual mentor. When Mikhail's side is defeated, rather than allowing him to escape, she takes on the role of a pitiless and incorruptible informer and denounces him to the Red authorities.

Perhaps the most extreme explication of the theme of political loyalty versus private desire is found in the short story *The Forty First* by Boris Lavreynov, where the rough and ungainly proletarian heroine, Maryutka, executes her aristocratic lover rather than surrender him to the White forces.[8] But unlike Liubov, who displays neither compunction nor regret at her deed, Maryutka is a poet at heart. Although her attempts at poetry are as crude as her lovemaking, at the end she is overcome with horror at her actions. Perhaps Lavreynov wished to emphasize the moral obloquy that invariably accompanies the death of desire.

The Women's Day plays in the 1920s, by contrast, were set in less heroic times. Deemphasizing the mythic future, these texts instead addressed the tensions inherent in redefining the female persona. These propaganda pieces fell into the genre of works described as agitprop. Feminist dramaturgy of this period was an instructive enterprise, and amateur theater brought to women what Brecht was later to call "pleasurable learning."[9] The plays provided the spectators with an analysis of the political and economic conditions of the NEP era, and presented them with new ideological categories with which to interpret the conditions of their daily existence. On a more personal level, these plays explored the sources of emotional stress and familial/social oppression inherent in the lives of Russian women, and offered tentative solutions.

Although the plays are formulaic and crafted within the canon of Bolshevik thought on the "woman question," a close reading of the subtexts reveals that the authors took considerable interpretive liberties and created diverse dramatic situations. Topically, they incorporate both social/familial and political issues. In fact, the very categories of private and public spheres were conceptually redefined since the easy percolation of state-sponsored ideas violated the liberal notion of the sacrosanct private sphere. Within the texts, an attempt is made to relate Bolshevik ideology to the domestic concerns of Russian women and to show that in a socialist state there is no separation between private existence and political participation. Themes of love, violence, and betrayal are randomly interspersed with the depiction of rebellion and revolution, the battle of the sexes, class conflict, gender solidarity, and the creation of communal life. Far from focusing on one exclusive theme, each of the plays broach such a variety of issues that the resolutions are weak and incomplete. What gives cohesion to these otherwise polyphonic plays is the authors' concern with depicting the process of personalization of politics and the politicization of the private sphere in a socialist state.

**Reprising Popular Initiative**

International Women's Day in the Soviet Union was a sacralizing ritual that commemorated the incorporation of women into the body politic. Holiday propaganda was especially aimed at peasant women, domestic servants, older women, and housewives, a sizable constituency that rarely came into contact with the state. The very act of participation in the festivities marked the rite of passage from the sphere of unenlightened individualism into the socialized nucleus. Similarly, within the plays, the hero/heroine was led from the dark periphery of ignorance and deviance into the inner moral community. In terms of dramatic technique, the plays follow a path of linear development: identification of the main characters, presentation of the problem, unfolding of the plot, and finally the resolution. But more important is the appearance of what Helen Keyssar calls "the strategy of transformation, of the theatrical manifestation of metamorphosis of contexts, actions and most crucially of character."[10] The denouement consisted of the heroine's transformation of self through the exercise of will. While the state reserved the right to define the notions of individuality and freedom, the heroine achieved liberation, not through patriarchal intervention by the state, but by the realization of her self-worth as a human being, empowered to restructure affective relationships and her social surroundings. Within the texts, notions of woman as object contest with the novel idea of woman as agent. But women's agency could find expression only within an acceptable range of state-approved activities.

During this period an emphasis on voluntarism and grassroots activism to solve the most pressing problems of women's existence was a dominant propaganda theme.[11] Given the material poverty of the state in the 1920s and the lack of political strength in the countryside, the Bolsheviks had no alternative but to advocate solutions that lay within the grasp of the population. But this trend was an important modification of the Bolshevik position on the "woman question." Formerly, Bolsheviks such as Lenin, Kollontai, and Bukharin believed that Soviet women would be liberated only when the state had built communal institutions to perform domestic tasks and provide child care.[12] Due to economic constraints during the NEP era, political theorists were rethinking the role of the state in women's emancipation and stressing the popular, rather than the government, initiative.[13] Leaders of the party such as Lenin and Trotsky, and organizations like the trade unions, subscribed to a notion of popular participation in officially sponsored "women's issues."[14] But it is important to remember that the state set the agenda and controlled the debate on voluntarism. As Lenin said, due to the war and low industrial production, there were few communal facilities (such as crèches, laundries, and dining halls) to liberate women from domestic servitude, and therefore it was imperative that women should concern themselves with the creation of such institutions.[15] The NEP era plays were a part of this ideological revisionism and represented a decided emphasis on personal/communal acceptance of responsibility for the improvement of the status of women, but the discourse on popular female activism was carefully set within the larger parameters of party goals and policies.

### Cast of Characters

The question of identity and what defined the New Soviet Woman formed the central issue in every text surveyed. The plays rarely included physical descriptions of the main characters, and the heroines were generally imaged as an edition of the Soviet "everywoman." It is interesting to see that in the Bolshevik world, the "typical woman" was perceived primarily as a wife and/or mother living within a family. This situationing of women in familial networks was repeated in other sources of Bolshevik propaganda directed especially at women. There were few references to single women, divorced women, abandoned women, or unemployed women. Single women, without the protection of an extended family, rarely appeared, but when they did they were usually past middle age and therefore untroubled by emotional and sexual complications. In an effort to control the liberalism and sexual permissiveness of the 1920s, Soviet propaganda adopted a distinctly conservative moral tone toward sexuality. While it was permissible for a heroine to overthrow the authority of a husband, mother-in-law, or community in pursuit of a state-approved political goal, we rarely find the equivalent of Seifullina's sexually liberated heroine, Vireneya.[16]

In popular propaganda in the 1920s, a sexually liberated or predatory woman was usually equated with a prostitute. In the short skit *Zhena v dvukh vidakh* (Two faces of women), the author provides a rather Manichean vision of women's liberation.[17] Contrasting the deviance of two "unsatisfactory" wives, the skit presents a clear picture of only two alternatives open to women. In the first instance, a woman tries to exploit her body in order to exchange an oppressive spouse for a rich man. In the second instance, since the woman's indifference to housewifery stems from her pronounced political consciousness, the husband eventually accepts her shortcomings on the domestic front. Ultimately, the second wife, as a good Soviet heroine, manages to preserve both her public life and personal life.

The skit opens with a wife complaining that her husband never takes her anywhere, and that he only comes home for his meals. The husband says truculently that if she hangs out at theaters and clubs, who will do the housework? She asks him if he will love her more if she dresses well and uses makeup. But before he can answer, she rushes out and the husband is left onstage, angrily regretting the absence of a peaceful atmosphere at home. His friend, who is the recipient of these confidences, replies that his wife is even worse. She is always at the Zhenotdel cell and often refuses to cook dinner. Once she even had the audacity to hand him the needle and thread so he could darn his own clothes. Both men agree that they should have married women who were not only physically attractive but possessed of all the skills of a competent homemaker.

Meanwhile, the hitherto meek housewife has undergone a complete transformation and enters, drawling affectedly. She is fashionably dressed, complete with makeup, sheer stockings, and high heels. She starts flirting with her husband's friend and invites him to take her to a restaurant. When her husband protests, she subjects his manners, clothes, material poverty, and his extremely boring personality to scathing criticism. Both the husband and the friend are appalled at the metamorphosis. The latter feels thankful that, despite his wife's predilection for political activism, she is not a painted trollop. The skit ends with the wife waltzing off the stage with the expressed intention of finding herself a rich man. Although the skit ends without a clear resolution, it contains an obvious message for conservative husbands: politically active wives may be indifferent housewives, but they are preferable to exploitative, petty-bourgeois women.[18]

In another dramatic sketch, *Tseremonia*, an extremely violent attitude is exhibited toward an adulterous wife. Katerina, after being abused by her peasant husband for years, hears about the new rights of women and sexual equality. Emboldened by these ideas, she leaves him for another man, Nikolai. Emelian, the husband, goes to the village soviet to complain of his wife's adultery. The soviet administration, not knowing what to do, arrests the guilty pair and calls a village meeting. Although the chorus criticizes the conservatism of peasants like Emelian, the head of the village soviet declares that when women act like Katerina, they shame all. As he asks rhetorically, "Why did we suffer through the revolution and through struggles with different generals?" In the end, the members of the village, in a parody of prerevolutionary wedding ceremonies, douse the adulterous pair with buckets of cold water and whip them with willow branches.[19]

Although there is no evidence that Valentin Kataev was familiar with the skit *Zhena v dvukh vidakh*, his enormously popular play *Squaring the Circle*, written toward the end of the NEP, also dealt with the similar theme of ill-assorted couples struggling with the new revolutionary codes of romance and marital ethics.[20] The play features two heroines, one petty-bourgeois and materialistic, the other dedicated and idealistic. Tonya, the serious-minded Komsomolka who disdains feminine frivolities and is unversed in the arts of dalliance and domesticity, marries Abram, an amiable but shallow man. Ludmilla, common and cloying, is paired with the sincere and simple worker, Vasya. By the end of the play the four are realigned in a more appropriate pairing and Vasya realizes that though Tonya is incapable of making cutlets, they can share a more equal relationship that is based on intellectual and ethical affinity.

Since most of the plays deal with the transformative and liberating impact of the October Revolution on the status of Soviet women, they were usually constructed around the temporal antiphonies of the past and the present. This is in consonance with the general Bolshevik predilection of evaluating the achievements of the revolution in contrast to the unrelieved misery and oppression inherent in the tsarist social order. Similarly, the plays are divided into the opening sad scenes of women's lives set in prerevolutionary or preliberation days, and usually end with a vignette of a happier and markedly Soviet present. Scenes from the past prominently feature three stock villains—the husband or lover, the mother-in-law and assorted old women, and, less frequently, the village priest.[21]

References to the use of physical violence against women were a popular dramatic device used to represent the degraded status of women in the past. The woman as an object of violence is a recurring motif in the plays, and physical vulnerability of women was an important hallmark in the Bolshevik construction of gender. The repeated references to wife beating within the plays as a "normal" mode of interaction between husbands and wives underscored the physical oppression of women in traditional Russian society. In contrast to his prerevolutionary counterpart, the Soviet hero not only abstained from using violence toward women, he treated them with respect and courtesy.

By presenting detailed scenes of wife beating, the writers probably wanted to elicit a visceral reaction from the audience. For example, in a *zhivaia gazeta*, written for Women's Day, wife abuse is singled out as one of the more terrible relics of the prerevolutionary past. In this living newspaper, when a woman leaves the house to listen to the accordion player on the street, her husband beats her savagely for her absence.[22] In the rhymed skit entitled *Den' rabotnitsy* (Day of the woman worker), the husband repeatedly threatens to hit his wife whenever she complains of her unbearable workload.[23] In the *instsenirovka Prosnis' krest'ianka* (Awake, peasant woman), the husband tells his wife that he beats her to get rid of the devil, and for his "good work" in chastising her, he'll go straight to heaven.[24] To the women in the audience, the dramatic treatment of the issue explained that the abuse that they suffered was neither "natural" nor socially sanctioned in Soviet society, as it was in tsarist Russia. Since the male characters who beat their wives were often shown to be counter-revolutionary elements, violence against women was represented as an anti-Soviet act.

Despite the "naturally" misogynistic tendencies that men displayed in these propaganda pieces, occasionally they were capable of moral regeneration and transformation as well. Through the use of public shaming, political re-education, and legal intervention, it was shown that it was possible to change the attitudes of some men toward women. And once the transformation in male consciousness was successfully effected, there was little danger of a relapse into prerevolutionary attitudes and mentality. The play *Vos'moe marta* presents a typical example of the ease with which a traditional Russian male could be recreated to fit the mold of the "New Soviet Man." Scene 1 opens to a loud disagreement between Sazhin, a factory worker, and his wife, Motya. Sazhin refuses to allow his wife to attend a Women's Day meeting. Not only does he think a special holiday organized solely for women is pointless, he also refuses to countenance ideas about gender equality. As he asks rhetorically, if women leave home, is he, Sazhin going to wash the clothes?[25] Kisina, an organizer of local women, who is both a witness to and a vigorous participant in this verbal exchange, decides that Sazhin needs to be taught a lesson. She prints a cartoon in the factory wall newspaper that prominently features Sazhin as a Tatar Khan, holding his wife in thrall.

Initially, Sazhin is furious because everybody in the factory refers to him derisively as Chengiz Khan. The imaging of Sazhin as an Oriental despot implies that those who are against women's liberation are by definition premodern, Asiatic rather than Western, and tyrannical. The public ridicule, however, brings Sazhin to the realization that he is mistaken in his attitude toward women's liberation. In the last scene, at a Women's Day meeting, Sazhin declares, "We often forget that our women are workers like us. Often we treat them as if we still lived in the past. I am also guilty of this crime. . . . Away with the wife who is a slave to her husband, I greet a new wife: a comrade in arms!"[26]

The short piece *Priatali kontsy, popali v otsy* (Concealing the evidence, they became fathers), provides a solution to male deviance in a slightly different fashion.[27] In this instance, women can seek justice not merely from the community through ritual shaming of the offender, but via legal means. The play opens with a man refusing to marry a woman he has just seduced. She declares that she is pregnant, but he is unmoved and claims refuge in cant phrases about free love. As she threatens to take him to court, he convinces his friends to testify that all of them have slept with her. He gambles on evading responsibility for child support by casting aspersions on her virtue. However, the trick fails as the judge, according to the Family Code of 1926, orders each of the four perjurers to pay a quarter of the share of child support payments.[28]

Husbands and lovers were not the only villains; the plays point out trenchantly that all those who cling to mores and morals of the past are invariably advocates of wife abuse. In F. Ilinskii's skit, *Baby ne raby* (Women are not slaves), we find three old women bemoaning the contemporary corruption of youth, their atheism, and the propensity of modern women to contradict their husbands. The women wax nostalgic for the past when it was "customary" for men to beat their wives and for women to accept their punishment uncomplainingly.[29] Old women were invariably presented as a drag on the revolutionary consciousness of the proletariat and the peasantry. They were shown to be the preservers of a feudal culture and a religious consciousness. Old women were usually beyond redemption as they had internalized the social and physical subjugation of women as natural and moral. Mothers-in-law were portrayed as socially useless and therefore fit only for housework. They usually sided with the village priests and encouraged their sons to exploit and mistreat their wives.[30]

The use of old women as a dramatic device symbolizing the prerevolutionary past dates back to the early days of the revolution. In the play *Eulogy to the Revolution*, performed in Voronezh in 1918, evil destiny was embodied in the form of old women. Intermittently throughout the production, three old women appeared on the stage, warning the audience that the revolution would only bring misery and counseling them to passively accept their fate.[31] The famous poster by the Soviet satirist Mikhail Cheremnykh, *Istoriia pro bubliki i pro babu* (Story of the baba and the bagels), related the story of a fat old woman whose arms are loaded with bagels. When a Red army soldier, off to fight the Poles, asks for a bagel, she refuses. However, she is later eaten up, bagel and all, by the Poles.[32] Sara Lebedeva, in her poster entitled *Razrukha*, used the image of an old crone with bony arms and legs, withered breasts, and a malignant expression on her shriveled face to epitomize the economic devastation of the country.[33]

The play *Leninka* has a character Agafiia, who is referred to as the "bazaar radio."[34] Obviously a counter-revolutionary element, both Agafiia's material and social activities are inimical to the values and norms of Soviet society. To begin with, she runs a small tavern near the workers' dormitory and sells *samogon* (moonshine). Situated on the outer limits of the workers' living space, she is a threat to its existence as she is the recipient of a major portion of the workers' pay packet. Second, as an incurable and inaccurate gossip, she is a continuous source of misinformation. She prophesies the imminent collapse of the Soviet regime and warns that there are secret police informers everywhere. She also reports that the emperors of China and Japan have threatened Zinoviev with economic boycott unless he restores capitalism. Being illiterate, her news is always wrong, and in one memorable exchange Marina, the protagonist, bests her in a political argument. Marina is a literate and articulate woman worker and therefore reads Soviet papers and knows the "real" news. Marina informs Agafiia that there is no emperor in China, and by implication casts doubt on the veracity of all her news. Because of her access to Soviet institutions like the factory political circles and newspapers, Marina is better informed than Agafiia, who as the typical village woman can only mindlessly repeat bits and pieces of gossip picked up in the course of her unlawful activities. Agafiia's political backwardness is contrasted sharply with Marina's modernity.

Agafiia's sins of omission and commission extend even further. She is also active in retarding the activities of legitimate Soviet heroines. In this instance, she teams up with Martha, Marina's mother-in-law, in order to hinder her attendance at factory meetings. The two old women criticize Marina's indifference to household chores and the needs of her children. But the end of the *instsenirovka* effectively vanquishes the two old women. Marina, due to her political abilities, is nominated to the factory committee and becomes a highly effective organizer of women. The family regularly eats at the factory dining hall, and her children are taken care of at the pioneer clubs. Finally, Marina leads a campaign against Agafiia and destroys her illegal tavern. She means to replace it with a cooperative store that sells fresh food. Agafiia is unrepentant. She has neither seen the error of her ways, nor does she start life afresh. Instead, at the end of the play, we find her muttering imprecations against Marina for destroying her trade.

Very few of the plays dealt with the transformation in the consciousness of mothers-in-law or old women.[35] In Soviet propaganda, the future was shown to be mainly a preserve of the youth. The energies of young women needed to be liberated from the pointless preoccupation with domesticity, and rechanneled toward socialist construction and political activism. If old women served any function at all, they could take the heroine's place in the kitchen and the nursery.

**Three Soviet Heroines**

The various dramatic personae that Soviet heroines assume in the plays makes it difficult to categorize and identify common characteristics without obliterating the range of differences. Three plays, however, are representative of the three phases in the process of liberation. The plays *Babii' vyigrysh* (Women's victory), *Fenia Travina*, and *Blokha* (The flea) are all set in the countryside and feature a peasant woman as the main character. Indeed, in the majority of the plays, women are shown as the more progressive element in the countryside, and seem far more susceptible to Soviet propaganda than men. The first play deals with the awakening of consciousness, that is, the tentative realization by the heroine of her subordination and the renegotiation of relations with her husband and community. The second treats the enormous opposition that a woman faces within the family and from society when she becomes aware of her individuality and tries to play a public role. The last one signals the appearance of the "woman triumphant"; she has not only triumphed over social and customary restraints but wields political power to redefine the nature of political authority.

In A. Goriachhi's *Babii' vyigrysh*, we are introduced to two women, Fedora and Khavronia.[36] They are depicted as "typical" peasant women, illiterate, uninformed, subservient, with little control over their children and accountable to their husbands for everything. In act 1, scene 1, we find Mitrich, the husband of Khavronia, agonizing over his wife's supposed infidelity. He visits his friend Repkin, Fedora's husband, and suggests to him that they should jointly mount surveillance on their errant wives. Repkin is at first outraged and warns Mitrich about casting unfounded aspersions on his wife's character. But he is soon convinced and says, "if I find that she is up to no good, I'll kill her on the spot. I'll tear her to pieces with my own hands: I will not leave a single piece of living matter."[37] The two men pretend to go on a trip but actually conceal themselves in the hut in order to catch their wives in the act. The future augurs ill for the women, as Repkin hides in a wooden chest in the hut and Mitrich lies behind the stove.

Fedora is delighted that her husband is out for the day and invites her female friends over. The women of her village have been wanting to meet and discuss certain political issues but have been frustrated by the lack of neutral space and privacy. All the women are annoyed by the poor selection of goods at the local consumer cooperative and want to elect someone from among themselves to the board. At the same time, they are terrified at their presumption of daring to interfere in the male preserve of politics. Khavronia relates how she was afraid to openly question her husband Mitrich, and had to trick him into revealing the date for the local cooperative elections.[38]

Aware of their ignorance and unsure of the validity of their cause, the women invite Matrëna, a Zhenotdel worker, to advise them.[39] The women treat Matrëna as a social superior, much to her obvious discomfort. While the women are discussing the necessity of having a female representative on the board of the cooperative, Repkin erupts violently from the chest where he has been hiding. One of the women had inadvertently sat on the chest that concealed him and nearly suffocated him by cutting off his air supply. The symbolism is flagrant. In Repkin's perception, the liberation of women is a direct and threatening infringement on male power.

The women are terrified when Mitrich appears as well and try to flee, but Matrëna convinces them to stay and face the consequences. Repkin and Mitrich are relieved at the 'innocent' nature of the their wives' activities. As Matrëna prepares to leave, she says that she will discuss the matter of women's representation with the local party cell. Mitrich is appalled and says that it is inconceivable that a woman could run the cooperative. Simple and easy domestic chores are all that need concern women. His wife Khavronia, emboldened by Matrëna's presence, offers to do his work in the field if he will complete her 'simple housework' for a day. Mitrich, confident that Khavronia will fail, rashly promises to let her stand for elections if she completes his work satisfactorily.

The next scene is an essay on the hilarious consequences of gender reversal. The audience watches Mitrich floundering in the kitchen, overwhelmed by the rigors of domesticity. His children run amok, the cow steps on his hand, the bread burns in the oven, the pigs get loose, he upsets a bucket of water in the hut, and finally neighboring women come in and criticize his housewifery. As one woman says, if Mitrich's housekeeping is an example of male management, it is not surprising that the affairs of the cooperative are in such a mess. Repkin, meanwhile, has radically changed his views and tries to convince his friend of the justice of the women's claims. Mitrich finally admits defeat and agrees that women have a right to put up a candidate for election.

The battle of the sexes in a socialist society is not a private affair, and the change of women's status within the family is immediately reflected in the public sphere. Women's emancipation is not a personal odyssey for self-fulfillment. Khavronia realizes her subordination only when she tries to step out of her designated role as wife and mother. But her desire for personal emancipation is stimulated by a public cause. At the same time, there is an attempt to demystify the public/political sphere. The cooperative is not an abstract entity, nor is it an alien imposition administered by professional bureaucrats. It is a communal organization run by the village for the benefit of its members. Over and over again the plays hammer home the message that in a socialist society state institutions have a purely communal character and that the exercise of popular control is the best guarantee for their efficient functioning.

In Goriachii's play, while the women are exhorted to enter the male domain of politics, there is no implication that men will help in domestic duties. For the moment, Khavronia has successfully demonstrated her capabilities to her husband. Having gained his respect, she has earned the right for all the women in the village to sit in on political assemblies. The last scene foreshadows the process of *samokritika* (self-criticism).[40] Mitrich, at a Women's Day celebration, confesses amid raucous public laughter and jeering his misguided attempts to incarcerate his wife.[41] But he has seen the error of his ways and admits ruefully that ever since Khavronia was elected to the cooperative, the quality of goods has improved.[42] In this play, as in others of this genre, there is a tacit assumption that the emancipation of women depends to a large extent on the redefinition of masculinity.

Khavronia's freedom is ultimately contingent on the changes in her husband's attitude. The fate of the New Soviet Woman is organically linked to the appearance of the New Soviet Man.[43]

P. Yarovoi, in *Fenia Travina*, deals with problems that liberated and politically active women face when their husbands remain trapped in traditional ideas about family life and the status of women.[44] This play is an interesting Bolshevik parallel to Russian folk plays that often revolved around the theme of the cuckolded husband. Except in this case Semën, the protagonist, is mistaken when he accuses his wife Fenia of infidelity. Fenia, as chairman of the village soviet, has business dealings with men on the board of the local institutions. Semën ostensibly directs his anger and jealousy at Pavel, the chairman of the cooperative, and also Fenia's coworker, but there is a deeper reason for his malaise. Unable to accept the fact that Fenia occupies a position of public prestige, he is bewildered by the complete reversal of gender roles. He makes Pavel a target of his anger because it is easier to accuse his wife of sexual infidelity. Mistrust and jealousy are familiar emotions in Semën's psychological world. Calling Fenia a whore or a bitch denigrates her political authority by reducing her once more to a habitual object of violence and abuse. Like Mitrich in the earlier play, Semën believes that a woman who plays a role in the public/male sphere has lost her virtue and her very desire to do so betrays a lack of "womanliness." The entire village is deeply interested in this ménage à trois and feel that Fenia's supposed sexual degeneracy is symptomatic of the moral corruption of Bolshevik politics and institutions.

Fenia, embarrassed by his insults and hurt by his mistrust, finally decides to leave Semën. Before she leaves, she asks Semën whether he considers her a horse or a human being and adjures him to find a fool to sleep with and dominate. In the next scene, Fenia is at the soviet office with the secretary and Pavel, the chairman of the cooperative. We see that Fenia's political elevation has sent shockwaves through the entire village and other men fear her as a source of pollution. Daria, a peasant woman, tells Fenia, "I do not understand what has happened to the men ever since you were elected chairman, my husband won't allow me to go to meetings or to rallies."[45] Just then, Semën comes in roaring drunk, attacks Pavel, and then tries to strike Fenia. The scene is poignant and underlines the basic physical insecurity of women. Fenia, despite all her political authority and intellectual superiority, is completely vulnerable to the exercise of force. Although she conducts herself with dignity and tries to reason with her husband, she is unable to defend herself. Fenia calls for the guard and has Semën arrested. At the end of the scene we find Pavel trying to convince Fenia that her husband loves her dearly but is enveloped in a miasma of jealousy and suspicion.

Unfortunately, the Soviet predilection for facile and happy endings trivializes the final scene of this otherwise powerful play. We see that Fenia has come home to pack up her things. She is deeply mortified by the fact that Semën has embroiled her in a public scandal. The shame of being the object of village gossip seems more painful to Fenia than Semën's shortcomings as a husband. Semën cannot believe that she actually wants to break up her marriage and tells her that she has changed and is no longer a human being. Fenia replies with irony that it is only now that she is truly a *chelovek* (individual). Semën alternately pleads with her, rails at her, and even threatens to kill her.

Providentially, Fenia's friend Grusha comes in and tells Semën that the village kulak (rich, peasant landowner) Titkin has alienated him from Fenia by concocting lies about her supposed affair with Pavel. According to Grusha, the "enemies of the people" hate the artel, hate Soviet rule, and regard women as horses. This remark seems to suggest that resistance to the liberation of women can be construed as a sign of political opposition to the regime. Semën realizes that he has been used as a pawn against Soviet power and begs Fenia for forgiveness. Fenia forgives him and they embrace.

From Khavronia to Fenia we see a clear line of development. Khavronia continues to be subject to her husband's authority and ultimately wins a small victory through stratagem. Fenia, on the other hand, seeks more than mere equality. She wants respect and demands total capitulation to her moral convictions and her political beliefs. But in both cases there is a vindication of the sexual purity of the women. The "public" nature of the women's civic responsibilities is no license for sexual autonomy. In the text, the platonic nature of Fenia's relationship with Pavel is repeatedly stressed. The line dividing the "public-minded woman" from the stereotypical "public woman" is thinly drawn, and the New Soviet Woman has to endure a public ordeal to prove her chastity. While men have to undergo a parallel mental transformation, the strength and resilience of the marital bond is also emphasized.

The third play, *Blokha*, is the only play among those that I have collected in which the heroine is depicted as a single woman. But her advanced age is stressed so as to preclude any sexual attachments.[46] The title named for the heroine Maria Blokha contains a wealth of allusion. Who is the parasitical flea? Is it Nikita the rich kulak shop owner, or his stooge the manager of the local cooperative? Or is it Maria herself, as her name implies? Maria, the old widow delegate, goads the male peasants like a flea, with constant references to their passivity in the face of exploitation.

The play borrows quite obviously from Alexander Neverov's famous short story, *Marya the Bolshevik* (1921), where the heroine, though physically larger and stronger than her puny husband, nevertheless submits to his petty demands and tyrannical acts in a docile manner.[47] But with the onset of the revolution, Marya undergoes a strange metamorphosis. She refuses to be subservient, refuses to bear children, and even learns how to read. She is then elected to a village council as a joke, but at the helm she displays exemplary management capabilities. Marya not only disrupts her own household and divorces her husband, but her enthusiasm for Bolshevism infects other women of the village. Marya starts a Zhenotdel cell where the women gather to talk and study. They in turn begin to start challenging the authority of their menfolk. The village is saved from Marya by the providential arrival of Cossacks and she leaves the village with departing Bolsheviks.

Maria Blokha in a sense represents the second phase of Marya the Bolshevik's career. The civil war is over, the external enemies are routed, and the Bolsheviks have to deal with the more mundane but equally important business of revolutionizing social life. Maria is represented as an archetypal village hag transmogrified into the epitome of the "New Soviet Woman." It is not merely her age that gives her certain customary latitude, she is also single and therefore physically free from male control. Moreover, Maria is a born leader and refuses to accept her sex as an inhibiting factor. In this play, the author plots the course of Maria's rise from a tiresome old scold to the role of a visionary leader. In the village where the play takes place, Kalupaev, the resident kulak, has through bribery and corruption placed his own men at the helm of the village administration. Maria, who has just returned from a political training seminar for women in the city, tries to rouse village opinion against this state of affairs. She proposes that they elect new candidates to the soviet.[48] At first the peasants ridicule Maria, then they threaten her with a beating. All her rational suggestions are ignored as she is just a *baba*. But finally, after much coherent argument, she convinces the peasants to call a general meeting. In a show of gender solidarity, the women of her village show up en masse at the village assembly, composed usually of male heads of households. Although the soviet chairman repeatedly tries to chase them away, they remain to support Maria.

At the assembly, Maria challenges the incumbents and accuses them of corruption and collusion with the rich peasants. The chairman of the soviet is horrified and instead of defending his record can only repeat that as a woman, Maria should concern herself with her children and refrain from meddling in affairs beyond her capabilities. But the village is impressed by Maria's reasoning and the scene ends with the people planning to turn over the chairman of the soviet and the manager of the cooperative to the local authorities for theft and corruption. While the people can unmask villains, only the state can administer justice and punishment.

In the last scene, Maria has been elected as chairman of the village. As Grigorii, an erstwhile skeptic of women's liberation, says, Maria has truly performed miracles. Under her leadership, the divided village has turned into a true community with labor artels and communal farming. She has worked with the local women to organize a system of cooperative dining halls and child-care facilities so the women are free for more productive labor. At the same time, these overworked peasant women, for the first time in their lives, have leisure time for education and entertainment.

But Maria's authority extends even further, as she invades the private sphere by serving as an arbitrator of village morals and sexual relationships. In the last scene we find her hectoring Taras, a young man who has seduced a village maiden. She threatens him with the People's Court unless he takes responsibility for the child he has fathered. In a similar manner, she roundly berates a peasant who refuses to send his daughter to school. Maria's authority is ubiquitous—she knows which men beat their wives and implores women to expose their husbands if they ill-treat them. She publicly denounces bootleggers, slackers, and other violators of labor norms. Maria accepts no limits to her power. The village is an extended family in which she rules as a loved but fearsome matriarch. She has substantially redefined the notion of political authority by simply eliminating the boundaries dividing the public and the private. In her view, civil society does not exist in contradistinction to the state; the two are vitally interrelated. She reserves for herself the right to remold private behavior and to define the categories of deviance for the sake of the public good.

Women's Day theater offered another dimension to and source for female iconography in the NEP era.[49] Bolshevik propaganda at the popular level did not merely formulate alien images of the defeminized, leather-coated commissar flouting the conventions of family and society. Rather, within the plays we find a complex vision of liberation formulated to appeal to women at different levels of political maturity. In the final analysis the consistent effort to convince spectators that Bolshevik ideas of women's liberation were functional within the existing Russian context could be translated into practice by women themselves without large-scale social engineering by the state. The New Soviet Woman was likewise depicted as a protean archetype with strong roots in popular culture rather than a single idealized entity. Finally, with the emphasis on sexual purity of women and stable marital relationships, we see the prologue to the Stalinist compromise. In the process of translation into popular discourse, abstract revolutionary idealism was mediated by the entrenched culture it tried to transform.

With the demise of NEP and the onset of the first Five-Year Plan, the party agenda for women changed radically. Women's Day publications detailed the various threats to the Soviet Union from foreign countries and exhorted women to strengthen the country by partaking in the goals of socialist construction and reducing the costs of production through the rationalization of labor.[50] In the countryside collectivization was pictured in gendered terms, the *kolkhoz* offering the ultimate haven for liberated women. As the Zhenotdel fought a rear-guard battle to preserve its vision of Soviet feminism, the department itself was dissolved. But the Five-Year Plan also brought full employment and an increasing array of social services for women. The Stalinist state co-opted much of the rhetoric of the Zhenotdel agenda, even though it was presented in different terms. Finally, the Soviet heroine moved from being the stepchild of the Soviet symbolic system to the center of Stalinist propaganda.

As the NEP era was superseded, the New Soviet Woman acquired other characteristics. The capacity to labor, always an important Bolshevik virtue, acquired both mythical and mystical qualities during this period as women were literally transmogrified through their participation in the production process. In addition, women's more overt dependence on the new welfare state which provided social services such as nurseries, kindergartens, laundromats, and communal dining rooms enabled them to work more effectively. While the theme of male counter-revolutionary behavior continued to feature a subtext of socialist patriarchy, it was simultaneously represented and strengthened by the existence of the wise party leader or the communist mentor in women's lives.

Anatole Glebov's play, *Inga*, which premiered during International Women's Day in 1929 at the Moscow Theater of Revolution, contained many of the new motifs and, not surprisingly, went on to enjoy considerable success thereafter.[51] The play showcases four very different women: Inga, who is strong willed and trenchantly feminist in her attitude; Glafeera, more traditionally tied to hearth and home; Mera, a remnant from the civil war days with a completely cynical attitude toward sexual morality; and Nastya, who resentfully accepts beatings from her husband out of fear of abandonment. The play hinges on the love triangle of Glafeera, her husband Dmitri, and Inga, the other woman, except that the author jettisons the standard plot of the nineteenth-century western novel with an ending in which both women emerge stronger and independent of the man. Inga, an intellectual and the manager of a clothing factory, falls in love with Dmitri, a worker and chairman of the factory committee. She displays little remorse at breaking up his family and justifies her right to personal happiness at the expense of others by citing her service to the revolutionary cause.

Dmitri is attracted to Inga because she is modern and politically conscious, unlike Glafeera. But as Somov, the party secretary, points out, he has done little to educate Glafeera and raise her to his intellectual level. As the play progresses, Inga refuses to put Dmitri ahead of her work and her duty, and wants to be a comrade rather than a traditional wife. At the same time, Glafeera, who is initially devastated at being abandoned by Dmitri, transforms herself into the New Soviet Woman through the redeeming power of factory labor. Somov urges her to put her daughter, Valka, in a nursery and begin a course of study. She refuses to accept alimony from Dmitri or child support for her daughter. At the end of the play when Dmitri wishes to return, she tells him clearly that she will survive with or without him. Moreover, like Inga, she will not permit him to stand in her path of progress. At the end of the play, while Dmitri appears confused and demoralized, Glafeera and Inga seem to have reached an instinctive understanding—they embrace and kiss. But it is made clear that Glafeera will not emulate Inga's casual attitude toward love, sex, and family. Glafeera's newly found confidence and sense of self is expressed through labor and selfless service to the community. At end of the play Inga too agrees with Somov that the personal has to be subordinated to the political: "everything which stands in the way of reconstruction . . . everything external, internal, personal, general, has to be swept away. . . . Sentiments are mobilized, too! Oh, you know that this is not easy! But however it may be, the personal life of Inga Rizzer will give you no more trouble!"[52]

five
# The Language of Liberation

As the decade of the 1920s drew to a close, the policies of the NEP were increasingly criticized by sections of the party and the populace.[1] The drawing up of the first Five-Year Plan, a savagely utopian scheme, had far-reaching consequences, not only for politics and the economy, but also for Soviet citizens. Ultimately, the success of Stalin's grandiose scheme of construction was dependent on the rapid creation of cadres of loyal and enthusiastic workers, shorn of the defects of the Russian national character. The creation of the New Soviet Man and Woman was an important part of the first Five-Year Plan, crucial to the success of rapid industrialization and collectivization.

In 1929, the Zhenotdel, though on the brink of disbanding, made an attempt to create a woman's agenda in keeping with the large-scale goals of the Five-Year Plan. The plan envisaged the elimination of female unemployment, the participation of women in the socialist reconstruction of industry and agriculture, the reduction of female illiteracy, both literal and political, and the creation of a network of social service institutions that would fulfill domestic duties. Despite this ambitious plan, historians have, for the most part, concentrated overwhelmingly on one aspect—the recruitment of women to industry. They have emphasized the fact that the extensive recruitment of women to industry in 1930 was a direct result of an unanticipated labor shortfall and was, as such, a production necessity that was later legitimated as the revival of the socialist vision of women's emancipation through participation in labor.[2] According to these scholars, the wives and mothers of workers were drawn into expanding industries in order to avoid greater housing pressure in cities that fresh reserves of men from the countryside would cause. Although the massive female unemployment of the 1920s was eradicated during the course of the first Five-Year Plan, the decrease in real wages prevented a concomitant improvement in the living conditions of women. And, these writers add, though the Soviet state increased the numbers of child-care institutions, communal dining halls, and laundries, they were of limited help to women because they were both inadequate in number and deficient in the quality of service they offered.

Another aspect of the Five-Year Plan has gone largely unnoticed in the western literature.[3] The *kul'turno-bytovoi pokhod*, or the campaign for the cultural reconstruction of daily life, was started with much publicity and fanfare on International Women's Day in 1929 by the Zhenotdel. It subsequently set the public agenda for state policies toward women in the 1930s. An analysis of the campaign highlights that the Zhenotdel was fairly powerless and depended on the cooperation of various ministries, factory administrations, trade unions, and local party cells to realize its mandates. Also, in the Stalinist system the distribution and duplication of duties among various organizations and at various levels frustrated the best intentions of planners at the central level. This campaign was partly a realization of the utopian ideas popular in the 1920s that called for the organization of individual families into living communes and artels. Here members would pool resources and labor in order to share domestic duties and child rearing.[4] The Komsomol was particularly enthusiastic about this and popularized ideas of communal living through articles in *Komsomol'skaia pravda*. From 1928 onward, worker families, from a few factories in Moscow and Leningrad, organized communes in buildings. But soon this issue became intertwined with the antiurban visionary town planning as advocated by Iu. Larin and L. M. Sabsovich. In 1930, the Central Committee of the party published a decree warning against the use of coercive measures to promote communalization. It also criticized the privileging of questions of daily life over economic tasks facing the country.[5] Subsequently, the campaign for communalization of daily life died down, but the idea that the state should provide social services continued to be an important element in Soviet thinking.[6] In 1930 the campaign was integrated into a drive to mobilize women for industry, and Women's Day celebrations during the first Five-Year Plan were organized mainly around the production priorities of the state. But despite its relative marginalization, one aspect of the campaign—the liberation of women from domesticity through state provision of social services—was acknowledged by the Soviet state as a quasicontractual corollary to the participation of women in the Five-Year Plan. As such, it formed an essential component of the Stalinist gender contract.

Two commemorative illustrations published on the occasion of International Women's Day in 1929 aptly illustrate the aims and limitations of the Soviet agenda for women. The first one presents a collage of Soviet women engaged in various socially useful activities, framed against a backdrop of industrial construction.[7] The cameos include a peasant woman speaking from a podium, a woman reading a book, women working in a factory, a group of preternaturally clean children sitting at dinner (presumably in a kindergarten), and a woman scientist peering into a microscope. The second is a cartoon entitled "Holiday and Everyday" and represents an insider's wry commentary on the actual position of women in Soviet society.[8] The top half of the cartoon is dominated by the massive figure of a smiling woman worker listening to accolades pronounced by a man. From his suit and tie one can infer that he is an upper-level factory administrator. The date prominently figured in the text is March 8. In the bottom half of the picture the date is March 9 and the figures are represented in inverse proportion. The woman no longer towers over the man, but is half her former size. The expression on her face is submissive and her head is bowed under the stream of invective that is flowing from the open mouth of the erstwhile adulatory factory administrator.

The artist captured more than the essential tokenism of International Women's Day when she represented the holiday as a carnivalesque moment, when the power structure allowed the temporary inversion of social relations in Soviet society. But the elevation of women on this one day, far from serving as a means of empowerment and social advancement, threw into dramatic relief the actual subordination of women in Soviet society and the inadequacy of the rites and rituals of Women's Day. But given this caustic assessment of Women's Day, does the second cartoon automatically negate the first collage, created in the spirit of socialist realism?

Fig. 2. "Prazdnik i budni" (Holiday and everyday). Izvestiia, Moscow: R.S.F.S.R., March 8, 1929, 1.

The texts represent both the extent and limits of the visionary aspirations of the Soviet agenda for women. The Soviet state, despite the low priority accorded to this goal, was dedicated to the idea of drawing women into socialist construction and turning Russian women into modern and productive members of society. The question was how to effect this transformation on a socially meaningful scale. Could Women's Day be transformed from the irrelevant hoopla of a single festive day, when the Soviet Union as a nation acclaimed and feted the achievements of their women, into a veritable revolution in the popular perceptions of femininity and

108  **The Language of Liberation**

gender relations? Could the propaganda campaign of March 8, which dealt with the themes of women's liberation, equality in the workplace, reconstruction of domesticity, and war on misogyny, be turned into sustained activity during the whole year? Finally, could state institutions be persuaded to take responsibility for translating the rhetoric of emancipation into deeds?

By 1929, Women's Day was coming under scrutiny from various quarters other than cartoonists. There was much confusion about the exact purpose and relevance of the holiday. Some claimed that the holiday propaganda was just an exercise in empty rhetoric that marginalized women even further by concentrating attention to their needs qua women to that one day of the year. An article in the *Komsomol'skaia pravda* noted that the question of women's liberation was raised occasionally, only on jubilees of International Women's Day, whereas Women's Day should be a year-long phenomenon.[9] The article went on to criticize the hyperbole of Women's Day propaganda that coexisted strangely with widespread administrative apathy and indifference to women's needs, in both the private sphere and on the shop floor.

When Aleksandra Artiukhina, the head of Zhenotdel, criticized the way in which the state-mandated policy for the promotion of women from low-paying jobs to responsible positions *(vydvizhenie)* was being violated by factories, she was calling for a similar accountability for party-speak.[10] It was not simply that a major credibility gap existed between rhetoric and reality, but sometimes the rhetoric of liberation was actualized and undermined simultaneously. The promotion of women from low-paid, unskilled jobs to positions requiring higher skills, or even administrative positions, was one of the more important commemorative rituals of Women's Day. Every year on Women's Day throughout the 1920s, newspapers would report approvingly that women had been promoted in factories and state institutions. The cumulative impact of such a policy would have been substantial, had it not been for the fact that most of these promotions lasted only for that one festive day of the year. In most cases women were asked to return to their former position the next day, or in some cases their male colleagues made it so difficult for them to continue their work that they often begged the administration for a demotion. A report on professional work conducted

**Fig. 3.** "Posle 8 marta" (After March 8). *Trud*, March 9, 1929, 1.

among women textile workers from April 4, 1928, revealed that promotions of women on Women's Day were fairly infrequent as women promoted by the trade unions often lacked qualifications; this led to bad feelings among co-workers. Another common Women's Day practice that frustrated the original intentions of the policy of *vydvizhenie* was to promote women to low administrative posts, where the pay was less than that earned on the shop floor.[11] A Women's Day cartoon, printed in 1929, offered a critical commentary on the issue of promotions. The cartoon featured a factory administrator irritably telling two women workers, "again you are raising the issue of promotion. What is the matter with you all, do you think everyday is Women's Day?"[12]

For those women who did not aspire to promotions, low-paid jobs on the shop floor were not without peril as there was little recognition by administrators of the various kinds of harassment that women had to contend with. *Komsomol'skaia pravda* carried a particularly noteworthy account of blatant administrative disregard in face of sexual harassment. The article targeted the irresponsibility of factory administrators who mouthed the mandatory rhetoric of liberation on Women's Day but—whether due to hypocrisy or a genuine misunderstanding of the language and ideals of liberation—failed to execute their promises.[13] Marusia Kozlova, a young peasant woman, was particularly nauseated by a speech at a Women's Day meeting in her timber factory at Dneprstroi. The paper reported that the orator in question spoke with eloquence and passion about the mobilization of housewives for participation in the reconstruction of the Soviet economy. The words recalled to Marusia her own experiences on the shop floor. As a young peasant recruit to the factory, she repeatedly came to the attention of four male co-workers who made crude and derogatory remarks to her. Matters came to a head when the men pinned her down and tried to raise her skirt to verify if she was truly a virgin. The girl was so humiliated and mortified that some co-workers took pity on her and complained to the administration. The manager studied the facts of the case and concluded that the men were merely dallying with her, and that they would be verbally reprimanded.[14] Harassment of women workers could often involve actual cases of rape, but rarely were the criminals charged with the offense or even taken to task by the factory administration, which more often than not tended to view such incidents as normal occurrences.[15]

As we know from Rose Glickman's study of women factory workers in late Imperial Russia, sexual harassment of women was a very common phenomenon in tsarist times. The fact that such practices continued in the Soviet Union is not surprising.[16] What was revolutionary in Soviet Russia was that this behavior was deemed inappropriate in a socialist society and was regarded as a situation that required attention and remediation. Women's liberation would not be achieved merely through government intervention in the economy; it required a cultural revolution in the manners and morals of Soviet society. This widespread belief, especially among members of the Zhenotdel, in the ability of the state to reshape the cultural physiognomy of the Soviet man and woman gave impetus to the *kul'turno-bytovoi pokhod* in 1929.

### Kul'turno-Bytovoi pokhod

The emphasis on the reconstruction of daily life had its roots in the works of Marxist theorists such as Bebel, Kollontai, and Lenin. They had identified the private household as a prison for women and had been particularly critical of domesticity, believing that housework forced women to waste time in socially unproductive labor, which in turn perpetuated their cultural and political backwardness. During the Five-Year Plan culture took on unprecedented significance as it was overtly linked to the functioning of the economy. The success of the first Five-Year Plan was contingent on raising the productivity of the Soviet worker, which in its turn was connected to upgrades in educational levels of the population. Indeed, possession of technical qualifications indicated the *kul'turnost'* (cultural level) of an individual.

In his speech to the Fifteenth Party Congress, Aleksei Rykov, chairman of the Sovnarkom (Council of People's Commissars), emphasized that industrialization and further economic development could not proceed without a parallel advance in the cultural level of Soviet society. This attitude was further illuminated in the resolutions adopted by the Congress that called for an "energetic struggle for the reconstruction of daily life, for culture . . ."[17] Subsequently, in 1928, Women's Day slogans emphasized that the recruitment of women to industry and their freedom from domestic duties was vitally connected to the re-creation of proletarian family life. However, it was not until 1929 that the *kul'turno-bytovoi pokhod* took on dramatic proportions and became part of a decisive battle in the ongoing cultural revolution.[18]

The Zhenotdel conceived the 1929 Women's Day campaign in part to compensate for the complete marginalization of women's needs and concerns during NEP. Accordingly, Zhenotdel proposed that Women's Day, instead of being a one-day event, should be extended to last until the beginning of April and beyond, as the need arose. Apart from the lengthy time period that the campaign was supposed to occupy, the goals of the campaign, in keeping with the bombast of the Five-Year Plan, were extremely ambitious. In journals and newspapers, Zhenotdel promoted the campaign as an all-out assault on *staryi byt'* (former lifestyles): on the backwardness of daily life, which included filth and the unsanitary conditions of working-class quarters and facilities such as baths, laundries, and dining halls; sexual exploitation of women and physical abuse in the home and on the shop floor; incorrect upbringing of children; drunkenness; and hooliganism. During the 1920s the party routinely attributed high rates of female unemployment to female illiteracy and lack of technical qualifications. The campaign therefore targeted the eradication of female illiteracy so as to draw women into production.[19] It also sought to increase female political activism by raising enrollments in trade unions, party organizations, and soviets.

In the Soviet Union women, through their monopoly of child care, were seen as the primary transmitters of culture. Indeed, in an ingenuous argument, an article in *Kommunistka* attributed the sexual harassment and rape of women on the shop floor to the incorrect upbringing of workers' children that made them prone to committing acts of violence and hooliganism.[20] This argument derived from Marxist notions of privileging the environment over heredity and represented the Soviet faith that it was possible to eradicate unwelcome aspects of proletarian culture through *vospitanie* (education) and indoctrination.

Apart from criticizing the practices of daily life, Zhenotdel also proposed that Women's Day be used to authenticate the workings of Soviet institutions dedicated to domestic work. This entailed verifying the conditions of crèches run by the Commissariat for Public Health (Narkomzdrav), factory administrations, and trade unions. In newspaper articles Zhenotdel advised Narkomzdrav to organize conferences to familiarize women with progressive maternal education and with the services provided by the Section for Maternity Protection. Zhenotdel also proposed that Narkompros should increase both the number and the quality of preschool institutions, especially in the countryside. Narpit was instructed to train cooks for communal dining rooms and to open a center in Moscow that would provide hot breakfasts for children of workers. Under the terms of the campaign, social service institutions were to be investigated by members of the *bytovoi-pokhod*. Unsanitary conditions, the rudeness of staff, and the exorbitant fees charged by these institutions were some deficiencies that required attention.[21] The Commissariat of Labor (Narkomtrud) was to arrange speeches on the significance of women's labor in International Women's Day conferences, and increase its efforts to send unemployed and underqualified women to technical training institutions.[22] The campaign also proposed to verify whether the new housing cooperatives were setting aside the mandatory 5 percent of their total budgets for the creation of laundries, baths, communal kitchens, clubs, Red Corners (rooms or parts of rooms containing Bolshevik educational material), and day-care centers.[23]

Both the Communist Party and the Zhenotdel believed that the success of the *kul'turno-bytovoi pokhod* would be achieved by a combination of administrative action and popular participation. Accordingly, the Central Committee of the party circulated instructions for the creation of Commissions for the Improvement of the Life and Labor of Working Women. These organizations were to be formed as adjuncts to soviets at every administrative level and also at various industries and ministries. As far as possible, these commissions were to be composed of women delegates from the Zhenotdel, and other women activists in the locality.[24]

In addition to these permanent commissions, Zhenotdel recommended that factories, trade unions, factory committees, communal farms, workers' apartment complexes and barracks create temporary commissions that would spearhead the *kul'turno-bytovoi pokhod* and investigate deficiencies in social service institutions and conditions of daily life. These commissions were not simply fact-finding research teams; they also served by example and gave practical advice on sanitation, child care, and the creation of communal lifestyles. The commissions were also to encourage women to enroll in literacy courses, and participate in trade union–sponsored social and political activities.

The decision to deploy the campaign was an indicator of party recognition of the special needs and concerns of women, and as such was intended as a reply to critics who deplored the diurnal nature of Woman's Day. In comparison, the *kul'turno-bytovoi pokhod* was planned as an investigative campaign that would give the Zhenotdel concrete facts and figures about the actual living conditions of Soviet women. But the fact that the commissions, both the ad hoc and the permanent ones, were to be composed primarily of women ensured their lack of power right from the beginning. Therein lay the roots of one of the two major problems of the campaign. The trade unions, ministries, and factory administrations could easily ignore the recommendations of an ad hoc commission composed of women.[25]

Another problem concerned the nature of purported solutions to the reconstruction of daily life, and on this issue the Communist party and the Zhenotdel were seriously divided. During the 1920s, the party had cited poverty and lack of material resources to explain the complete absence of institutions that were supposed to liberate women from domesticity.[26] The solution the party adopted during NEP was to transfer responsibility onto the women themselves. In journals such as *Klub, Rabotnitsa, Kommunistka, Krest'ianka*, and others, and in propaganda plays and delegate meetings, the party exhorted women to create their own cooperative institutions such as crèches, communal kitchens, and work artels.[27] This had been a major propaganda theme during the NEP years, when in the absence of both resources and initiative, the party tried to elicit popular female participation for the fulfillment of state goals regarding women.

Although the Zhenotdel had advocated the party line of voluntarism in public, in meetings and congresses it consistently contradicted the party's position that women should achieve their own liberation through cooperative efforts at the grassroots level. Artiukhina argued that this was an unrealizable goal, and women would be truly free of domestic drudgery only when the state invested in the necessary infrastructure. At the Fifteenth Party Congress, she asserted that women were steadfast in their support for the party and the Five-Year Plan, but the country lacked the institutions that would allow women to participate in the fulfillment of these plans. Artiukhina added that the liberation of women from domesticity could not be the work of women alone, but required substantial assistance from the state and the party. Vera Lebedeva, head of the Section for Maternity Protection (OMM) in the women's conference held in Moscow in 1927, was similarly critically about the inherent limitations of voluntarism:

"a network of daycare centers cannot be created on the charity of a population. . . . The daycare centers must be permanently entered in the budgets of district executive committees."[28] Therefore, while the party stressed cooperative and local solutions to women's issues, the Zhenotdel called for state regulation, interference, and investment. But rather than blame the party itself, Artiukhina used a disingenuous explanation that was a variation on the traditional Russian theme of the good tsar and bad ministers. In this instance, the party, especially the Central Committee, was the good tsar who was committed to the liberation of women, while the trade unions, local party cells, and other organizations were subverting the promises of the revolution by refusing to provide services that were hitherto the responsibility of the family.[29]

To what extent was this true, and to what extent was it convenient to scapegoat local institutions, is difficult to answer. But the growing scholarship on the Stalin era testifies to the extreme inefficiency and chaos inherent in the system, and the complete failures in the operation of vertical chains of command between the central party organization in Moscow and the administrative units in the provinces.[30] Moreover, deeply ingrained misogynistic Russian attitudes helped in the flouting of party instructions. It was a relatively simple matter for the harassed factory administration to concentrate on oratorical fervor and profundity on the occasion of Women's Day, and to ignore the implementation of practical welfare measures for the rest of the year.[31]

Moreover, from the sources it is apparent that there was considerable disagreement between local party cells and the Zhenotdel about the purported goals of the Women's Day campaign. A circular of the Trekhgorniaia Manufactory party cell in Moscow in 1929 encouraged members to concentrate on fulfilling the industrial plan, formation of women's shock brigades, and liquidation of the kulaks in the countryside, instead of stressing the importance of the *kul'turno bytovoi pokhod*. The circular emphasized that the imminent dissolution of the Zhenotdel was to be discussed at Women's Day meetings, and there was even a suggestion that a delegation of women workers should request Stalin to appear at the holiday celebrations.[32]

Despite the lack of unity in aims, the initial reports of the 1929

Women's Day festivities were impressive and reflected the increasing public participation in the holiday. The *kul'turno-bytovoi pokhod* was deployed on a fairly wide scale, even in areas as desolate and brutish as the Urals and Siberia. In Tver, for example, almost a thousand women were recruited for a week-long investigation into the condition of more than 250 institutions, crèches, and clubs. In Moscow, several crèches, kindergartens, and workers' sanatoria were opened on Women's Day.[33] In numerous barracks and clubs, Red Corners were created for women and children. In the factory Rabotnitsa in Leningrad, women workers organized a competition for the cleanest and best-dressed children. Another factory, Krasnyi Tkach, presented *agitsudy* (dramatized mock trials) on the topic of wife beating.[34] It appears that institutions had considerable independence in deciding the format of Women's Day festivities, and the only event common to all were standardized Women's Day lectures publicizing the goals of the first Five-Year Plan and the ways that women could help in its successful realization. As expected, the state's production goals were given more prominence than the cultural revolution aims advanced by the Zhenotdel.

While newspapers such as *Pravda* and *Izvestiia* tended to stress the festive and celebratory aspects of the holiday and enumerated the number of social service institutions opened on that day, the journal of the Zhenotdel, *Kommunistka* and internal trade union communiqués presented a more complicated assessment of the campaign. These reports tended to alternate between enthusiastic self-congratulation and more sober details of the terrible conditions of worker's lives and the widespread indifference to the objectives of the campaign, even in Moscow.[35] A report from the Tver Profsovet announced that the decrees concerning Women's Day published by the VTsSPS and the Central Committee of the party had been followed to the letter. Unions of metal workers, textile workers, and others with a large proportion of female members had created special commissions for Women's Day. Streets, clubs, and factories had been festooned with placards and slogans exhorting women to participate in socialist construction. From the middle of February, conferences were held in barracks and clubs. Libraries arranged exhibitions on women's achievements and published lists of literature suitable for women to read. On Women's Day itself, there were large demonstrations and rallies at factories. During the evenings, clubs organized family evenings with orchestral music and other light entertainment. Nine women were promoted in textile factories and another thirteen graduated from literacy schools *(likpunkty)* on the occasion of Women's Day. Finally, in the province of Tver, 1,125,882 rubles had been assigned from the Fund for the Improvement of Workers' Lives to upgrade social services for women.[36]

The Ural Profsovet reported similar activities in 1929. In addition, a major effort was made to clean the women workers' barracks in celebration of Women's Day. In the Urals region eleven children's institutions opened; these included crèches and medical consultation centers. But although, compared to previous years, there seemed to have been more agitational work done by trade unions to popularize Women's Day, there were several shortcomings. Trade unions of textile workers, forestry workers, medical workers, and Narpit failed to send in their reports to VTsSPS on measures taken on Women's Day in the Urals. Large-scale industrial plants, employing huge numbers of workers, had taken no measures whatsoever in improving living conditions in barracks.[37]

From other trade union reports, moreover, it was quite apparent that crèches and dining halls in industrial centers were insufficient in number, and in most cases were very expensive while providing poor service. Some crèches could charge almost twenty to thirty rubles a month per child. A survey of crèches in Leningrad revealed that some of them had no beds or toys, and served bad food and watery milk. Investigations into workers' dining halls in the asbestos industry revealed that the meals were both expensive and tasteless.[38] Although the Zhenotdel had always advocated communal dining rooms as a way to relieve tired women workers after their shifts, estimates for as late as 1929 show that even in large urban areas such as Leningrad and Moscow only 6 to 12 percent of the population ate in state-run cafeterias.[39]

It was not surprising that investigation into proletarian quarters revealed a glaring absence of libraries, clubs, crèches, dining halls, and living space; but more unexpected was that the campaign also produced interesting observations on the alleged sexual and social anarchy reigning in proletarian barracks. The narratives reflect a predominantly bourgeois, Victorian moral repugnance toward the violence, immorality, and unnatural familial relationships prevalent in workers' lives. While trade union reports tended to be terse and referred only in passing to shocking examples of men and women sharing sleeping quarters in overcrowded and filthy barracks, *Kommunistka* carried a series of detailed articles that provide an interesting commentary on the attitudes of both the observers and the observed.

**Private Lives of Workers**

On one level, the excessive detail of the *Kommunistka* articles seem symptomatic of a prurient voyeurism thinly disguised by an attitude of sociological inquiry. On the other hand, the articles might have been aimed at rousing the state to strong action since they included intimate details of workers' lives, complete with names and residential information. Strangely enough, the reports contain few solutions; instead, they serve as a sad commentary on the state of affairs in Russia and are ultimately more revealing of the fears and anxieties of the observers when confronting sexual and familial anarchy.

The condition of Soviet children was a particularly sensitive issue during this period. Not only had the state failed to cope with the massive problem of *bezprizornost'* (orphaned children) in the country, but the workers seemed completely unaware of bourgeois notions of child care and upbringing.[40] To the horror of the investigators, the unhealthy-looking children in worker barracks were growing up bereft of parental supervision. They ran around in crowded and filthy corridors, listening to the swearing and cursing of the adults around them and watching the fighting, the "hooliganism," and the drunken cavorting of men and women.[41] The modern notions of childhood as a separate stage of human development seemed alien to Russian proletarians, whose children were saddled with adult responsibilities at a very early age. In a culture that had little concept of privacy, shielding children from the struggle and strife of daily living seemed unnecessary and physically impossible to achieve. As N. Alekseeva, commenting on the lives of working-class children, observes, "It seems as if neither the Pioneers, the Komsomol, nor the Zhenotdel have been able to introduce anything from the principles of socialism."[42]

Women workers seemed completely impervious to the advice on maternal education that these organizations tried to offer. Furthermore, even though reorganization of life on the principles of communal existence promised to ameliorate the lot of women workers, they refused to espouse the rational and communitarian social attitudes that Zhenotdel workers sought to inculcate. Women workers would spend four to seven rubles a month on a nanny, but for some reason incomprehensible to the investigators, they declined to pool their resources for cooperative day care, or even prepare their meals in rotation.[43] On the rare occasion when they cleaned their rooms, women would toss garbage into the corridor and refuse to take responsibility for the cleanliness of the rest of the premises.

Of even deeper concern was the exploitative nature of the parent-child relationship. A member of the investigating team in the small industrial town of Shuia reported the story of Nina, a fifteen-year-old prostitute. At the age of twelve Nina had been sold by her mother in exchange for a bottle of vodka. As the investigator said, "The most disgraceful thing about this affair is that it happened in the country of the dictatorship of the proletariat, where the sale of humans is punishable by law as the most criminal of deeds."[44] Not only did the deed go unpunished and unnoticed but the child was prostituted several times thereafter until she finally took a hand in the commerce and exploited her body for her own gain. When she got pregnant, the mother who lived off her earnings beat Nina so badly that she miscarried. Nina's older sister was also a prostitute and both of them supported the drunken mother.

This unfortunate story was offensive at various levels. It showed the unnatural relationships of the Benderskii family, in which the mother acted as a pimp instead of nurturing her children. The children continued in their self-exploitation, and their "commercial" activities pointed to the lack of alternatives in a socialist society and made a mockery of the Marxist analysis of prostitution as a product of capitalism. Finally, it showed the ephemeral impact of the October Revolution on the everyday life of the proletariat.[45]

In the same building, there was another case of a fifty-year old woman, Lemeshova, who resided with her eighteen-year-old lover and her grandson in perfect amity. An older woman as an active sexual agent obviously offended the sensibilities of the observer. Even worse was the fact that the able-bodied young man was perfectly content to be maintained by a woman. Finally, to the special concern of the investigator, the five-year-old grandson obviously understood the sexual nature of the relationship between the adults. The author concluded his report by calling for material help for unemployed Soviet women and increased cultural work in such dens of iniquity. Other reports from villages in the Urals spoke of the prevalence of widespread sexual anarchy among the youth and concluded that there had to be a revolution in social attitudes toward women.[46]

## Official Conclusions and Prescriptions

The results of the investigations created a widespread negative self-assessment and the realization that as far as women were concerned the revolution had failed to deliver its most basic promises. In response to pressure from the Zhenotdel, perhaps, the Central Committee of the Bolshevik party published a statement on the general goals of the party for women workers and women peasants.[47] Changing sexual morals and mores was difficult and, with the exception of the Zhenotdel, the party had other priorities. Instead of focusing on sexual deviance, parental indifference toward children, and widespread misogyny, the statement reiterated the old tautology that only full employment would lead to the emancipation of women. Despite their continued emphasis in the press on cultural reconstruction and the communalization of daily life, the party continued to advocate socialist labor as the panacea for all evils. They hoped that the Five-Year Plan for industry and agriculture would wipe out female unemployment and other attendant vices of proletarian existence.[48]

The statement is interesting and deserves more than casual perusal. It outlines the methods of work that party and soviet organizations had to undertake in order to mobilize women for industrial labor, agricultural construction, and fulfillment of the mandates of the projected cultural revolution. It reflects the typical schizophrenia of party mentality in that women were represented as both a threat to socialist reconstruction and as a valuable resource if their energies could be properly channeled. On the one hand, the report read, "the attraction of the wide mass of working women to active participation in socialist construction has acquired primary significance." On the other hand, "in the conditions of sharpening class struggle ... anti-Soviet elements could use women against the Party goals."[49]

Making a leap, the document admits that in order for women to work it was necessary for institutions such as Narkompros, Narkomzdrav, VTsSPS, cooperatives, Narkomzem, and housing authorities to invest in building social welfare institutions. This was a classic Bolshevik line, and its verbalization reaffirms the obligations of the Soviet state toward women, not as a charitable system reaffirming gender dependency—as the language of welfare in the West intimated—but as a recognition of the rights of Soviet women as productive members of society. But at the same time, in addition to fulfilling labor obligations, women were supposed to participate enthusiastically in the creation of these institutions. This was the central dilemma of the socialist state that all too often tried to fuse local initiative in the service of a state-sponsored goal. This reliance on local initiative in order to create social services for women provided a perfect exit line for lower bureaucratic organizations that exploited the productionist elements of party policy and ignored the humanistic elements as far as they were related to the reconstruction of the private sphere.

The contradictory characterizations continue. The document claims that only through participation in labor would women's cultural standards be raised. And therefore, the document advises Soviet organizations such as Gosplan, VSNKH, and Narkomtrud to facilitate the entry of women into all branches of industry and to make a special case for the promotion of women to positions of responsibility. It would seem that the party's advocacy of female involvement in industry, collective farms, and politics served as recognition of the special interests of a needy political constituency, but this rhetoric of liberation is indiscriminately interwoven with the language of cost-benefit analysis. In the last sentence, the authors note that the mobilization of women is crucial to the success of the Five-Year Plan, both politically and economically. Not only did the party require labor cadres for the construction of industry, it also required "the education of women communists in the spirit of Bolshevik *partiinost'* (party-mindedness) was imperative so that they could effectively combat all deviations from the general Bolshevik party line."[50]

Loyal party member, tool for anti-Soviet elements, uncultured and uneducated symbol of Russian backwardness, crucial constituency for the success of the Five-Year Plan, the document of the Central Committee exemplifies the anxieties and disjunctures in Soviet propaganda and its inability to create a coherent discourse or a unified imagery as far as women were concerned. Soviet policy, however, was more focused and followed a resolute course toward increasing the percentage of women in the labor force. This was reinforced and rendered urgent by the unanticipated labor shortage in industry in 1930.[51]

## Women in Socialist Labor

The initial projections of the first Five-Year Plan envisaged a modest increase in female employment, from 27 percent in 1927–28 in all economic divisions, to 32.5 percent by 1932–33. By July 1929, despite the inception of the Five-Year Plan, the proportion of women among the unemployed reached 49.5 percent. This was primarily due to the orientation of the economic expansion toward heavy industry in which women were traditionally underrepresented. B. Marsheva, an economist, voiced concern that the Five-Year Plan actually worked to the disadvantage of women.[52] By 1930, however, there was a widespread labor shortage in the Soviet union, and on Women's Day 1930, *Za industrilizatsiiu*, the organ of the VSNKH, published articles attacking the domestic hearth as the last bastion of the bourgeoisie and called for the liberation from the kitchen of the 5.5 million housewives in Soviet cities. Elsewhere in the same issue, an article averred that the prejudice against the employment of women in industry had to be eradicated, but to do so women had to overcome their illiteracy and raise their technical qualifications.[53] On September 8, 1930, *Izvestiia* published a series of instructions from the party to Narkomtrud. They called for a list of trades and professions to be reserved predominantly for women, instructed Narkomtrud to increase the number of seats for women in vocational schools and to draw up plans to improve social services. That same year Narkomtrud outlined a plan for women's labor, and by 1931 the large-scale mobilization of women workers into industry was outlined as one of the principal goals of industrialization.[54] This was reaffirmed by the publication on October 1, 1931, of the decrees of the third session of the TsIK SSSR that called for increasing the rate of mobilization of women. In

1931, the party decided that the principal slogan for Women's Day should be "the attraction of 1,600,000 women workers to industry, *sovkhoz*, and *kolkhoz* construction."[55]

With the increasing pressure on housing and food supply in cities during this period, the use of unemployed women workers from worker families already living in the city was deemed a practical move. As Serebrennikov said, "such recruitment of local reserves was naturally cheaper and simpler than recruiting of outside labor in other districts."[56] However, the propaganda that unfolded on Women's Day stressed a different series of reasons tying the "woman question" directly to the fulfillment of the Five-Year Plan. During Stalin's revolution a fundamental shift in the phrasing of the "woman question" occurred. In actuality the position of women did not improve dramatically in the 1930s; however, in public pronouncements the liberation of women was directly connected to the central concerns of the state. The neglect of women's issues was represented as a rightist deviation and could even be interpreted as deliberate wrecking. Formerly, the liberation of women was perceived as a long-term process whose resolution was seen in terms of restructuring the private sphere. The liberation of women from the domestic sphere was upheld as one of the many desirable objectives in the progress toward socialism, but even the massive female unemployment during NEP and its catastrophic impact on women's living standards was not perceived as a matter of national emergency.

During the 1930s, however, the emancipation of women was directly related to questions of national importance such as industrialization and the defense of the country. Women's Day propaganda depicted in gruesome detail the worsening economic crisis in the West. As capitalism became mired in ever-widening circles of contradictions, capitalists naturally sought to deflect attention from internal troubles by planning a massive assault on the Soviet Union, which due to its unprecedented growth rates was attracting the envy of all and sundry. As capitalistic intervention was becoming increasingly inevitable, it was necessary for the Soviet Union to industrialize at a rapid rate and complete the goals of the Five-Year Plan in four years. This was impossible without the widespread mobilization of women. Moreover, in case of war it was imperative that women be trained and prepared to take over the positions of men in industry and agriculture. This message formed the central theme of all Women's Day speeches and addresses in 1931. Newspapers and journals, in their articles on Women's Day, stressed these ideas in sensational and dramatic prose.[57]

The VTsSPS, in instructions to trade unions, *zhensektory* (women's groups), clubs, factory committees, and Komsomol cells, advised that at Women's Day rallies speakers should explain the worsening international situation and mobilize women both to strengthen the defense potential of the country and to fulfill the Five-Year Plan in record time. It was imperative to increase the number of women in educational establishments, women's shock brigades, and actively raise the number of women employed in machine building, metallurgical, fuel, and electrical industries. The campaign was to be aimed especially at the Ukraine, the Northern Caucasus, the Urals region, Azerbaijan, the northern provinces, the Lower Volga, and Central Asia. This basic message was to be reiterated and elaborated in meetings of housewives, in clubs, dormitories, barracks, and children's matinees.[58]

Members of the VTsSPS who had been sent out as emissaries to various parts of the Soviet Union to verify the progress of the 1931 Women's Day campaign, however, reported widespread administrative hostility and complete disregard of instructions regarding the mobilization of women. It appeared that lower organizations interpreted instructions in a very selective manner. They chose to celebrate Women's Day rather than use it as a means to recruit women to industry. Reports from Moscow, Leningrad, and the northern regions suggested that factory committees and agitation sections of various trade unions had indeed invested resources and time in organizing Women's Day rallies, festive meetings, children's matinees, plays, concerts, teas, orchestras, film shows, and literary evenings. Female shock workers *(udarnitsy)* were given bonuses. Brigades were formed to clean up workers' barracks for Women's Day and to inspect social service institutions as an integral part of the ongoing *kul'turno-bytovoi pokhod*. Wall newspapers, with articles featuring exemplary women, were specially printed for the occasion.[59]

These activities, however, were peripheral to the Women's Day campaign, whose real purpose was to raise the numbers of women in industry. It seemed that while the party had succeeded in popularizing Women's

Day, it was unable to use the holiday in service of state goals. While women's employment grew in 1931, it was nowhere near the mandated goals. In fact the mobilization of women into industry was completed despite the noncooperation of factory administration and trade unions. Despite the immense labor shortages, factory managers felt little compunction in disregarding party orders about the mobilization of women. The recruitment of women into industry represented in microcosm a classic clash between deep-seated Russian cultural values and the efforts of the Soviet state to industrialize and modernize, and thereby became an arena for testing the limits of state control.

The Soviet media represented the conflict not as a power struggle between the party and economic institutions, but as the gradual and progressive erosion of misogyny in Russian society. Through the enlightened policies of the party—which constantly represented itself as the champion of women and the guarantor of their upward mobility—and the determination of the women themselves to prove their mettle in the teeth of male prejudice, there was little doubt as to the eventual outcome. The story of Agafiia, published in *Za industrilizatsiiu*, exemplifies the gradual acceptance of women in technical positions on the shop floor. Agafiia wanted to work as a lathe operator, so the factory committee sent her to the director of the plant, who in turn sent her to the engineer. The first day at work proved particularly traumatic for Agafiia as the shop floor was composed exclusively of critical males who jeered constantly at her mistakes. But, this being a Soviet story, she naturally mastered the techniques in a week and soon was accepted as one of the boys.[60] This story is a good example of 1931 Women's Day propaganda, which promised both the eradication of the labor shortage and the eventual resolution of the battle of the sexes in the Soviet Union. The story held out hope to women and, at the same time, served as an example to factory administrators who, in real life, were very different from Agafiia's boss.[61]

As reports came into the VTsSPS, they almost unanimously admitted that trade unions and factories had, on the occasion of Women's Day, outlined no plans for the recruitment of women. Most of the influx of women into industry was random and unplanned. Investigators sent out by the VTsSPS came back with stories of widespread neglect and administrative apathy. For example, in Novosibirsk and Omsk it appeared that not a single organization was even aware that the Women's Day campaign of March 8 was supposed to be used to recruit women to industry. Trade unions in Ukraine and Azerbaijan exhibited similar ignorance. It seemed that the VTsSPS was partly to blame insofar as it failed to send out instructions to various unions detailing precise measures to be adopted for the recruitment of women.[62]

In Magnitogorsk women were recruited haphazardly at various construction sites. When hired, they were subject to constant abuse. In one case, a woman was set to work a night shift loading bricks with five hundred men. The men spat in her face and tried to assault her physically. When she complained about the treatment, a male worker told her that she had only herself to blame. The unfortunate woman endured this treatment until the morning and then appealed to the director of the factory to transfer her to the day shift. The director interpreted this request as a sign of laziness and lack of desire on her part to continue working. He promptly fired her. In other instances, women were asked to load and carry heavy things like gravel, bricks, desks, and sleepers while men were given much lighter work. Investigations into factories in Leningrad, Ivanovo, Ukraine, and the Urals all revealed the antiwomen feelings of managers, trade union workers, old workers, and even party members.[63] Husbands were equally opposed to the idea of their wives working in factories, and in some cases resorted to physical violence to prevent them from seeking employment.

B. Marsheva railed against the opportunistic leadership of Narkomtrud, who completely overlooked the importance of drawing on reserves of female labor. She also criticized the conservatism of trade unions, lower party workers, and other labor organizations that, despite party instructions, failed to realize both the social and economic implications of the mobilization of women workers. Marsheva argued that on one hand the employment of women would serve as the realization of the promises of the October Revolution. On the other hand, the underrepresentation of women in heavy industry would have adverse repercussions on the defense potential of the nation.[64]

Given widespread labor shortages the party was at a loss to understand why the percentage of women in industry, though increasing, fell far short of the numbers envisaged. There was a concerted propaganda effort to prove that women workers were as good as if not better than men.[65] Reports and articles stressed that the work discipline of women was much higher than that of men and that fluctuation among the female labor force was much lower. For example, at the Putilov factory, supposedly the turnover rate among men was 57 percent, while among women it was only 11 percent.[66] These facts were publicized in the hope that factory administrators would change their attitudes toward women workers.

However, apart from the conservatism of the factories and trade unions, there were other reasons for the slow growth in women's employment. The continuation of the *kul'turno-bytovoi pokhod* during the Women's Day campaign in 1931 revealed that matters had scarcely improved since 1929. The creation of institutions such as dining rooms and child care centers had not kept pace with the ambitious targets envisaged in the first Five-Year Plan. According to the initial projections of the first Five-Year Plan, by the end of five years all workers would consume their meals at state-run dining halls. But even in factories like Krasnyi Bogatyr, where 80 percent of the employees were women, the factory dining rooms were charging nearly ninety kopecks for a meal that included meat. Given that the wage of senior women workers was roughly 138 rubles a month, the dining room represented a luxury rather than a service that women could depend on. If in 1927–28, 107,000 children were enrolled in kindergartens, then according to the Five-Year Plan, by 1931–32 they were supposed to accommodate 217,000. In reality, at sites of new construction projects like Magnitostroi and Traktorstroi, there was a terrible absence of living quarters, kindergartens, and crèches.[67] A VTsSPS survey of child-care institutions in 1931 revealed that the number of workers' children serviced by factory day-care facilities was very low.[68] Moreover, the cost per child could run as high as thirteen to fourteen rubles a month.[69]

### The Language of Soviet Welfare

At a Women's Day celebration in 1931 in Moscow at the factory Metron, a woman worker seated in the audience commented, "You only talk about the fact that we are growing, in reality we have nothing, only lines. We have no crèches, we have nowhere to put our children, nothing to eat."[70] This remark throws light on the nature of the ritual of Women's Day. If ritual provides a window on cultural patterns, then Women's Day highlighted both the convergence and dissonance in Soviet society. On the one hand, the observer's remark showed the emptiness of Soviet ritualized rhetoric. But, simultaneously, by condemning the absence of social services for women, the observation emphasized the expectations of Soviet women as citizens. The critic was castigating the state's failure to honor its promises, but she was neither questioning the welfare functions of the state nor its arrogation of certain duties and obligations to itself. In Soviet propaganda, the state was represented as the purveyor of social services. Whether or not this was the purported objective of the Stalinist state, Soviet propaganda unwittingly created areas for the state discourse to be contested by the citizens.

Soviet welfare policies were formulated in strict contradistinction to the welfare measures instituted in the West, especially in the United States during the Depression, and in Europe after the Second World War, where state and private agencies tended to distinguish between worthy and unworthy recipients of government assistance. The idea of a welfare state responsive to women's needs as working mothers was a novel political innovation, especially compared to Western countries which often considered welfare policies a temporary and charitable gesture toward distressed citizens or, more commonly, intended them to strengthen the patriarchal family and keep women out of the wage-labor market.[71] In the Soviet Union, government assumption of services formerly provided by families was integral to the vision of the October Revolution. The fulfillment of these duties was not perceived as charity to citizens fallen on hard times, but as the rights of Soviet women as citizens. The debate over the mobilization of women into industry was phrased in contractual terms. There was a public admission that in order for women to fulfill state plans the state would, in its turn, have to fulfill certain obligations.

A decree of the All-Union Soviet of Housing Cooperatives, passed in April 1931, underlined the need to create crèches and dining rooms in cooperative houses. It specified that 20 percent of the kitchen space in cooperative houses be set aside for communal dining rooms. Housing cooperatives were instructed to set up sixteen-hour crèches. The Commissariat of Labor would meet the costs of day-care centers and dining halls by deducting 10 percent from each person's rent and by advancing long-term loans. A strongly worded decree of the Central Committee ordered Gosplan and Narkomzdrav to ensure that 100 percent of all workers' children in large industries be enrolled in crèches and kindergartens by 1932. Party concern was further reflected in the larger appropriation of funds toward social services in the second Five-Year Plan.[72]

Finances did not appear to be the major problem. Of the 38,961,000 rubles assigned to the territory of RSFSR for the construction of crèches in 1932, almost half remained unused by the end of the year. Construction of buildings progressed very slowly, even in areas like the Moscow and Leningrad provinces, where the largest sums had been allocated. Furthermore, few concrete plans had been drawn up for the precise allocation and division of resources and responsibilities for construction among the various state bodies. From some reports, it appears that trade unions and insurance organizations (Sosstrakh) believed that they were being unfairly assigned all the burden of new crèche construction, and complained that Narkomzdrav and housing and consumer cooperatives should invest more resources and render more help. Narkomzdrav, in its turn, blamed the industrial administration and factory management for the delay in construction. This endless abrogation of responsibility, so characteristic of the Stalinist system, caused further confusion and delays.[73]

The instructions of the party were fulfilled and overfulfilled, according to Soviet statistics. The number of crèches for infants increased from 257,000 in 1928 to 5,143,400 in 1934; kindergartens for children expanded from 2,132 in 1927–28 to 25,700 in 1934–35.[74] In reality, many of the so-called new crèches were hastily revamped old buildings such as schools or former living quarters. As late as 1937, despite fixed Gosplan estimates of construction, the cost of building crèches varied widely from province to province, creating anarchy.[75] The conditions of kindergartens were even worse due to lack of funds for buildings and the intermittent cessation in food supply. Premises were often highly congested and unhygienic; linen supply was inadequate, and furniture such as cots and desks was almost completely missing. Children were badly clothed and dirty, and there were few efforts to quarantine sick children. Furthermore, the employees at these institutions were usually untrained and poorly qualified.[76] The irony was complete: the state had set out to acculturate Soviet women into the norms of socialized existence, and had wound up creating exemplary institutions whose conditions resembled to a frightening degree the unreconstructed and erstwhile working-class life.

Given the widespread indifference and hostility to the mobilization of women, and the inadequate services, it was surprising that between 1930 and 1931, 422,900 new women entered the workforce, and the percentage of women in heavy industry jumped from 22 percent to 42 percent. Women workers made unprecedented gains in the male-dominated sectors of construction such as railroads, mining, metallurgy, and machine production.[77] Historians have argued that the real reason for the sudden influx of women into the workforce in 1930-31 was due to a catastrophic drop in real wages and falling family incomes.[78] But in the state propaganda, the mobilization of women for industry was depicted as popular affirmation and enthusiastic support for the party goals of industrialization.[79]

In Soviet literature, the first Five-Year Plan did not merely result in the industrialization of a peasant nation, but also the modernization of a female population that hitherto was perceived as backward and uncultured.[80] The gendered dimensions of industrialization were figured in the reimaging of the Soviet woman as a liberated, reconstructed person who symbolized and simultaneously served as a yardstick for Soviet progress. Marxism had always claimed that only women's participation in the public sphere would truly liberate them. Stalin's revolution had dragged the Soviet woman into the public sphere; the first step had been completed. All that remained was the further education and acculturation of the erstwhile private prisoner. Education—especially technical education—*udarnichestvo* (shock work), and later *stakhanovism*, held the key to future upward mobility. Although the Soviet government had always aspired to the provision of universal education, only during the first Five-Year Plan were there dramatic upgrades in female literacy percentages.[81] Following the February 1929 government decree that reserved 20 percent of the seats for women in higher educational institutions, the number of women enrolled increased rapidly. The number of seats reserved for women was raised to 25 percent beginning in September 1930.[82]

Women's Day propaganda in the 1930s stressed the nexus between per-

Fig. 4. "8 Marta tret'ego goda piatiletki" (March 8: Third year of the Five-Year Plan). Hoover Institution on War, Revolution, and Peace. Moscow: Izogiz, 1931, RU/SU-1751.

sonal and state goals. If *udarnichestvo* meant heightened worker productivity and better quality of goods, it also translated into bonuses and possible promotions into administrative positions.[83] During these years, Women's Day festivities began to focus primarily on rallies by female shock workers, singling them out for praise and reward.[84] Shock work brigades (made up of workers who overfulfilled norms of production) were formed in factories, and women were encouraged to publicly declare themselves *udarnitsy* as part of a new celebratory ritual for Women's Day.[85] Trade unions were ordered to arrange exhibitions of the production results of the shock work brigades, and individual exemplary women workers were publicly ac-

132  **The Language of Liberation**

Fig. 5. "Obshchestvennomy pitaniiu-bol'shevistkie tempy i vysokoe kachestvo" (For the social food supply—Bolshevist tempo, and high quality). International Institute for Social History. Ogarkov and Liubimov, 1931, BG E5/587.

claimed. In 1933, Women's Day was officially declared the day of the *udarnitsa*.

As society became more complex, specialization and technical training separated the masses from the elite in the factories. At Women's Day ceremonies, shock workers were rewarded with silk blouses, radios, sewing machines, and cash bonuses. The growing pervasiveness of the idea of woman as both a qualified wage earner and consumer underscored the essential modernity of the New Soviet Woman. Few would contest the fact that the New Soviet Woman, as she was presented at home and abroad, had a modern persona, but modernity in Stalinist Russia meant something different

Fig. 6. "Delegatka, bud' vperedi" (Delegate, take the lead!). International Institute of Social History, 1931, BG E5/578.

than what the term implied in the West. In the last chapter I dissect the identities of Stalinist heroines in order to identify the various component parts that constituted the public face of Soviet women. In the process I also reveal the troubled and gendered nature of the discourse on Soviet modernity.

six

# The Public Identity of Soviet Women

The Stalinist revolution had a decisive impact not only on the material status of Soviet women but also on the state discourse reserved for them.[1] During the 1930s the narrative structures and symbolic imagery used to represent Soviet women in the public sphere underwent important modifications. Perhaps the most prominent feature in the process of reimaging public female identity was the creation of Soviet heroines, women who had supposedly penetrated the bastions of male primacy and excelled in positions hitherto considered unsuitable for them. Soviet heroines were fêted and lavishly promoted by the media in a language peculiarly overladen with Stalinist hyperbole. The process of heroicization, to coin a cumbersome noun, lay at the epicenter of the Stalinist discourse of women, and served as a legitimizing myth in a society of uncertain social values and cultural forms.[2]

One could argue that the transformation of the Russian woman from a symbol of backwardness to one of modernity in Soviet propaganda served to justify Stalinist policies in the 1930s. While the propaganda surrounding heroines familiarized Soviet women with the mores and morals of becoming modern, to the Soviet men it offered telling clues about the nature of new gender relations. Finally, Soviet modernization was a complicated phenomenon that differed substantially from the Western model.

While the symbolic revamping of woman's image carried implications of a modern society constructed on the basis of gender equality, the heroines' overt dependence on the state and the abject gratitude that they publicly expressed toward Stalin, the father figure, reinforced premodern notions of personal subjection and political subordination, rather than the

Fig. 7. "Proshloe, Nastoiashchee" (In the past and in the present). *Pravda*, March 8, 1933, 2.

autonomy of a modern citizen.[3] The Soviet system urged modernization, but its repressive policies constituted in themselves the biggest obstacle to the evolution of a civil society—a fundamental component of modernity. Or, as John Gray, a political theorist, says, "there is an inherent paradox in totalitarianism in that it deploys modern ideology in the service of an antimodernist project."[4]

Modernization and modernity are problematical terms that have a complicated genealogy. Beginning with the artistic leaders of the Romantic movement, other nineteenth-century intellectuals such as Marx, Nietzsche, Durkheim, and Weber were deeply ambiguous in their characterization of

136   The Public Identity of Soviet Women

Fig. 8. "Trudiashchiesia zhenshchiny vsekh stran! Stanovites' v pervye riady bortsov protiv voiny, protiv fashizma, protiv kapitalisticheskoi eksploatatsii! Da zdrastvuet 8 Marta mezhdunarodnyi kommunisticheskii zhenskii den'" (Long live the 8th of March, International, Communist, Women's Day). Hoover Institution on War, Revolution, and Peace, RUSU/1820. Moscow: OGIZ-IZOGIZ, 1937. Artist: Buev.

the successes and failures of the modern age. Following the Second World War, modernization theories enjoyed an unprecedented popularity in positing a universal experience of modernity, but this waned again due to the poststructuralist and postmodernist critiques leveled against them in the 1980s and 1990s.

The key ingredients of modernization, (setting aside the value judgments about modernity) include the transformation of societies by the industrial revolution, the primacy of secular and scientific knowledge, and the growth of a bureaucratic welfare state that engages in rational planning.[5] Some scholars, such as Jurgen Habermas, see the evolution of civil society and the attendant public sphere as one of the main characteristics of modernity.[6] According to Habermas, the public sphere came into existence at the same time that the state became the locus of depersonalized authority, and it was marked by free communication and a spirit of criticism that helped the transition from absolutist monarchies to parliamentary regimes.[7] The Soviet Union fulfilled many of the conditions of modernization while creating institutions that were unique. By the 1930s it was well on its way to becoming an industrialized nation under the disciplinary impetus of a bureaucratic welfare state. At the same time, however, the state, far from being an impersonal locus of power, was almost medieval in the staged performance of authority that was embodied in the public persona of Stalin and a few key figures, and presented endlessly before a captive audience.

Although the Soviet Union lacked a civil society, it had a public sphere wherein citizens were expected to both consume propaganda and display their familiarity with state discourses. Meetings, demonstrations, and holiday festivities provided ideal arenas within the public sphere where citizens could articulate their new Soviet identities and weave their personal histories into the narrative of the nation. If the exclusion of women from the public sphere was a distinguishing feature of both liberalism and fascism, in the 1930s the Soviet state claimed to have resolved the *zhenskii vopros* (woman question), and eliminated gender disparity.[8] The Stalinist rhetoric of feminist liberation did not directly translate into improved living standards, or even the diminution of misogynistic attitudes in private. But in the world of public utterances, Soviet officials were loath to utter sentiments that could be construed as antiwomen. Soviet propaganda, therefore, became a means of self-censorship, much like the category of "political correctness" in the United States.

Moreover, the propaganda associated with Soviet women served primarily to legitimize the regime. Soviet identity was created against an imagined European identity, both liberal and fascist. Soviet accomplishments were repeatedly contrasted with the shortcomings and deficiencies of the more "advanced" countries of Western Europe. In this dialogue the New Soviet Woman served as the embodiment of Soviet belief in gender equality and the welfare state. She also served as a justification for the creative and innovative nature of the Stalinist revolution. Under Stalin, or so the propaganda claimed, material conditions had changed so dramatically that Soviet superwomen were to be found in every corner of the nation—in collective farms, the military, institutions of higher learning, factories, the sports arena, even down in the tunnels of the Moscow subway system. In the 1930s the morally ambiguous and complex heroine models of the preceding decade, such as Dasha Chumalova, the heroine of Gladkov's novel, *Cement*, were replaced by Stalinist heroines, identifiable prototypes of modernity, and proof of the innate superiority of Stalinism over all other political and economic models of development.[9] In *Cement*, Dasha appears both pitiless and pitiful. Her ideological convictions are so strong that she condemns her daughter to an almost certain death by insisting that she share the privations of other Soviet children in a state-run institution. In a similar manner, she destroys her bourgeois home—complete with lace curtains—and channels all her energies toward political goals. But Dasha's sacrifices are too epic, too tragic, and she seems curiously unprepared to deal with daily life in the aftermath of the revolution. Stalinist heroines, in comparison, revel in the quotidian and overcome obstacles with ease. They combine motherhood with career obligations and also find time to volunteer their services to the state and society.

**Stalinism and the Woman Question**

As we have seen in the last chapter, the inception of the first Five-Year Plan in 1928 created a huge labor shortage in the country. For the first time in Soviet history, women were recruited into industry in significant numbers, even though factory conditions were appalling.[10] Women made some modest gains in the agricultural sector, which barely compensated for the extensive dislocation and trauma caused by collectivization.[11] Women were encouraged to join technical schools and colleges. Also, the state started spending precious resources on the construction of child-care centers, kindergartens, and medical facilities, but as noted previously, these facilities were inadequate in number and the quality of services left much to be desired. Despite party hyperbole, little was done to substantially relieve women of domestic tasks. But the discussion about state-sponsored social services created a vocabulary of rights and expectations for Soviet women. Finally, the 1930s saw the unprecedented upward mobility of women in such discrete fields as aviation, defense, agriculture, industry, arts, and sports.

Statistically, this cohort of Soviet heroines was not significant, but the publicity that surrounded them fostered the creation of a heroine myth that is revealing of certain social values and prescribed gender relations promoted by the Stalinist state.[12] From this pool of upwardly mobile women, a few were selected as heroines and celebrated in the media. The narrative about Soviet heroines, although rarely based on material reality, was an important element in Stalinist discourse, as it served as a gendered justification of the modernity of the regime, and upheld the Stalinist monopoly of socialist miracles. The heroines were memorable chiefly as repositories of state-mandated values, and their testimonies fleshed out the bare bones of Stalinist historiography.

The life histories of Soviet heroines were described by journalists, narrated by themselves on public occasions, and published in compendiums of biographical sketches of women, a genre that became especially popular in the 1930s.[13] The lives of real heroines had an eerie resemblance to the lives of fictional heroines, a testament to the ubiquitous power of the tropes of socialist realism.[14] The conventions governing this literature were fairly simple and included a straightforward narrative style, the transformation of consciousness through the retelling of one's life history, and personal redemption through identification with the goals of the Stalinist state. The protagonists were often the heroines of the middle level, extraordinary for their times but not necessarily national celebrities like Maria Demchenko, the *stakhanovka*, or Polina Osipenko, the aviator, or Pasha Angelina, the tractor driver. Nor were they the tried-and-true old female Bolshevik party activists. Rather, they were women from poor families who had achieved a measure of success under the Stalinist system and were in turn promoted by the state as the privileged recipients of Stalinist policies. But in structure and content the stories of the lesser heroines were similar to those of the national celebrities, and this testimonial literature served a political purpose.

### International Women's Day in the 1930s

Women, who were for the most part absent in Soviet public discourse, became the center of attention around March 8. The Stalinist period was no exception, and despite the greater prominence of female imagery in Soviet rhetoric and visual propaganda during this time, Women's Day celebrations continued to be the central showcase for Soviet women and their miraculous feats. The Central Committee journal *Sputnik agitatora* published biographical sketches of Soviet heroines in order to provide local agitators with concrete examples and detailed information for their Women's Day speeches. Regional and local party organizations were instructed to shower special attention and honors on women heroines on Women's Day.[15]

In the early part of the 1930s trade unions were asked to spotlight *udarnitsy*, women directors of factories, and women engineers as heroic examples and single them out for bonuses, promotions, and labor awards at Women's Day celebrations. Trade unions were also instructed to arrange production results of female shock work brigades and hold rallies where exemplary women workers were held up for public approbation. Beginning in 1935 media and trade union attention shifted to women *stakhanovites*. Women and their achievements were glorified in song, verse, and drama. Local and national journals and newspapers printed commemorative holiday issues prominently featuring accomplishments of Soviet women. Party leaders wrote newspaper articles and used this opportunity to remind women of the benefits that the socialist regime showered on them.[16]

In keeping with the growing *kul'turnost'* (refinement) of the Soviet population in the 1930s, Women's Day festivities took on an élan that was strangely reminiscent of prerevolutionary leisure pursuits. All this was consonant with the state-sponsored gaiety in Stalinist Russia that took its cue from Stalin's statement, "life has become better comrades, more joyous."[17] During the 1930s, especially after 1935, celebrations, carnivals, and public amusements punctuated the depredations wreaked by the widespread, state-sponsored repression of the Soviet people in which millions were executed and even larger numbers imprisoned. For example, on August 5 and 6, 1937, the Moscow Trade Unions organized grandiose public carnivals at the Gorky Park of Leisure and Culture. Hundreds of thousands of costumed and masked revelers danced the waltz, the tango, and the fox-trot. They admired torch-lit processions and gorged on abundant food and drink. The Moskva River brimmed with decorated boats, and the night sky was illuminated with fireworks and lights. Traditional fairground attractions offered to the visitor an eclectic range of amusements.[18]

In 1935, the Trekhgorniaia factory in Moscow threw a lavish party on the occasion of Women's Day. *Udarnitsy* arrived at the ball garbed in costumes of parachutists, Red sisters, skiers, snipers, aviators, and representatives of male-dominated professions. Members of a Red Army cavalry unit that patronized the civilian defense unit of the factory were invited to the party to squire the women on the dance floor.[19] Lesser institutions treated women to traditional Russian feasts, dancing, and speeches reminding them of the benefits that Stalin and the Soviet state had given them. Women's Day celebrations were often suffused with the apprehension of terror that ranged around but were nonetheless festive occasions.[20]

In 1936 a reception was held at the House of the Soviets to honor the heroines of the fatherland. Over seven hundred notable women, most of whom had been awarded Soviet decorations, were invited to the gala. These included women directors of state enterprises, *stakhanovites*, artists, doctors, scientists, parachutists, singers, and actresses.[21] Women graced the occasion "clad in elegant evening gowns adorned with corsages of snowdrops, violets and mimosa. After the concert and the supper, one could hear sounds of the orchestra that signaled the beginning of the evening dance. Confetti rained, paper streamers and balloons wafted through the evening air."[22] Factories across the nation arranged commemorative evenings for their outstanding women workers and rewarded them with cash bonuses and other expensive gifts. Movie theaters displayed placards and slogans commemorating Women's Day, and *udarnitsy* were allowed to buy tickets at a discount without standing in line.[23]

In contrast to this untrammeled gaiety, a festive meeting at the Bolshoi Theater in Moscow at which the upper echelons of the Communist party were well represented marked the political nature of the holiday.[24] Similar celebratory meetings were held in provincial capitals of the Union on Women's Day at which exemplary Soviet women were invited to speak about their achievements.²⁵ These included women pilots, directors of collective farms, transport workers, *stakhanovites* in industry, scientific personnel, and of course veteran female Bolsheviks such as Krupskaia, Artiukhina, Smidovich, and Ulianova. Women delegates were invited from abroad to participate in these meetings. Their presence was intended to mark the internationalism of Soviet ideology, and their speeches about the suffering women in capitalistic countries provided a dramatic mise-en-scène for the supposedly joyous and glorious life of Soviet women.²⁶

At these ceremonial events, Soviet heroines were asked to address the august audience and recount their life histories.²⁷ The heroines spoke in an edited voice, and the conjuncture between state propaganda and these autobiographies is quite remarkable. Nonetheless, these accounts reveal a depth of information about the construction of a public female identity in Stalinist Russia. Unfortunately, they tell us next to nothing about private identities of this period.

### Soviet Heroines in the Public Sphere

In public discourse, the crux of female identity in the 1930s was formed by the heroine's attachment to work.²⁸ The mystical attachment to norm fulfillment that many of these heroines exhibited was in part the realization of the Marxist prophecy of unalienated labor. Free from "exploitation," the heroines I researched toiled in factories, farms, railway yards, and combat units. They worked for the greater glory of Stalin and for the good of the country. If this dedication to one's work was a state-approved theme, at a more subtle level we find that exemplary labor output was a means to upward social mobility and to material wealth. Maria Isaakovna, an employee at a book printing factory, saw her pay rise from six rubles to eight to nine rubles a day after she became a *stakhanovka*. She lived in a three-room apartment along with her husband, mother, and three children. The fact that she was a party member and also served on the factory committee must have helped her attain these goals.²⁹ Nonetheless, professional success gave women financial independence, a certain level of prestige in society, and helped in the renegotiation of power relationships within the family. Therefore, it was not surprising that women defined themselves primarily in terms of their occupations.³⁰

Smirnova, a chairwoman of a *kolkhoz* in the Moscow *oblast*, was invited to speak at the Bolshoi Theater in Moscow at a Women's Day celebration in 1936.[31] The guest list for the function included Khrushchev, Bulganin, Stasova, and Ulianova, to name only a few of the VIPs present. Stalin himself graced the event midway through the meeting, along with Molotov, Kaganovich, and Ordzhonikidze.[32] Smirnova was no pastoral maiden sporting on the sylvan green, a character so dear to fiction writers in the 1930s, but forty years old, palpably aware of her self-worth, and quite overcome at the miraculous nature of her achievements.[33] In her account of her life, Smirnova stressed her incredulity that she, a farm worker, was addressing the heads of the Soviet state. As she said, this rarely happened anywhere in the world, and it was especially surprising in Russia where the village woman was a notorious symbol of oppression and backwardness. Smirnova described her situation: "Look at me a kolkhoznitsa . . . I have come to this hall and am speaking with the bosses, the administrators of Moscow."[34] From her account it appears that Smirnova was a simple peasant woman, but the collectivization of land opened new opportunities for her. She worked hard, proved herself, and was appointed the chairman of a *kolkhoz*. As she said, "before I was nothing, now I am a heroine of labor and I was awarded the Red Banner of Labor."[35] In contrast to her previous insignificance, the recognition of her services by the state gave her life a measure of meaning. Smirnova's identity, therefore, was deeply intertwined with her occupation, her skills, and her power in the *kolkhoz*.[36]

Creation of female identity was closely tied to the chronology of the revolution.[37] The Soviet press in the 1930s was replete with Cinderella stories of women born to poor peasant families who, in the wake of collectivization, rose to responsible positions within the *kolkhozes*. Even the noted director, Sergei Eisenstein, developed this theme in his film, *Staroe i Novoe* (Old and New). The film *Member of the Government* (1939), by A. Zarkhi and I. Kheifits, dealt with the story of an uneducated and downtrodden farm worker, Aleksandra Sokolova, who eventually became the head of the collective farm and a delegate to the Supreme Soviet.[38] These Soviet heroines, unlike the mass of the Russian *baby* (old women), who were violently opposed to collectivization, realized that the *kolkhoz* would free them from their miserable dependence on their husbands and fathers. An article in

*Krest'ianka* polled women in the Northern Caucasus as to why they joined local *kolkhoz*. While the majority of the women described their initial antipathy to the *kolkhoz*, a couple of them declared that they joined the collective farm of their own volition, and one took the initiative of joining against the will of her husband.[39] From the very inception of the campaign, they worked energetically to convince the *temnye* (uncultured) and backward women in the village to join the collective farms, even when most of their exhortations fell on deaf ears. Often these heroines were cursed and taunted by other village women for their efforts. During a conversation with Kalinin, a *kolkhoz* worker recalled how the village women spat at her and called her the apostle of the Antichrist when she tried to persuade them to join the *kolkhoz*. Sometimes these women became the objects of vile rumors and were harassed in their communities. In one extreme case, class enemies wrongfully sentenced an exemplary agricultural worker named Khitrikova from the Kurgansk District in the North Caucasus to one year's hard labor.[40] Contrary to expectations, most of these collaborators were neither party nor Komsomol activists, but local women with ambition and foresight whose alliance with the party worked to the mutual benefit of both sides.

This basic theme of the lone heroine pitted against a foolish and improvident village formed a master narrative for the biographies of Soviet heroines. Their stories were constructed around the axis of prerevolutionary oppression and postrevolutionary liberation. But more often than not, the crucial moment in women's lives was not the October Revolution, but the Stalinist revolution. Propaganda in the 1930s strove to rewrite the chronology of the revolution, and the years of the first Five-Year Plan seem to be the decisive time period for the liberation of Soviet women.[41] The story of Matrena Doroshenko, a poor peasant woman from the Northern Caucasus, offers a good illustration of the Stalinist version of women's history. The October Revolution did not make any substantial change in Matrena's situation as a dependent housewife, and she suffered at the hands of her husband and his cruel family during the 1920s. But during collectivization, she sided with the party even though her husband's family was part of the *kulak* counteroffensive. She testified against her brother-in-law, Iosif Doroshenko, recounting his affiliation with the Whites during the civil war. She also denounced the *kulaks* that had gained control of their collective farm. Matrena suffered murderous reprisals: her home was burned down and she was physically attacked and hospitalized for a couple of weeks. But the state rewarded her for her collaboration and soon she was appointed chairman of a *kolkhoz*, Krasnyi Donbass.[42] The moral of the story was fairly obvious: devotion to the family was a waste of emotion, but devotion to state interests brought rich dividends.[43] Such stories sanitized the brutal record of collectivization by associating terror and violence with class enemies while reserving the modern means of persuasion—reason and legal testimony—for party activists.

Although these "exemplary" women were demarcated sharply from the rest of the backward women, this was a temporary hiatus, and this device of disjuncture was used exclusively in the period of collectivization. During the 1930s, the reverse was true, and the notion of sisterhood formed a crucial element in female identity. Sisterhood served a variety of functions in the Soviet Union, and in the press there are repeated instances of women turning to one another for support, for sustenance, for friendship, and for help. An article about Halima Apa Kasakova, an administrator of the Women's Club in Tashkent, describes the caring relationships that she maintained with the women of the city. Whenever she appeared in the club or on the streets, local women clustered around her with cries of "Mother," shook her hand, and complained about conservative and recalcitrant husbands. Halima Apa always responded with affectionate concern and sound practical suggestions.[44] At a time when the purges were literally tearing the country apart and atomizing Soviet society into a collection of suspicious strangers, it was important for the media to stress the theme of a socialist *gemeinschaft* in order to offset the effects of terror. Soviet society was described in familial metaphors, and ties between citizens were represented as bonds of kinship.[45]

During the 1930s, Women's Day stories about heroines emphasized the fact that these were not lone pioneers, but belonged to a nucleus of caring and like-minded women. Thus, the ten young women skiers from an electric factory, who skied the 1,400 kilometers from Moscow to Tiumen in 1936, referred to their close and friendly relations with each other. The skiers helped each other on the way, especially when one of them showed signs of tiring. They also spoke eloquently about the warmth and hospitality that they received on their journey from various *kolkhoz* workers, railroad workers, and Red Army soldiers.[46] In a similar manner, the women's miner brigade in the eighteenth shaft of the Moscow Metro was enthusiastic about the harmony that prevailed in their labor group. Not only did the miners work together, they also shared common interests in the arts and theater. On occasion they even joined forces in their quest to reform uncouth and lazy male comrades.[47]

Women workers at the L. M. Kaganovich ball bearing factory in Moscow took the kinship metaphor one step further. According to the leader of the group, their unit literally functioned as a surrogate family for one of their co-workers who had a little baby boy. No one referred to Masha Krokhotkina's husband, but her female co-workers in essence adopted her baby, showered her with gifts and advice on child rearing, relieved her from the night shift, and helped take care of the infant so the mother would not be overwhelmed by the double shift.[48]

Sisterhood could, in many instances, stretch across international boundaries, and although the Stalinist state had abandoned the principles of proletarian internationalism, gender ties were able to surmount hostile relations between nations. A gripping saga published in 1937 recounted the story of the Soviet patriot Praskov'ia Efimovna and her bravery during her incarceration in prison in a foreign land. Efimovna was shipwrecked along with her four-year-old son on the coast of Japan in 1936, captured as a Soviet spy, and subsequently tortured by the Japanese authorities. Poor Japanese women sympathized with her plight and helped keep her alive by throwing food to her surreptitiously through the prison bars.[49]

If the female sense of self was created in relation to other women, at the same time it was articulated in sharp contradistinction to the archetypal Russian male. There were two elements in this antagonistic relationship with men. In the first instance, men, husbands, and fathers were invariably portrayed in the literature as a brake on women's cultural and professional development, and as a reactionary presence that served to stultify their personal growth.[50] This was a complete reversal of the earlier Bolshevik propaganda in which women were characterized as a drag on the revolutionary consciousness of proletarian men, and as an apolitical and profoundly counter-revolutionary force.[51] In the second instance, heroines such as Smirnova apparently displayed great satisfaction at the reversal of power relationships within the family, which was invariably predicated on the greater earning power of the women vis-à-vis their husbands.

In numerous stories there are references to husbands who try to prevent women from achieving their personal ambitions, male co-workers who refuse to accept a female overseer, or even casual passersby who display traditionally misogynistic attitudes. Describing a train journey, a reporter wrote that a seaman was entertaining his fellow travelers with stories about life on the high seas. A woman passenger seemed particularly interested, but the seaman was quite curt with her and said that it was easy for women to be excited by tales of exotica, but that life on the sea was very arduous. Later it turned out that the woman in question, Barbara Mikhailovna, had served on various kinds of ships, sailed in distant seas and oceans, and had been in a ship that had been torpedoed twice in the Mediterranean Sea.[52] Ollennikova, a *stakhanovite* worker, and the first female railroad controller in her section, recalled at the 1936 Women's Day conference in Moscow that she faced a lot of hostility at the workplace. Men flouted her authority and her orders. Once a machinist came up to her and said that he wanted to meet the controller, and when she identified herself, he replied: "What kind of a controller are you, I can hear a woman's voice, get me the controller."[53] But finally, with the help of the party and due to her own perseverance, her male co-workers accepted her authority.

Flight navigator Marina Raskova, lecturer at the Zhukov Air Force Academy, recalled how her husband tried his best to prevent her from becoming a pilot. Naturally, she paid little attention to his entreaties and went on to have successful career in the air force.[54] Similarly, Agafiia Durniasheva, a *stakhanovite* worker at the Trekhgorniaia Manufactory in Moscow, teacher at a technical school, party worker, and mother of five, revealed that she had been hindered in every step of her career by her husband. In her interview she stated that the fact that she earned more than her husband and was a party member, had created problems in her marital relationship.[55] Initially, when she had wanted to attend trade school, her husband sought to dissuade her, citing their large number of children as the main deterrent. She ignored this advice, completed the apprenticeship courses, joined the party, and was rewarded with a spacious apartment for her large family.[56]

In her Women's Day address, Smirnova's feelings of superiority toward her husband were an important part of her perception of self. She exhibited certain contempt for her husband and the men on the *kolkhoz*. She said that during the years of collectivization the men ran away and left them in the lurch, and when they returned, the women didn't really need them.[57] This was perhaps the most disingenuous explanation on record of the forced deportations of millions of peasants, one that reduced the tragedy of collectivization to the farce of coy gender conflict. Smirnova was obviously pleased with the transformation of her status from subordination to one of relative super-ordination. Savoring the irony of role reversal in her family, she said,

> I am the chairman of the *kolkhoz*. . . . And all the men submit to my authority [laughter in the audience]. I am the chairman of the *kolkhoz* while my husband is a simple laborer. I give him orders and point out all his shortcomings. I converse with him like he is just another worker, not my husband—. Before when my husband went to the *skhod* [village assembly] and later I asked him about the proceedings, he would reply that it was none of my business. Now I come and tell him all that we decided and he listens to me, now he is humble. I am decorated and he is not.[58]

Smirnova's recital contained the new prescriptive mores for gender and marital interaction. But one wonders if she had internalized them, or whether she was merely quoting from an approved script.

### Soviet Heroines in the Private Sphere

The discourse on motherhood and maternalism constituted an important element in women's public identity in the 1930s. There was a substantial difference in the Stalinist construction of motherhood and maternalism. Here I use the term *motherhood* to refer to the act of reproduction, while *maternalism* denotes notions of parenting and the idealized relationship between the mother and child that is often enforced by the state and society. For example, in postrevolutionary America, although women were denied political rights, they were nonetheless exhorted to raise good republican children. Similarly, women in nineteenth-century Western Europe were supposed to seek fulfillment through reproduction and discharge civic obligations by transmitting to children appropriate social and moral values. In Russia, however, there was little historical precedent of limiting women's functions to child rearing, and the nineteenth-century Western notions of women fulfilling their destiny exclusively through domesticity were fairly uncommon.[59] While the Russian aristocracy routinely trusted the care of children to servants, peasant women and factory women could not afford the luxury of personally raising their children. These children were, for the most part, abandoned to the supervision of older children and old women unfit to work in the fields.[60] Despite their animosity toward bourgeois culture, the Bolsheviks, following the October Revolution, tried to inculcate typically bourgeois notions of child rearing in its citizenry.

Throughout the 1920s and 1930s, magazines for women such as *Rabotnitsa*, *Krest'ianka*, and *Obshchestvennitsa* carried simple articles explaining modern methods of child rearing and information on obstetrics. In Red Corners in factories, doctors and nurses held seminars on infant care, personal hygiene, and the importance of regular cleaning of living quarters. The Section for Maternity Protection (OMM) printed popular tracts on hygiene, nutritional information on children's diets, and articles on pre- and postnatal care.[61] Parents were encouraged to pay attention to children's homework, inculcate good reading habits, and take an interest in their social development. In Women's Day speeches in the 1930s, Party leaders stressed the responsibilities of parents to their offspring and exhorted them to supervise their children's development. However, at the same time, it was repeatedly emphasized that maternal functions were only supposed to consume a fraction of women's time, the rest of which was to be spent in socialist labor and community-oriented activity.[62]

The discourse on motherhood, too, was created along statist lines. By reproducing, Soviet women were fulfilling the prime obligation of good citizens. Mothers of large families exemplified civic virtue and social conscience. Unlike the Victorian construction of maternalism, which exhorted women to fulfill their feminine and therefore essentially biological destiny by reproduction—within the holy bonds of matrimony—in the Soviet Union, motherhood was presented as a public act. When a Soviet woman had a child she fulfilled an important national function—she ensured the reproduction of a future generation of socialists who would work for the fatherland and protect the motherland from the aggression of fascists and capitalists. It was an investment in the future on par with the investment in heavy industry. As Stalin said, "The Soviet woman has the same rights as the man, but that does not free her from a great and honorable duty which nature has given her: she is a mother, she gives life. This is not a private affair, but one of great social importance."[63]

Soviet discourse on motherhood was not self-contained; instead it was created in reference to both the "decadent" bourgeois West and the infinitely more demonized fascist order. While the nationalization of women's reproductive and productive capacities was part of a pan-European phenomenon, Soviet propaganda strove to distinguish the modernity of its pronatalist policies from the "retrograde" nature of those pursued in the West.[64] Of the various images used to contrast the vigor and vitality of the young Soviet Union with the degenerate and effete West, birth rates ranked among the most popular one.

Popular articles extolling motherhood cited comparative mortality and fertility figures that contrasted the Soviet Union favorably with the West.[65] In this instance, Soviet publications merely echoed the demographic anxiety that was being expressed in countries such as France, Spain, Scandinavia, Italy, and Germany in the 1930s. Propaganda claimed that while mortality rates were declining and birth rates were rising in the Soviet Union, they were dropping precipitously in France, England, Italy and Germany.[66] This was because the fascists in Germany were practicing a most sinister and ingenious form of eugenics. Birth centers across Germany were being closed, as fascists demanded that that the "natural" process of giving birth be carried out within the domestic space. But this romantic Nazi yearning for premodern German society, where women would be restored to their "natural" functions, concealed a form of class oppression. The Soviets alleged that by closing down birth centers and by denying working mothers access to doctors and medical pre- and postnatal care, the fascists were trying to control the growth of the proletarian population in Germany. According to Soviet medical opinion, the number of suicides among women in Germany was the highest in the world.[67]

In the Soviet Union, by contrast, state propaganda claimed that as biological reproduction was both a social act and a civic obligation, the health and welfare of pregnant women were public and state concerns. If motherhood was celebrated as a public duty, and as an act of patriotism in Stalinist Russia, the image of a caring and paternalistic state order was given equal visibility in the media. Thus, Maria Il'inichna, mother of ten children, in an interview on the occasion of Women's Day, highlighted the fact that three of her children went to a nursery, one to kindergarten, and the older one attended school. Moreover, having given birth, women were not asked to sit at home and take care of their children. There was a constant tension implicit in the construction of maternalism. On the one hand, Soviet women were being taught to become modern mothers. They were told to replace age-old Russian practices of child rearing with modern and scientific advice on nutritious diets, daily hygiene, appropriate clothing, and stimulating intellectual surroundings. But at the same time, women were not perceived purely as caregivers, nor was reproduction their only function. Soviet children were citizens in their own right, and the Stalinist state promised to provide adequate medical care and child-care services. Inflated facts and figures on social service organizations accompanied the rhetoric extolling motherhood.[68]

Despite remarkable expansion in state social services, barely a dent was made in the demand for assistance during the 1930s. Strangely enough, these problems were openly acknowledged in the popular press.[69] The volunteer movement of the "Wives of Industrialists and Engineering-Technical Personnel" (obshchestvennitsy), organized by Sergo Ordzhonikidze, the commissar for heavy industry, was intended to utilize the services of this privileged cohort of women to compensate for shortcomings in state-funded social services.[70] A large number of articles in the women's press focused on the limitations of Soviet child-care services, dining halls, housing, and medical organizations, and instructed obshchestvennitsy how to supplement these services through voluntarism and community action.[71]

The argument was circular: since the state provided ideal social circumstances that were conducive to promoting motherhood, there was no compelling need for Soviet women to limit the size of their families. At the same time, due to the availability of social services, there was no reason why women should spend all their time on child care. As Agafiia Karpovna explained when asked how she managed to be a mother of five, teacher, worker, and social activist, she replied that it was all a matter of time management. A Women's Day film clip from 1937 showed women moving effortlessly from mothering at home to working in the factory to socializing in clubs with their children. The film clip presented a brief vignette of a female professor at the Military Engineering School, who was also a mother and a skilled seamstress.[72] Notions of efficient ordering of time evoked images of modernity. The multiple roles that Soviet women were expected to play in both the public and the private sphere were represented, not as a burden or double shift, but as a testimonial both to the Bolshevik "can do" spirit, and to the innate superiority of Soviet women over their international counterparts.[73] Although women privately acknowledged that the double shift was overwhelming, in public discourse the progressive efficiency of Soviet women was used to valorize the Soviet state. The 1930s diary of Galina Vladimirovna Shtange, an *obshchestvennitsa*, details her exhaustion in trying to complete her domestic and public duties. But at the same time, she appears very reluctant to give up her community activity and devote herself full-time to the care of her family.[74]

Abortion, naturally, represented a threat to images of joyous fecundity, and the arguments against abortion were constructed along the same lines that sought to promote motherhood. The abortion decree of June 27, 1936, carried several supplementary conditions in addition to the restrictions on abortions. These included the rendering of material assistance to pregnant women, growth in number of child-care centers and consultation clinics for children, increase in alimony payments to divorced wives with large families, and strict punishment of defaulters of alimony payments.[75] Once again, the abortion decree was used to contrast the limitations of the October Revolution with the achievements of the Stalinist revolution. It was argued that abortion had been reluctantly allowed in the 1920s because of the material poverty of the country and due to the desperate plight of its citizens. Even during the 1920s abortion was perceived as a necessary evil, and the Zhenotdel, the OMM, and doctors in nursing homes fought against granting permission for abortions.[76] But in the 1930s, because of the better living conditions and the social services provided by the state, there was little need to deny women their natural right to the joys of motherhood.

The abortion decree, however, unleashed a storm of protest from Soviet women across the nation. Although public acrimony was soon stifled, the number of illegal abortions in the cities of Leningrad and Moscow rose dramatically in 1937 and 1938. The Sovnarkom (Council of People's Commissars) sought to deflect blame for the growing number of illegal abortions by claiming that the methods used by the procurator's office to weed out illegal abortion centers were inadequate, and that the doctors and old women who performed abortions were not being punished appropriately. Also, Narkomzdrav, Narkomzem (Commissariat of Land Affairs), and Narkompros were criticized for the lack of material help rendered to pregnant women, terrible conditions at nursing homes, shortage of trained medical personnel, slow construction of day-care centers, and limited popularization of information on child care and the perils of abortion.[77] During these years, the strictures of Sovnarkom notwithstanding, a modest propaganda campaign was waged that celebrated motherhood and warned against the evil repercussions of abortions. Articles, purportedly written by doctors, warned that abortions invariably led to barrenness, loss of health and vigor in women, premature aging, hemorrhaging, and internal bleeding.[78] Soviet propaganda stressed that women who resorted to back-alley abortions were reverting to the mores of a presocialist and premodern peasant Russia. Since old women lacking scientific skill and knowledge principally performed them, it was inconceivable that the modern Soviet women would patronize such butchers, according to the propaganda. In 1938, the paternalistic provisions of the 1936 abortion decree were further expanded. The Central Committee decrees published on Women's Day of that year declared that the constant concern of the party for Soviet mothers and children was reflected in the increased state funding for the construction of nursing homes and day-care centers.[79]

In stark contrast to the nurturing role of the party, males, especially husbands and lovers, were cast in the role of the evil seducers who urged girlfriends and wives to have abortions in order to escape the consequences of their irresponsible sexual behavior. An article in *Molodaia gvardiia*, analyzing letters written by women in response to the abortion decree, concluded that in most instances men were guilty of forcing women to have abortions. While women's agency in motherhood was stressed, abortion was represented as an infringement on women's free will and modernity. During this period, in consonance with the other clauses of the abortion decree, there was a statewide crackdown on errant husbands who refused to pay alimony or child support.[80]

A popular short story by M. Shoshin from 1938, "A Rendezvous," weaves the theme of negligent fathers and triumphant daughters in a naive but matter-of-fact manner.[81] As a young mill worker in prerevolutionary Russia, Ivan had been an ambitious man who had jilted his proletarian girlfriend in order to marry a rich older woman. However, twenty years later, he realizes that wealth has brought him little joy. As he contemplates his meaningless existence, he finds out that he has an illegitimate daughter, Nadia, a famous shock worker in the textile industry. Ivan proposes a meeting, and at the rendezvous Nadia appears poised, energetic, and confident while the father is remorseful and uneasy. She treats him kindly, without recriminations or tears, and is indifferent to his pathetic attempts to make reparations, both monetary and emotional. While Nadia, her daughter, and her mother Maria have woven a resilient family circle based on loving relationships and solid achievement, Ivan appears pitiful in his loneliness. In the final analysis, Ivan's alienation resulted from his willful flouting of the values of Soviet society, and the story shows that there can be no meaningful existence outside those normative boundaries.

### Stalin and the Soviet Heroine

In this classic struggle of the sexes, propaganda stressed that it was the Stalinist state that supported the heroine and ensured her success in every sphere of existence. The *trudoden'* (work day) system in the *kolkhoz* made peasant women financially independent of husbands or fathers, and for the first time rewarded her materially for her labor input. Masha Scott, in an interview with Pearl Buck, recalled that her mother used to wave her collective farm card in her husband's face and taunt him, "'You always said you supported me. Now you see I am earning as much as you,' she declared. 'So I have as much to say as you have, don't I? You had better not say anything more to me.'"[82] According to Stalin,

> Only collective farm life could have destroyed inequality and put woman on her feet.... The collective farm introduced the work-day. And what is the work-day? Before the *trudoden'* all are equal—men and women. Here neither

father nor husband can reproach a woman with the fact that he is feeding her. Now if a woman works and has *trudodni* to her credit, she is her own master . . . and that is just what is meant by the emancipation of peasant women; that is just what is meant by the collective farm which makes the working woman the equal of every working man.[83]

It was reiterated repeatedly that only the party nurtured the hidden talents of women peasants and helped them become opera singers and parachutists. *Vecherniaia Moskva* carried a story of a young peasant girl from Siberia who, thanks to the Komsomol, became a student at the Moscow conservatory as an opera singer and even appeared as a soloist at the Bolshoi Theater.[84] The party created circumstances in which women could advance to high administrative positions and admonished Soviet men who held traditional attitudes toward women and wanted to limit them within the confines of domesticity.[85] In a letter to the journal *Obshchestvennitsa*, a wife of an engineer at Magnitostroi complained that despite her youth and willingness to work, her husband wanted her to remain at home and minister to his every need. She feared the engineer's temper and wanted advice from the editors of the journal on how to engage in some meaningful occupation without suing for divorce. The tone of the letter implied that her husband was mistaken in harboring such antimodern sentiments toward women, and the writer seemed confident that the authorities would intervene on her behalf. In public, the party subscribed to the modern notion that marriage was founded on the equality between men and women. Men were urged to help in child care and housework.[86] In a story about an exemplary worker, Kriuchikhin, the writer of the story, stressed the fact that Kriuchikihin always helped his daughters with their homework.[87] Finally, it was repeatedly claimed that the party upheld women's rights to motherhood against the depredations of husbands and evil quacks. Men were publicly admonished to overcome their bourgeois attitudes and treat women as equals. The hyperbole surrounding the Soviet heroine was used to buttress the myth of upward mobility in the Soviet Union. Here, the traditional social and cultural stigma surrounding Russian women was especially useful. The creation of a Soviet hero was less miraculous in a society long accustomed to the myths of strong male rulers and valiant knights. But the transformation of the illiterate, uncultured, and counter-revolutionary

Russian woman was an achievement of far greater magnitude. The capacity to create the Soviet heroine not only conferred legitimacy on the Soviet regime, but through association with the heroines, Stalin, and by extension the Soviet Union, was guaranteed immortality.

The conversion of the *baba* to a civic subject constituted a revolution of unique social dimensions, and was represented in Soviet ideology as one of the more triumphant results of Stalinism. A speech by Stalin at the Seventeenth Party Congress which underscored both the functional attributes of the New Soviet Woman and her symbolic importance:

> Women represent half the population of our country, they represent an enormous army of labor, and their mission is to bring up our children, our future generation, that is to say, our future. That is why we must not permit this huge army of toilers to remain in darkness and ignorance! That is why we must welcome the growing social activity of our toiling women and their promotion to leading posts, as an undoubted indication of the growth of our culture (*kul'turnost'*).[88]

The cover of the February issue of *Krest'ianka* in 1931 shows a picture of two women *kolkhoz* workers poring over the decisions of the 1930 December Plenum of the Central Committee of the party.[89] The photograph associated women with modernity, political consciousness, literacy, and culture. Formerly, peasant women were thought to be entirely devoid of such characteristics. As Stalin said on several occasions, such a Soviet woman "could never have existed in previous times." Orators echoed the dictum that only a socialist country could produce such remarkable women.[90] Thus, in the ultimate analysis, Soviet women owed everything to the Stalinist Five-Year Plan in industry, and collectivization in agriculture.

The extensive literature thanking Stalin that emerged in the 1930s as an integral ritual of Women's Day celebrations exemplified this symbiotic relationship between Stalin and Soviet heroines. The narrative structure of the letters was essentially the same. With few exceptions, most of them were constructed around similar themes: The women letter writers addressed Stalin with the familiar *ty* (you), rather than the more formal *vy* (thou). Stalin's name was prefixed with the adjective *rodnoi* (one's own) to underscore the familial relationships that bound Stalin and the Soviet women. The women thanked Stalin for the extraordinary improvement in their cultural and material position, and for fulfilling the promises of October. The extensive concern for women's welfare that Stalin was accredited with was in consonance with the public imaging of the dictator as a paternal champion of women's rights and the sole guarantor of their upward mobility to positions of power and prestige.[91]

Thus the modernity of the New Soviet Woman was deeply compromised. If in her dedication to work and upward mobility, gender equality, efficient time management and nationalism, the Soviet heroine exemplified the modern citizen, her pronatalism, reliance on sisterhood, and devotion to Stalin was redolent of a premodern era. Finally, the statist orientation of the category revealed its ambiguous nature. Soviet heroines were completely dependent on the state to uphold their authority in both the public and the private sphere. This dependence, coupled with the atmosphere of repression and fear, bespoke political allegiance from the women. But at the same time, these heroines posed little threat to the political system. Their power was based on the artificial support extended by the state, not grounded in any fundamental change in the social order or popular attitudes. Also, since Soviet heroines rarely occupied positions of political power or strategic party posts, they could not form a serious pressure group for women's rights within the system. The heroines' claims to fame rested on the fact that they engaged in occupations traditionally reserved for men and by doing so lent credibility to the alleged Soviet commitment to women's liberation. At the same time, the miraculously transformative power of Stalinism was revealed. Not only had Russia modernized almost overnight into an industrial giant, but the *baba*, the most benighted expression of Russian backwardness, had been transmuted into a modern, confident, politically mature citizen, in short a *chelovek* (human being).[92]

# Epilogue

In conclusion, I present two vignettes that contain, in embryonic outline, the reconstructed Soviet woman of the 1930s. In a letter to Mikhail Kalinin, president of the Central Executive Committee of the Soviets, a young woman from Tashkent was deeply critical of the June 1936 ban on abortion. She claimed that, given her materially straitened circumstances, she could not afford to have another child. Nor did she have the energy after a full day's work to spend time with her child, or accompany her to various cultural functions. As a member of the Komsomol, and born of poor peasant stock, she hoped that her letter would not be interpreted as the opinion of a class enemy, but rather be taken as the *cri de coeur* on behalf of the majority of Soviet women. She was deeply critical of the attitudes of doctors who refused to grant permission to sick women for abortions, and warned that many women were forced to seek the help of old women, or induce abortions themselves. As she said, "this was not the liberation of women, but rather the enslavement of women, ultimately we are reverting to becoming birth-giving machines, that give birth every year."[1]

Although the letter was a complaint against Soviet decrees, the letter writer identified herself completely in terms of the New Soviet Woman, including the customary denunciation of her fictive predecessor, the fecund peasant mother. She represented herself as a product of the Soviet system, and apparently embodied its values of upward mobility. Although of peasant stock, she was not only literate, she was also a member of the Komsomol, and thereby exhibited a degree of political consciousness. She held modern attitudes about parenting, and was aware that it entailed more than the act of giving birth. Moreover, her letter implied confidence that the Stalinist system was sympathetic to the plight of women and would alleviate the poor conditions of hospitals, which included the hostile attitudes of the medical staff to those seeking abortions.

In the second instance, in response to an investigation into the quality of child care afforded to children at a tobacco factory in 1935, Comrade Kempe, an older woman who had worked in the factory for twenty-five years, said that her parents never even had the right to think of child-care facilities at the factory. Her daughter previously attended a kindergarten, and subsequently was a disciplined student at a primary school. The younger women workers, however, with fewer memories of the prerevolutionary past, were deeply critical of the conditions in the factory-run kindergarten. Prokof'eva, a woman worker who had worked at a tobacco factory for only six years, was happy that her child had been taught the elements of hygiene at the kindergarten. But at the same time, she felt that due to the unsanitary conditions of the kindergarten, the drafty building, and insufficient food, the children tended to fall sick far too often.[2]

The difference in the responses showed both the successes and the failures of the revolution. On the one hand, the revolution had completely failed to create the welfare utopia that it had promised and continued to promise. In the late 1930s restrictive laws on divorce and abortion, the glorification of the nuclear family, and elevation of the function of motherhood all pointed to the declining power of the visions of liberal feminism. Stalinism did not fulfill the ideals of the October Revolution in that gender parity remained an abstract dream throughout the life of the Soviet Union. But Stalinism did complete one part of the Bolshevik gender project; it managed to semiotically reencode the category of "woman" in Soviet public discourse. Officially, Soviet women were rarely reviled as politically immature or backward. Instead, Soviet heroines embodied the tortured nature of Soviet modernity.[3]

The relationship of women to the state had undergone a seismological shift in terms of the political imaginary. In public propaganda Soviet women, unlike their counterparts in tsarist Russia, subscribed to the vision of the welfare state. They expected the Soviet state to provide certain social services, employment, and educational opportunities. Women identified themselves in terms of their professional achievements, as do citizens of a modern state. At the same time they expressed a quasifeudal sense of gratitude to the state, personified as a male patron or mentor. Indeed, woman's selfhood could only be expressed through her interaction with the ideology, practices, and institutions of the state.

The state for its part, through the production of propaganda intended for female consumption, marked women as a political entity with singular needs and privileges. Soviet discourse articulated a female subject who was endowed with a distinctive voice, and could narrate her own story coherently through the medium of time. In the Soviet media women exhibited a modern consciousness of the self, as a being situated in time and subject to the forces of history. The crude division contained in women's stories between the oppressive prerevolutionary past and glorious future helped perpetuate a historical consciousness of being time-bound. The notion of time was imagined in segments of national history, rather than in the idealized ebb-and-flow of traditional female lives. Intimate episodes such as childhood, youth, marriage, and childbearing were grafted onto the larger ongoing national drama. The periods of revolution, civil war, collectivization, and industrialization were more than organizational devices used by politicians and historians. Indeed, as I have tried to show, they were temporal markers that structured female narratives and anchored the vicissitudes of fates suffered by individuals.[4]

Finally, the revolution inured women to the exigencies of change, an integral part of modernity. Indeed, the one constant amid the many discourses about the New Soviet Woman was the ability of the women to grapple with rapid change and domesticate the most extraordinary circumstances. Marx described the modern environment in his *Communist Manifesto:*

> All fixed, fast-frozen relations, with their train of ancient and venerable prejudices and opinions, are swept away, all new-formed ones become antiquated before they can ossify. All that is solid melts into air, all that is holy is profaned, and man is at last compelled to face with sober senses his real conditions of life, and his relations with his kind.[5]

The above paragraph can be read as an epitaph for Stalinist history. If the revolution had taught women one thing, it was to take little for granted, and nothing as constant.

# Notes

**Introduction**

1. On folk beliefs, see Linda Ivanits, *Russian Folk Belief* (New York, 1989); Eve Levin, *Sex and Society in the World of the Orthodox Slavs, 900–1700* (New York, 1989); Joanna Hubbs, *Mother Russia: The Feminine Myth in Russian Culture* (Bloomington, Ind.: 1988); and Cathy Frierson, *Peasant Icons: Representations of Rural People in Late Nineteenth-Century Russia* (New York, 1993). For a literary analysis of the virtuous woman in nineteenth-century Russian literature, see Barbara Heldt, *Terrible Perfection: Women and Russian Literature* (Bloomington, Ind., 1987). On women and modernity, see Nikolai Chernyshevsky, *What Is to Be Done?* trans. Michael R. Katz (Ithaca, N.Y., 1989); Richard Stites, *The Women's Liberation Movement in Russia: Feminism, Nihilism and Bolshevism* (Princeton, 1978); and Richard Stites, "M. L. Mikhailov and the Emergence of the Woman Question in Russia," *Canadian-American Slavic Studies* 3 (summer 1969): 178–99. On gender mythology, see Marina Ledkovsky, "Avdotya Panaeva: Her Salon and Her Life," *Russian Literature Triquarterly* 9 (spring 1974): 423–32; Lina Bernstein, "Women on the Verge of a New Language: Russian Salon Hostesses in the First Half of the Nineteenth Century," in *Russia–Women–Culture*, ed. Helena Goscilo and Beth Holmgren (Bloomington, Ind., 1996), 209–24; Linda Edmondson, *Feminism in Russia, 1900–1917* (Stanford, 1984); Barbara Engel, *Mothers and Daughters: Women of the Intelligentsia in Nineteenth-Century Russia* (Cambridge, 1983). For an elaboration of the gendered interpretation of liberalism in Russia, see Laura Engelstein, *Keys to Happiness: Sex and the Search for Modernity in Fin-de-siecle Russia*, (Ithaca, N.Y., 1992).

2. Joan B. Landes, "Marxism and the Woman Question," in *Promissory Notes: Women in the Transition to Socialism*, ed. Sonia Kruks, Rayna Rapp, and Marilyn B. Young (New York, 1989), 15–28.

3. This neglect was approved by leading Menshevik and Bolshevik women such as Elena Stasova and Vera Zasulich, who viewed work among women as a distraction from the "real" goals of revolution. Aleksandra Kollontai, "Avtobiograficheskii ocherk," *Proletarskaia revoliutsiia*, 3 (1921): 275, writes how Zasulich was critical of the women's club Kollontai had organized in St. Petersburg, and dismissed it as a "superfluous enterprise." For an overview of Bolshevik work among women prior to 1913, see Barbara Evans Clements, *Bolshevik Women* (Cambridge, 1997).

4. D. M. Genkin, *Massovye prazdniki* (Moscow, 1975); James von Geldern, *Bolshevik Festivals 1917–1920* (Berkeley, 1993); Victoria E. Bonnell, *Iconography of Power: Soviet Political Posters Under Lenin and Stalin* (Berkeley, 1997); see esp. chap. 3. Christel Lane,

*The Rites of Rulers: Ritual in Industrial Society–The Soviet Case* (Cambridge, 1981).

5. Jules Michelet, *History of the French Revolution*, trans. Charles Cook (Chicago, 1967); Albert Mathiez, *Les origines des cultes revolutionnaires, 1789–1792* (Paris, 1904); Mona Ozouf, *Festivals and the French Revolution*, trans. Alan Sheridan (Cambridge, Mass., 1988).

6. On an elaboration of the concept of female backwardness, see Elizabeth Wood, *The Baba and the Comrade: Gender and Politics in Revolutionary Russia* (Bloomington, Ind., 1997).

7. Clifford Geertz, *The Interpretation of Cultures* (New York, 1973), 92–93; *Negara: The Theater State in Nineteenth Century Bali* (Princeton, 1980), 122–23, 136. David Cannadine, "Introduction: Divine Right of Kings," in *Rituals of Royalty: Power and Ceremonial in Traditional Societies*, ed. David Cannadine and Simon Price (Cambridge, 1987), 1–19, also argues against the posing of symbolic acts against the "real" workings of power.

8. Nancy Ries, *Russian Talk: Culture and Conversation During Perestroika* (Ithaca, N.Y., 1997).

9. Mary Buckley, *Women and Ideology in the Soviet Union* (Ann Arbor, Mich., 1989); Wood, *The Baba and the Comrade*.

10. E. Kamenka, "Public/Private in Marxist Theory and Marxist Practice," in *Public and Private in Social Life*, S. I. Benn and G. F. Gauss (New York, 1983); see also *Gendered Domains: Rethinking Public and Private in Women's History*, ed. D. O. Helly and S. M. Reverby (Ithaca, N.Y., 1992).

11. For a good discussion of the various definitions of the public and the private, see Jeff Weintraub, "The Theory and Politics of the Public/Private Distinction," in *Public and Private in Thought and Practice: Perspectives on a Grand Dichotomy*, ed. Jeff Weintraub and Krishna Kumar (Chicago, 1997), 1–42; Dena Goodman, "Public Sphere and Public Life: Toward a Synthesis of Current Historiographical Approaches to the Old Regime," *History and Theory* 31, (1992): 1–20; Benjamin Nathans, "Habermas's 'Public Sphere' in the Era of the French Revolution," *French Historical Studies* 16 (1990): 620–44.

12. Sheila Fitzpatrick, *Stalin's Peasants: Resistance and Survival in the Russian Village After Collectivization* (New York, 1994); Lynne Viola, *Peasant Rebels Under Stalin: Collectivization and the Culture of Peasant Resistance* (New York, 1996); Leslie A. Rimmel, "Another Kind of Fear: The Kirov Murder and the End of Bread Rationing in Leningrad," *Slavic Review* 66, (1997): 481–99; Stephen Kotkin, *Magnetic Mountain: Stalinism As Civilization* (Berkeley, 1995); Jochen Hellbeck, "Fashioning the Stalinist Soul: The Diary of Stepan Podlubnyi (1931–1939)," *Jahrbücher für Geschichte Osteuropas* 44, (1996): 344–73.

13. Hayden White, *Content of the Form: Narrative Discourse and Historical Representation* (Baltimore, 1987).

## Chapter 1

1. Sara E. Melzer and Leslie W. Rabine, ed., *Rebel Daughters: Women and the French Revolution* (New York, 1992); Candice E. Proctor, *Women, Equality and the French Revolution* (New York, 1990); Olwen Hufton, *Women and the Limits of Citizenship in the French Revolution* (Toronto, 1992); Lynn Hunt, *The Family Romance of the French Revolution* (Berkeley, 1992).

2. Alan Dundes uses the term "folk ideas" to describe "the building blocks of worldview." I use ideograms in a similar sense. See his "Folk Ideas as Units of Worldview," in *Towards New Perspectives in Folklore*, ed. Americo Paredes and Richard Bauman (Austin, 1972), 93–103.

3. Friedrich Engels, *The Origins of the Family, Private Property and the State* (New York, 1972). See also Karl Marx and Frederich Engels, *German Ideology*, in Karl Marx, *Selected Writings*, ed. David Mclellan (New York, 1977), 159–191.

4. This was the central argument of Aleksandra Kollontai's *The Social Bases of the Woman Question* (St. Petersburg, 1909). Kollontai (1871–1952) was the most famous Bolshevik advocate for female emancipation. She lectured and wrote prolifically on various issues relating to women, socialism, and revolution. After 1917 she served as the head of Zhenotdel before being marginalized in the diplomatic service for supporting the Workers' Opposition.

5. Stalin, "On the Draft Constitution of the USSR, 1936," in *Women and Communism: Selections from the Writings of Marx, Engels, Lenin, and Stalin* (Westport, Conn., 1975), 50. In his speech in 1925 Stalin argued that "International Women's Day means winning the women's labor reserves to the side of the proletariat" in "Greatest Reserve of the Working Class," in *Women and Communism*, 44.

6. On reproduction guaranteeing the existence of the labor republic, see Kollontai, *Sotsial'nye osnovy zhenskogo voprosa* (St. Petersburg, 1909), 230; preface to *Society and Motherhood* (1916), in Aleksandra Kollontai, *Selected Articles and Speeches*, trans. Cynthia Carlile (New York, 1984), 97–111; "Labor of Women in the Revolution of the Economy," in *Selected Writings of Alexandra Kollontai*, ed. and trans. Alix Holt (Westport, Conn., 1977), 142–49. Lenin, in his pronouncements on women's issues, was particularly vicious in his denunciation of domesticity and the deleterious impact it had on women's consciousness. See his speech at the First All-Russian Congress of Women Workers, Nov. 19, 1918, in *Women and Communism*, 43. See also his articles, "International Women's Day, 1918," ibid., 46, and "A Great Beginning, June 28, 1919," ibid., 55–57.

On views of postsocialist society, see August Bebel, *Women Under Socialism*, trans. Daniel de Leon (New York, 1917); V. I. Lenin, *The Emancipation of Women* (New York, 1934), 63, 69; Karl Marx and Friedrich Engels, *Communist Manifesto* (Middlesex, England, 1984), 100–101, 105; Leon Trotsky, *Women and Family* (New York, 1972).

7. See Nikolai Bukharin and E. Preobrazhensky, *The ABC of Communism* (Ann Arbor, Mich., 1966), 178–79, 234–35; I. Armand, "Osvobozhdenie ot domashnego rabstva," in *Kommunisticheskaia partiia i organizatsiia rabotnits: Sbornik statei, rezoliutsii i instruktsii* (Moscow, 1919), 31–34.

8. Alfred Meyer, "Marxism and the Woman's Movement," in *Women in Russia*, ed. Dorothy Atkinson, Alexander Dallin, and Gail Warshofsky Lapidus (Stanford, 1977), 91; Alexandra Kollontai, *Love of Worker Bees*, trans. Cathy Porter (Chicago, 1978); Alexandra Kollontay, *A Great Love*, trans. Lily Lore (Freeport, N.Y., 1971).

9. Eric Naiman, *Sex in Public: The Incarnation of Early Soviet Ideology* (Princeton, 1997), 208–35.

10. *Vasilisa Malygina*, in Kollontai, *Love of Worker Bees*.

11. *Autobiography of a Sexually Emancipated Communist Woman*, trans. Salvator Attansio (New York, 1975), 7; N. K. Krupskaia, *Zhenshchina-rabotnitsa* (Moscow-Leningrad, 1926), 22–23; on women's monetary independence, see V. I. Lenin, "Razvitie kapitalizma

v Rossii" (1899), *Polnoe Sobranie Sochinenii* 3:352–54; on the code of laws, see "The Original Family Law of the Russian Soviet Republic," in *The Family in the U.S.S.R.*, ed. Rudolph Schlesinger (London, 1949), 37–38.

12. Krupskaia, *Zhenshchina-rabotnitsa*, 31–32; see Zetkin's speech to the Social Democratic Party Congress in Gotha, 1896, in *Clara Zetkin: Selected Writings*, ed. Philip S. Foner (New York, 1984), 79; Kollontai's quote from "Towards a History of the Working Women's Movement in Russia," in *Selected Writings*, 40.

13. P. F. Kudrina, "Natashiny sny," *Rabotnitsa* (Feb. 23, 1914): 11–15.

14. See, for example, biographical sketches of exemplary Bolshevik women in collections such as *Revoliutsionerki Rossii* (Moscow, 1983) and *Slavnye Bol'shevichki* (Moscow, 1958). For an analysis of the qualities of the Bolshevichki, see Barbara Evans Clements, *Bolshevik Women* (Cambridge, 1997).

15. See Zinoviev's speech, "Rabotnitsa, krest'ianka i sovetskaia vlast'" (Petrograd, 1919).

16. When Dybenko, Kollontai's husband, fell afoul of party authorities for his ill-disciplined behavior, Kollontai protested vigorously and resigned from the party. See Richard Stites, "Alexandra Kollontai and the Russian Revolution," in *European Women on the Left*, ed. Jane Slaughter and Robert Kern (Westport, Conn., 1981), 114. For her comments on motherhood, see "The Labour of Women in the Revolution of the Economy," in *Selected Writings*, 142–49.

17. Karen Honeycut, "Clara Zetkin: A Socialist Approach to the Problem of Women's Oppression," in *European Women on the Left*, 36; Barbara Evans Clements, "The Birth of the New Soviet Woman," in *Bolshevik Culture: Experiment and Order in the Russian Revolution*, ed. Abbott Gleason, Peter Kenez, and Richard Stites (Bloomington, Ind., 1985), 220–37.

18. This sentiment had precedent in classical Marxism. According to Marx, paraphrasing Fourier, "the change in a historical epoch can always be determined by women's progress towards freedom, because here, in the relation of woman to man, of the weak to the strong, the victory of human nature over brutality is most evident. The degree of emancipation of woman is the natural measure of general emancipation." Quoted in Lise Vogel, *Marxism and the Oppression of Women: Toward a Unitary Theory* (Brunswick, N.J., 1983), 42.

19. Lenin, *Women and Communism*, 46, 52, 57, 58.

20. I. F. Armand, "Rabotnitsy vo II internatsionale," in *Stat'i, rechi, pis'ma* (Moscow, 1975), 155, 158. A. Kollontai, *K istorii dvizheniia rabotnits v rossii* (Kharkov, 1920), 22.

21. E. Bochkareva and S. Liubimova, *Svetlyi put'* (Moscow, 1967), 41; V. Bil'shai, *Reshenie zhenskogo voprosa v SSSR* (Moscow, 1956), 78–82; S. Serditova, *Bolsheviki v bor'be za zhenskie proletarskie massy* (Moscow, 1959), 84–99; S. Liubimova, *50-leti'e mezhdunarodnogo zhenskogo dnia* (Moscow, 1960), 5–10; S. V. Karavashkova, *Konkordiia Nikolaevna Samoilova* (Moscow, 1979), 26–32; L. Katasheva, *Natasha: A Bolshevik Woman Organizer* (New York, 1934), 22–37.

22. Clara Zetkin, *The International Socialist Congress at Stuttgart, August 18, 1907* (Berlin, 1907), 40–47; for Zetkin's stance on suffrage, see also Amy Kathleen Hackett, "The Politics of Feminism in Wilhelmine Germany, 1890–1918" (Ph.D. diss., Columbia University, 1976), 206, 210–12.

23. A. Kollontai, *Mezhdunarodnye sotsialisticheskie soveschaniia rabotnits. I. Shtutt-*

*gart 1907. II. Kopengagen. 1910* (Moscow, 1918); *Report of the Socialist Party Delegation and Proceedings of the International Socialist Congress at Copenhagen, 1910* (Chicago, n.d.), 21.

24. Elena Blonina (Inessa Armand), *Rabotnitsy v Internatsionale* (Moscow, 1920), 20.

25. Phillip S. Foner, *Women and the American Labor Movement: From World War I to the Present* (New York, 1980), 158–59; Madeline Provinzano, "It All Began Right Here," *Daily World*, March 6, 1980.

26. Aleksandra Kollontai, "Avtobiograficheskii ocherk," *Proletarskaia revoliutsiia*, no. 3 (1921): 283.

27. Anne Bobroff, "Bolsheviks and the Working Women 1905–1920," *Soviet Studies*, no. 26 (1974): 549–55; A. Kollontai, "I v Rossii budet zhenskii den'," in *Izbrannye stat'i i rechi* (Moscow: 1972), 125–27; Rose Glickman, *The Russian Factory Woman 1880–1914* (Berkeley and Los Angeles, 1984), 274; Barbara Evans Clements, *Bolshevik Feminist: The Life of Aleksandra Kollontai*, (Bloomington, Ind., 1979), 76.

28. On backwardness of proletarian women, see N. Benikova, "Znachenie zhenskogo dnia," *Rabotnitsa* no. 1–2 (Feb. 3, 1914): 3. P. F. Kudelli, *Bor'ba za zhenskii den'* (Leningrad, 1928), 5. Praskov'ia Frantsievna Kudelli (1859–1944) was a member of the party since 1903. Prior to the revolution she worked in various cultural-educational organizations used by the Bolsheviks for illegal political work. In February 1917, she returned to St. Petersburg and worked for *Pravda* and subsequently for *Rabotnitsa*. From 1922, she was the head of the St. Petersburg *Istpart* and edited the journal *Krasnaia letopis'*. L. P. Zhak and A. M. Itkina, eds., *Zhenshchiny v revoliutsii* (Moscow, 1968), 226–36.

29. Another reason for organizing women might have been due to the resolutions taken at the Cracow Meeting of the Central Committee of the RSDRP, Dec. 26, 1912 to Jan. 1, 1913, that instructed Bolsheviks to broaden and intensify agitation among the masses and encourage all forms of revolutionary action. *KPSS v rezoliutsiakh i resheniakh s"ezdov, konferentsii i plenumov TsK*, part 2, 1898–1924 (Moscow, 1924), 287–300.

30. N. K. Samoilova, *V ob'edinenii zalog pobedi. K mezhdunarodnomu sotsialisticheskomu dniu rabotnits, 8 marta* (Moscow, 1921), 3. See also the general tone of N. K. Samoilova's pamphlet, *K mezhdunarodnomu sotsialisticheskomu dniu rabotnits* (Petrograd, 1918); Cecelia Bobrovskaia, *Twenty Years in Underground Russia* (New York, 1934), writes, "it never occurred to us to carry on work among them (women); the job seemed such a thankless one" (109).

Konkordiia Nikolaevna Samoilova (1876–1921) became a party member in 1903; she was co-opted as a member of the St. Petersburg Committee of the RSDRP in 1909. Secretary for the editorial staff of *Pravda*, she was also active in workers' educational circles. After the February Revolution, she conducted agitation among women and during the Civil War and was involved in party work in the Ukraine. In 1920 she was appointed the head of the political department of the agitational train, *Krasnaia zvezda*. On its second journey down the Volga, she caught cholera and died. See L. P. Zhak et al eds., *Zhenshchiny russkoi revoliutsii* (Moscow, 1968), 398–413; *Zhenshchiny v revoliutsii*, ed. A. V. Artiukhina (Moscow, 1959), 104–07; *Skvoz' vremia* (Moscow, 1968), 263–84; S. V. Karavashkova, *Konkordia Nikolaevna Samoilova* (Moscow, 1979).

Part of Samoilova's doubtful appraisal of the political reliability of women workers may have been derived from her personal experiences in Baku when during the course of her work among oil field workers she was physically assaulted by their wives. According to the author of the memoir, Samoilova was upset by this incident and she, like most other party members of the time, saw proletarian women as an impediment to the workers' movement. At the same time, the author speculated that probably the unpleasant incident also inspired in Samoilova a desire to work with women. L. Sosnovskii, "Iz vospominanii o K. N. Samoilove," in *Borets za raskreposchenie rabotnitsy, K. N. Samoilova* (Moscow, Leningrad, 1923), 30. P. Kudelli confirms this incident in *K. N. Samoilova-Gromova (Natasha) 1876–1921* (Leningrad, 1925), 40.

31. V. I. Lenin, "Chto delat'," published in *Sochineniia* (Moscow, 1931), vol. 4, 56. See also J. L. H. Keep, *The Rise of Social Democracy in Russia* (Oxford, 1963), 67–106, for the development of Lenin's views on the revolutionary potential of the proletariat.

32. S. T. Liubimova, *50-Letie mezhdunarodnogo zhenskogo dnia;* V. Bilshai, *Reshenie zhenskogo voprosa;* E. Bochkareva and S. Liubimova, *Svetlyi put;* S. Serditova, *Bol'sheviki v borb'e za zhenskie proletarskie massy 1903g-fevral' 1917* (Moscow, 1959), 84; P. F. Kudelli, *Bor'ba za zhenskii den',* 6–8.

33. Accordingly, on January 5 there was a mass meeting of women workers in the Vyborg region of St. Petersburg to popularize the idea of Women's Day. A similar meeting was held among weavers and tailors to discuss the day's format. Another meeting was held the same day on Vasilevskii Island, with about thirty domestic servants. Various issues were discussed pertaining to laws and insurance for domestic workers, electoral rights for women, union rights for domestic workers and the celebration of Women's Day. See *Pravda,* Jan. 20, 1913, 3.

34. On Bolsheviks not involving themselves with women, see A. Kollontai, *K istorii dvizheniia rabotnits v Rossii* (Kharkov, 1920), 21. The Bolsheviks endorsed woman's suffrage as a matter of principle but never took it up as a separate issue; see *Pravda,* Jan. 5, 1913, 3. Quote from *Pravda,* Jan. 15, 1913, 2.

35. *Pravda,* Jan. 20, 1913, 3.

36. Kudelli, *Bor'ba za zhenskii den',* 11. But Kudelli might have been intentionally misleading in her reporting more than fourteen years after the event. According to Linda Edmondson, Ianchevskaia was actually a Bolshevik. See Linda Edmondson, "Women's Rights, Civil Rights and the Debate over Citizenship in the 1905 Revolution," in *Women and Society in Russia and the Soviet Union,* ed. Linda Edmondson (Cambridge, 1992), 87.

37. *Zhenskii vestnik,* no. 2 (Feb. 1913): 33–35. Maria Pokrovskaia was a doctor who practiced among the St. Petersburg workers and was especially concerned with women workers. In 1905 she formed her own Progressive Party and published the influential *Zhenskii Vestnik* until 1914. She despised both the socialists and the liberals for ignoring specific women's demands and was a strong iconoclastic voice in the medical debates on prostitution, wherein she called for male self-control. For an analysis of her political stance, see Laura Engelstein, *Keys to Happiness: Sex and the Search for Modernity in Fin-de-siecle Russia* (Ithaca, N.Y., 1992).

38. In November 1912, a joint meeting of feminists in St. Petersburg attracted a large audience, and a second meeting, sponsored by Pokrovskaia's Progressive Party, produced a packed hall and near riots. *Zhenskii vestnik,* no. 12 (Nov. 1912): 273–74. Also, in response to pressure from the feminists the Duma had designated International Women's Day a holiday in 1913. See R. Ellwood Carter, *Inessa Armand: Revolutionary and Feminist* (New York, 1992), 105.

39. *Zhenskii vestnik,* no. 2 (Feb. 1913): 33–35. Finally, adducing the example of the

English socialists, whose purportedly antifeminist stance had pushed the English working woman into the arms of the suffragists, Pokrovskaia cautioned the Bolsheviks that if they did not include "feminist" demands in their platform, they would suffer the fate of their English comrades.

40. Moreover, the Social Democrats were not unaware of the subordination of women within the family, but they realized that it was a function of an exploitative capitalist society rather than patriarchal attitudes of the Russian proletariat. See *Pravda*, Feb. 15, 1913, 1.

41. Inessa Armand, "Rabotnitsy vo II Internatsionale," *Stat'i, rechi, pis'ma* (Moscow, 1975), 146–47, stressed that the growing numerical strength of women in the proletarian ranks made it necessary for Social Democrats to start recruiting women as an important political force.

42. *Pravda*, Jan. 26, 27, 29, 1913. See also *Pravda*, June 14, 1912, 4. Bolsheviks sidestepped the issue of oppression of women by male colleagues by saying that as workers became more conscious they would realize that it was useless to fight against the employment of female labor. The evidence suggests that the Bolsheviks truly believed that once women became more of a permanent fixture in the public domain, gender hostility would disappear.

43. *Pravda*, Feb. 17, 1913, 1–3.

44. For examples of hostile interactions between women workers and women revolutionaries, see Lidiia Dan's memoirs in *The Making of Three Russian Revolutionaries: Voices from the Menshevik Past*, ed. Leopold Haimson (New York, 1987), 80–82, 86, 95; *Zhenshchiny goroda Lenina* (Leningrad, 1963), 25.

45. Aleksandra Nikolaevna Grigor'eva-Alekseeva was by profession a textile worker. As far as I can piece together, Kudelli met the speakers at the Sampsonievskii Society for Education in the Vyborg region, a workers' club, and recruited them for Party work. See A. D. Sokolova-Sarafannikova, "Sampsonievskoe obschestvo obrazovanie," in *Zhenshchiny goroda Lenina*, 49–57.

46. GARF, f. 9601, op. 1, ed. khr., 133, l. 3; GARF, f. 102, op. 243, d. 5, ch., 57 (tom 1), ll. 17, 21; "K istorii prazdnovaniia mezhdunarodnogo zhenskogo dnia v Rossii," *Krasnyi arkhiv*, 2 (87) (1938): 6, 8–9; *Pravitel'stvennyi vestnik*, Feb. 17, 1913. According to another source, *Luch* was levied a fine of five hundred rubles for this infraction. See A. Elizarova, "Zhenshchiny-rabotnitsy i ikh dvizhenie do mirovoi voiny v Rossia," in *Mezhdunarodnyi den' rabotnits* (Moscow, 1925), 37.

47. *Pravda*, Feb. 19, 1913, 3.

48. A. N. Grigorievna-Alekseeva, "Zhenskoe utro," in *Zhenshchiny goroda Lenina*, 65–69.

49. *Pravda*, Feb. 20, 1913, 3.

50. Rose Glickman, *Russian Factory Women, 1880–1914*, (Berkeley, 1984), 141–43, provides examples of molestation of women by factory administrators.

51. Margulies-Aitova, a physician and a radical feminist, was active in the Zhenskii Politicheskii Klub. In 1911 she helped found a clinic called Pomosch' Materiam. See Rochelle Goldberg, *The Russian Women's Movement*, 338 n. 197. *Pravda*, Feb. 22, 1913, 2.

52. *Zhenshchiny goroda Lenina*, 68.

53. *Pravda*, Feb. 19, 1913, 3. Students at the Pollak course held a "Literary Morning" to commemorate Women's Day and entertained and instructed the workers in the audi-

ence with revolutionary songs and lectures. *Rech*, Feb. 18, 1913, 2. On sensitive issues, see *Pravda*, Feb. 24, 1913, 3.

54. The Third Women's Club had been formed in 1907 by a group of Social Democrats in the Taganka area on Semenovskii Street. It came under Bolshevik control in 1912 and was led by E. P. Krzhizhanovskaia and S. P. Nevzorova-Shesternina. The club was very popular among the working class and by the time it was closed down in November 1913, it boasted a membership of more than nine hundred people. See G. A. Arutiunov, *Rabochie dvizhenie v Rossii v period novogo revoliutsionnogo pod'ema 1910-1914* (Moscow, 1975), 102, 154; P. V. Barchugov, *Revoliutsionnaia rabota Bol'shevikov v legal'nikh rabochikh organizatsiakh*, (Rostov-na-Donu, 1963); T. Sapronov, *Iz istorii rabochego dvizheniia po lichnym vospominaniiam* (Leningrad, 1925).

55. On Ekaterina Kuskova, see M. Tikhomirova, "Zhenskii klub," in *Zhenshchiny v revoliutsii*, ed. A. V. Artiukhina, 112–16. On various celebrations, see S. Serditova, *Bol'sheviki v bor'be za zhenskie proletarskie massy* (Moscow, 1959), 89. On Kiev meetings, see P. F. Kudelli, *Bor'ba za zhenskii den'*, 17 and *Rech*, Feb. 24, 1914, 1.

56. See *Pravda* issues from Feb. 17 and 19, 1913.

57. *Novoe Vremia*, Feb. 18, 1913; see *Rech*, Feb. 18, 1913.

58. "K istorii prazdnovaniia mezhdunarodnogo zhenskogo dnia v Rossii," in *Krasnyi arkhiv*, 8–9; A. Mans'tova, "Pervyi zhenskii den' russkikh rabotnits," *Zhenskii vestnik* (March 1913): 86; M. I. Pokrovskaia, in article in the following issue of *Zhenskii Vestnik*, added that while feminists did not deny that women were exploited for their labor, women workers were also oppressed on account of their sex, and should join other women to fight male privilege. M. I. Pokrovskaia, "Kak rabochie ponimaiut feminizm," *Zhenskii vestnik* (March 1913): 67–68.

59. E. Bochkareva and S. Liubimova, *Svetlyi put* (Moscow, 1967), 43; Okhrana quote from GARF, f. 102, op. 244, d. 5, ch. 57 (tom. 1), l. 39.

60. On Menshevik's proposals, see A. Kollontai, "V Rossii budet zhenskii den'," 125–27; S. Serditova, *Bor'ba za zhenskie proletarskie massy*, 98; Inessa Armand, *Stat'i, rechi, pis'ma*, 159. On Kudelli, see A. F. Bessenova, "K istorii izdaniia zhurnala Rabotnitsa," *Istoricheskii arkhiv* (July–Aug. 1955), docs. 5, 7, 32–35; on Bolshevik's plans for Women's Day, see *Listovki Petersburgskikh bol'shevikov 1902–1917* (Leningrad, 1939), 2:93–94

61. On Lenin as inspiration, see, for example, Vera Drizdo, "Slova iasnoe, prostoe i glubokoe," in *Vsegda s vami. Sbornik posviashchennyi piatidesiatiletiiu zhurnala "Rabotnitsa"* (Moscow, 1964), 29. On Inessa Armand, see N. K. Krupskaia, *Memories of Lenin* (New York, 1934), 2:124; R. C. Elwood, *Inessa Armand*, 106–24, confirms the view that Inessa took the initiative in starting the journal. On Lenin's sister, see A. Elizarova, "Zhurnal 'Rabotnitsa' 1914 g," in *Iz epokhi 'Zvezdy i Pravdy', 1911–1914* (Moscow, 1923), 3:63. On Krupskaia's letter, see A. F. Bessenova, "K istorii izdaniia zhurnala Rabotnitsa," docs. 1, 28–29.

62. See, for example, N. Sibiriakova [pseud. K. N. Samoilova], "Pochemu rabotnitsam nuzhna svoi zhurnal," GARF, f. 1167, op. 3, d. 5157, ll. 2, 3, 4.

63. Rabotnitsa, no. 1–2 (Feb. 23, 1914): 4–5; *Rabotnitsa*, March 16, 1914, 9; *Rabotnitsa*, May 24, 1914, 2–3, 13–14.

64. A. F. Bessenova, docs. 5, 15, 19, 20, 32–34, 43–44, 46–47; Inessa Armand, *Stat'i, rechi, pis'ma*, 160.

65. In her letter to the St. Petersburg police dated Feb. 9, 1914, Samoilova requested permission to hold a meeting to discuss the "woman question." See GARF, f. 1167, op. 3, d. 5573, l. 3.

66. GARF, f. 93, op. 1, d. 170, l. 32; GARF, f. 102, op. 244, d. 5, ch., 57 (tom. 1), ll. 39, 40; "K istorii prazdnovaniia mezhdunarodnogo zhenskogo dnia v Rossii," *Krasnyi arkhiv*, 8; Z. B. Nikandrova, "Nash drug," in *Leningradki. Vospominania, ocherki, dokumenty* (Leningrad, 1968), 57; GARF, f. 102, op. 244, d. 5, ch. 57 (tom. 1), ll. 40, 41, 43, 66a, b.

67. Liudmilla Rudol'fovna Menzhinskaia (1876–1933) was a former teacher who had been introduced to socialism by Elena Stasova. A member of the party beginning in 1904, she worked with *Pravda* and *Rabotnitsa*. After the revolution she worked for Narkompros and Zhenotdel. See *Zhenshchiny russkoi revoliutsii*, 249–60, 564.

68. *Kommunistka*, no. 8–9 (Jan.–Feb., 1921): 14.

69. Ibid., 13.

70. GARF, f. 9601, op. 1, ed. khr. 62, l. 17.

71. GARF, f. 9601, op. 1, ed. khr. 133, l. 33.

72. Subsequently, a bitter controversy arose as to who was responsible for publishing the journal under such adverse circumstances. In her later account of the day, Samoilova waxed sentimental about the "dear male comrades" who brought out the first copy of *Rabotnitsa*. See *Kommunistka* 8–9 (1921): 14. But Elizarova took great exception to this needless piece of mythologizing. As she pointed out, it was inaccurate to say that the entire editorial board was arrested and that only the "dear male comrades were able to put out the first number of the journal."

73. Emilia Solin-Alekseeva, member of the Ispolkom of the Vyborg committee of Bolsheviks, helped to distribute copies of the journal among the women workers in the factories of St. Petersburg. By profession a telephone operator, she later worked in the factory Novyi Aibaz. She joined the party in 1910 and was one of the party organizers on the Vyborg side. She was arrested and exiled to Siberia in 1915 but returned to play an important role in 1917. She fell prey to White Guards during the civil war and was killed. See *Zhenshchiny v revoliutsii*, 102–03.

74. A. Elizarova, *Kommunistka*, no. 10-11 (March–Apr., 1921): 51; I. Armand, *Stat'i, rechi i pis'ma*, 161, corroborates Elizarova's version. See also Elizarova's letter to Krupskaia in A. F. Bessenova, doc. 14; L. Stal' recalled that male comrades at this point actually questioned the need to have a separate woman's journal, *Pechat' i zhenskoe kommunisticheskoe dvizhenie* (Moscow, 1927), 14.

75. *Rech*, Feb. 24, 1914, 2; *Novoe vremia*, Feb. 24, 1914, 4; GARF, f. 93, op. 1, d. 170, l. 32; *Pravda*, Feb. 25, 1914, 2; RGASPI, f. 456 op. 1, ed. khr. 8, l. 16.

76. P. F. Kudelli, *Bor'ba za zhenskii den'*, 24; *Rech*, Feb. 24, 1913, 2; "K istorii prazdnovaniia mezhdunarodnogo zhenskogo dnia," *Krasnyi arkhiv*, 10–11.

77. *Rech*, Feb. 24, 1914, 2; *Put' pravdy*, Feb. 25, 1914, 2; P. F. Kudelli, *Bor'ba za zhenskii den'*, 26.

78. Later, there were even some dramatizations of the Women's Day celebrations of 1914. See the short plays, "Vosmoe marta," in *8 marta: Materialy k provedeniiu mezhdunarodnogo dnia rabotnits i krest'ianok v derevne* (Omsk, 1925); "Vosmoe marta prezhde i teper'," in *Mezhdunarodnyi den' rabotnits* (Moscow, 1924).

79. *Put' pravdy*, Feb. 25, 1914, 2.

80. *Put' pravdy*, Feb. 25, 1914, 3, Feb. 28, 1914, 4; March 2, 1914, 2Z. Igumnova,

*Zhenshchiny Moskvy v gody grazhdanskoi voiny*, 8; *Zhenskii vestnik*, no. 3 (1914): 89; *Zhenskoe delo*, March 15, 1914, 18.

81. Linda Edmondson believes that the divide between the socialists and the feminists was not absolute at this point but gives little evidence to the contrary. See *Feminism in Russia, 1900–1917*, 154. In St. Petersburg, the members of the Feminist Progressive Party led by Maria Pokrovskaia organized a Women's Day meeting at which, in strict contradistinction to socialist goals, the main theme of the lectures was the extension of suffrage and the participation of women in the local city government.

82. "K istorii prazdnovaniia mezhdunarodnogo zhenskogo dnia v Rossii," *Krasnyi arkhiv*, 16.

83. *Sankt-Peterburgskie Vysshie Zhenskie Bestuzhevskie Kursy* (Leningrad, 1973), 67–68.

84. *Listovki Peterburgskikh, bol'shevikov*, 2:143, 198–200; L. Stal', *Pechat' i zhenskoe kommunisticheskoe dvizhenie*, 20–25.

## Chapter 2

1. Jane McDermid and Anna Hilyar, *Midwives of the Revolution: Female Bolsheviks and the Women Workers in 1917* (Athens, Ohio, 1999). McDermid and Hilyar provide a much needed corrective to the traditional historiography and reprises the role of female Bolsheviks and women in the February Revolution. The authors argue that the actions of women workers were not merely "apolitical" or "spontaneous," but crucial to the success of the revolutionary events of that year.

2. Leon Trotsky, *The Russian Revolution*, trans. Max Eastman (New York, 1959), 104.

3. Ibid., 105.

4. Ia. A. Iakovlev, "Fevral'skie dni," in *Proletarskaia revoliutsiia*, nos. 2–3 (1927): 61–62, asked precisely the same question. For dissenting views, see Richard Pipes, *The Russian Revolution* (New York, 1990), 272–337, who dismisses the pretensions of workers and socialists in claiming leadership during the February Revolution, and instead argues that it was primarily a mutiny of peasant soldiers, starting on February 28, that brought down the tsarist regime.

5. A Bolshevik participant in the revolution, A. M. Zotov later recounted that although women workers started the demonstrations on February 23, only after the men joined them did the strike action become organized. RGASPI, f. 70, op. 3, ed. khr. 568, l. 3.

6. In her speech to the Conference of Women Workers in Petrograd on November 18, 1917, K. N. Samoilova unfavorably contrasted the ill-disciplined actions of women in the February events to their organized participation in the October Revolution. See P. Kudelli, *K. N. Samoilova-Gromova (Natasha)* (Leningrad, 1925), 67. Later, she wrote in *Rabotnitsy v rossiskoi revoliutsii* (Moscow, 1920), "in contrast to the February Revolution, in which women's activities were poorly organized and elemental, during the October Revolution, women workers, together with the working class, led a bitter but a most well-organized struggle against their class enemies" (8). See also Borisov, *Fevral'skaia i oktiabr'skaia revoliutsiia i rabotnitsa* (Moscow, 1926); *Ot fevral'ia k oktiabr'iu. (Iz anket uchastnikov velikoi oktiabr'skoi sotsialisticheskoi revoliutsii)* (Moscow, 1957).

7. *Pravda*, March 10, 1917, 3.

8. Writing in 1918, Kollontai, *Rabotnitsa za god revoliutsii* (Moscow, 1918), testified to

the courageous and massive participation of the St. Petersburg women in the February Revolution but did not include any mention of Bolshevik organization or control of women's actions.

9. Aleksandr Shliapnikov, *Semnadtsatyi god* (Moscow, 1992), 2:69, "Fevral'skie dni v Peterburge," *Proletarskaia revoliutsiia*, no. 1 (1923): 80–81.

10. V. N. Kaiurov, "Dni fevral'skoi' revoliutsii," in *Krushenie tsarizm* (Leningrad, 1986), 237.

11. I. D. Chugurin, "Iz avtobiografii," in ibid., 252.

12. David Longley, "Iakovlev's Question, or the Historiography of the Problem of the Spontaneity and Leadership in the Russian Revolution of February 1917," in *Revolution in Russia: Reassessments of 1917*, ed. Edith Rogovin Frankel, Jonathan Frankel, Baruch Knei-Paz and Israel Getzler (Cambridge, Mass., 1992).

13. *V dni proletarskoi revoliutsii* (Soviet Union, 1937), 11. Subsequently, we find the same viewpoint in other Soviet accounts: *Petrogradskie bol'sheviki v trekh revoliutsiiakh* (Leningrad, 1966), 152; I. P. Lieberov and S. D. Rudachenko, *Revoliutsiia i khleb* (Moscow, 1990), 70; S. Serditova, *Bol'sheviki v bor'be za zhenskie proletarskie massy* (Moscow, 1959), 125–29; E. Bochkareva and S. Liubimova, *Svetlyi put'* (Moscow, 1967), 51–52.

14. Ermanskii, editor of the Petrograd United Workers Cooperative journal, *Trud*, dedicated the second edition of the journal as a commemorative issue for Women's Day. It was not a clarion call to arms; instead, it rather grandiloquently harkened to a future when there would be no enslavement of either men or women. Since I have been unable to locate a copy of the journal I have to rely on O. A. Ermanskii, *Iz perezhitogo* (Moscow, 1927), 141. The Inter-District Committee or Mezhraionka was formed in November 1913 by leading Bolshevik conciliators, followers of Trotsky and Plekhanov, and the Menshevik Internationalists, to foster party unity.

15. On February 23, A. M. Itkina addressed a massive Women's Day meeting at the People's House of Panin. The People's House had been a traditional place for Women's Day celebrations and other socialist inspired activities in the prewar years. The Mezhraiontsy also organized a Women's Day meeting at the Petrograd factory, Aibaz. Rakhil Kovnator, a young student at the Psychoneurological Institute at Petrograd, also a Mezhraionka, smuggled commemorative Women's Day literature into the Putilov factory. See *Bez nikh my ne pobedili by* (Moscow, 1975), 14. Rakhil Kovnator later joined the Bolsheviks. A Women's Day meeting was also organized at the Psychoneurological Institute in Petrograd with the help of Mezhraionka Berta Ratner. See I. Iurenev, "Mezhraionka," *Proletarskaia revoliutsiia*, no. 2 (1924): 133–34.

16. Michael Melancon, "Who Wrote What and When? Proclamations of the February Revolution in Petrograd, 23 February–1 March 1917," in *Soviet Studies* 40 (1988): 479–500.

17. "Fevral'skaia revoliutsiia v dokumentakh," *Proletarskaia revoliutsiia*, no. 1 (1923): 282, 283.

18. The Bolsheviks, who attached enormous significance to the written word, excused their inability to bring out a Women's Day poster by referring to a malfunctioning printer. See Shliapnikov, *Semnadtsatyi god*, 2:69.

19. N. N. Sukhanov, *Zapiski o revoliutsii* (Berlin, 1922).

20. Stites, *The Women's Liberation Movement in Russia*, 290–91; David Mandel, *The*

*Petrograd Workers and the Fall of the Old Regime* (New York, 1983), 63; Tsuyoshi Hasegawa, *The February Revolution: Petrograd, 1917* (Seattle, 1980), 216; Moira Donald, "Bolshevik Activity Among the Working Women of Petrograd in 1917," in *International Review of Social History* 27, pt. 2 (1982): 130–31.

21. N. D. Karpetskaia, *Rabotnitsy i velikii Oktiabr'* (Leningrad, 1974), 30.

22. Male Bolsheviks, such as V. N. Kaiurov and A. Taimi, actually addressed a crowd of women workers at a Women's Day meeting in the Lesnyi district of the city. V. Kaiurov, "Shest' dnei fevral'skoi revoliutsii," *Proletarskaia revoliutsiia*, no. 1 (1923): 158. A. Taimi, *Stranitsy perezhitogo* (Petrozavodsk, 1955), 171. Other Bolsheviks, such as S. L. Lapshin and Valikov participated in a Women's Day meeting at the metal factory, Phoenix, that was situated on the Vyborg side of the city. For evidence of male Bolshevik involvement, see *V ogne revoliutsionnikh boev* (Moscow, 1967), 129; *Petrograd v dni velikogo oktiabr'ia* (Leningrad, 1967), 32.

23. N. F. Agadzhanova and Maria Vydrina-Sveshnikova addressed a meeting on the themes of "War, inflation and the position of the women worker," at the Novyi Promet. Tolmacheva, a student of the prestigious Bestuzhev Women's college, spoke to a gathering of workers at Staryi Lessner. Vinogradova lectured a gathering of women workers at the chocolate factory, Konrad, on the eve of the holiday. I have drawn information on the activities of these female Bolsheviks from a number of sources. *Leningradki. Vospominaniia, ocherki, dokumenty* (Leningrad, 1968), 189; *Kommunistka*, no.10 (1927): 25, 26; *Oktiabriem mobilizovannye* (Moscow, 1987), 153; *Geroi Oktiabria* 1: 41, 258; N. P. Lieberov, *Na shturm samoderzhaviia* (Moscow, 1979), 118.

24. According to *Oktiabriem mobilizovannye*, shortly after an impassioned speech by N. F. Agadzhanova on the repressive nature of autocracy and the costs of war at the factory Novyi Promet, three thousand workers soon went on strike (152).

25. On meetings at factories, see GARF, f. 111, op. 5, ed. khr., 669, l. 171, 290; *V ogne revoliutsionnikh boev* (Moscow, 1967), 140; Leiberov, *Revoliutsiia i khleb*, 71. On rumors of strike, see *Kommunistka*, no. 10 (1927): 25. On new female recruits, see V. D. Perazich, *Tekstili Leningrada* (Leningrad, 1927), 5–11.

26. On privations caused by World War I, see Stites, *Women's Liberation Movement*, 287, 288; Alfred G. Meyer, "The Impact of World War I on Russia's Women," in *Russia's Women: Accommodation, Resistance, Transformation*, ed. Barbara Evans Clements, Barbara Alpern Engels, and Christine D. Worobec (Berkeley, 1992), 208–24. On workforce statistics, see Karpetskaia, *Rabotnitsy i velikii Oktiabr'*, 19; G. L. Sobolev, *Proletarskie avangard v 1917 godu* (St. Petersburg, 1992), 11–21. On textile industry, see S. A. Smith, *Red Petrograd: Revolution in the Factories 1917-1918* (Cambridge, 1983), 23. On life-threatening nature of work, see E. L. Broido, *Zhenshchina-rabotnitsa* (Petrograd, 1917); see *Rabotnitsa*, nos. 1 and 2 (1917), for accounts of working conditions in factories. On length of workday, see Karpetskaia, *Rabotnitsy i velikii Oktiabr'*, 24. On wages, see Smith, *Red Petrograd*, 48.

27. Lars Lih, *Bread and Authority in Russia, 1914-1921*, (Berkeley, 1990), argues that the major characteristic of the Russian national collapse, from 1914 to 1921, was the problem of food procurement and distribution: "One of the central features of this whole period of war, revolution, and civil war was a food supply crisis that was both symptom and intensifier of the overall dislocation and then breakdown of national economic and social life" (1). For detailed information on the strategies that women workers used in their

quest for food in the Central Industrial Region, see Anne Bobroff, "Working Women, Bonding Patterns, and the Politics of Daily Life: Russia at the End of the Old Regime" (Ph.D diss., University of Michigan, 1982), 2: 553–639. On price of bread, see Stinton Jones, *Russia in Revolution: Being the Experiences of an Englishman in Petrograd During the Upheaval* (New York, 1917), 68–69; on prices of other essentials, see Hasegawa, *The February Revolution*, 201.

28. Z. Lilina (Zinovieva), *Soldaty tyla, zhenskii trud, do i posle voiny* (Petrograd, 1918), 69–70. Iu. A. Kirianov, "Massovye vystupleniia na pochve dorogovizny v Rossii. (1914–fevral', 1917g)," *Otchestvennaia istoriia* (May–June, 1993): 5.

29. V. I. Lenin, *Polnoe Sobranie Sochinenii* (Moscow, 1962), 30:232–33.

30. *Bol'sheviki v gody imperialisticheskoi voiny. 1914–fevral' 1917* (Leningrad, 1939), 43, 44; *Listovki Peterburgskikh bol'shevikov. 1902–1917*, (Leningrad, 1939), 2:43, 198, 199, 200; "Fevral'skaia revoliutsiia v dokumentakh," *Proletarskaia revoliutsiia*, no. 1 (1923): 283.

31. Iu. A. Kirianov, "Massovye vystupleniia na pochve dorogovizny v Rossii (1914–fevral', 1917g)," 11.

32. *Krasnyi arkhiv*, no. 1 (1926): 28–29.

33. *Krasnaia letopis'* no. 1 (1927): 44.

34. GARF, f. 111, op. 5, ed. khr., 669, l. 306.

35. Perazich, *Tekstili Leningrada v 1917*, 11–12. Working women at the Neva Cotton Mills on the morning of the 23rd heard the noise from the streets and cries of "Stop work." The thread spinners threw open the doors and surged into the street. See *Leningradskaia pravda*, March 12, 1926.

36. Shliapnikov, *Semnadtsatyi god*, 2:69; *Kommunistka*, no. 5 (Oct. 1920): 25; RGASPI, f. 70, op. 3, ed. khr. 563, l. 4; RGASPI, f. 17, op. 10, ed. khr. 34, l. 22; *Krushenie tsarizma*, 238.

37. *Iz boevogo proshlogo. 1914–1918gg* (Moscow, 1957), 56; *Krushenie tsarizma*, 252.

38. N. F. Riabov, *My s Vyborgskoi storony* (Moscow, 1961), 20.

39. Shliapnikov, *Semnadtsatyi god*, 2: 87.

40. GARF, f. 7952, op. 4, d. 170(1), l. 2.

41. *V ogne revoliutsionnikh boev*, 376, 396; GARF, f. 102, op. 247, d. 341, ch. 57, l. 10b; Shliapnikov, *Semnadtsatyi god*, 2: 7.

42. Ermanskii, *Iz perezhitogo*, 140; Shliapnikov, *Semnadtsatyi god*, 2:75; *Bez nikh my ne pobedili by*, 52.

43. *Bez nikh my ne pobedili by*, 52. The female staff of the Vasilevsky Island Trolley Depot, sensing the unrest on Women's Day, asked of the neighboring 180th Infantry regiment if they would shoot at them if they went on strike. The soldiers gave the women a safe conduct, and the women workers went on strike. *Zhenshchiny goroda Lenina* (Leningrad, 1963), 87–92. See also *Vsegda s vami* (Moscow, 1964), 100–101.

44. "Doloi' samoderzhavie. Doloi' voiny," *Rabotnitsa*, no. 2 (Feb. 1923): 28.

45. *Krushenie tsarizma*, 278.

46. M. V. Rodzianko, *Krushenie Imperii* (New York, 1986), 298.

47. *Zhenshchina goroda Lenina*, 89. Other women participants also recalled the excitement of the revolutionary events; see T. Slovacheskaia, *Povest' rabotnitsy i krest'ianki*, 23.

48. *Zhenshchiny russkoi revoliutsii* (Moscow, 1968), 91.

49. M. G. Pavlova, "Dom na Sverdlovskoi," *Leningradki. Vospominaniia, ocherki, dokumenty* (Leningrad, 1968), 30–41. The Mezhraionka, Rakhil Kovnator, was asked to make a red banner with appropriate political slogans. Unable to find any red cloth, she finally borrowed a skirt from her friend and made banners with the words, "Down with Autocracy, Down with War and Long Live the Revolution." Rakhil Kovnator, "Nakanune fevral'ia," *Revoliutsionnoe iunoshestvo 1905–1917* (Leningrad, 1924), 188.

50. *Krushenie tsarizma*, 281.

51. *Pravda*, March 8, 1917, 3.

52. A. I. Kruglova, *Ne zabyvaemoe* (Leningrad, 1963), writes that when the prisoners were freed from prison, despite her fierce appearance and a revolver stuck in her belt, she had to control herself lest she start howling like a woman *(po-bab'i)* from sheer happiness (85).

53. Z. D. Iasman, "Goluboglazaia Nune," *Leningradki: Vospominaniia, ocherki, dokumenty*, 193.

54. Elena D. Stasova, *Stranitsy zhizny i bor'by* (Moscow, 1960), 88–89.

55. Kruglova, *Nezabyvaemoe*, 83.

56. See, for example, Robert Edelman, *Proletarian Peasants* (Ithaca, N.Y., 1987), 157; Dorothy Atkinson, *The End of the Russian Land Commune, 1905–1930* (Berkeley, 1983), 367–68; Petro G. Grigorenko, *Memoirs*, trans. Thomas P. Whitney (New York, 1982), 35.

57. Trotsky, *The Russian Revolution*, 105.

58. Aleksei Tarasov-Rodionov, *February 1917*, trans. William A. Drake (New York, 1931), 46–47.

59. Kruglova, *Nezabyvaemoe*, 84.

60. Perazich, *Tekstili Leningrada v 1917*, 16–17. Similarly, women workers from the Franco-Russian factory helped to propagandize the sailors on the cruiser *Aurora*, and encouraged them to take over the command of the vessel. A. Ionov, *Bor'ba Bol'shevistskoi partii za soldatskie massy petrogradskogo garizona v 1917* (Moscow, 1954), 35.

61. N. F. Riabov, a lathe operator, and subsequently general lieutenant in the Soviet army recounted that on February 27, during a confrontation between a detachment of ensigns and a group of workers in the Okhtinskii area, a group of women workers and housewives surrounded the soldiers and begged with tears in their eyes to refrain from shooting and join the revolutionaries instead. The ensigns soon joined the workers and helped to set fire to a police station. See his *My s Vyborgskoi storony*, 32; Kaiurov, "Shest' dnei fevral'skoi revoliutsii," 163.

62. According to Okhrana reports, in one encounter with the police on Vasilevsky Island, a woman called out, "don't rejoice too long, soon your heads will roll." See GARF, f. 111, op. 5. ed. khr. 669, l. 12. See also l. 350 of the same fond where a woman was arrested for insulting an ensign and disrupting public order near the Nikolaevsky Bridge; GARF, f. 7952, op. 4, d. 170(1), l. 7. On women disarming officers, see Kruglova, *Nezabyvaemoe*, 84. On the death of the colonel, see RGASPI, f. 70, op. 3, ed. khr. l. 5; Karpetskaia, *Rabotnitsy i velikii Oktiabr'*, 32. On fierceness of women, see K. G. Arshavskii, "Svoboda, Brat'ia! Vykhodite!," *Petrograd v dni velikogo Oktiabria* (Leningrad, 1967), 37.

63. Perazich, *Tekstili Leningrada v 1917*, 17–18; on sacking Protopopov's apartment, see the testimony of Vasiliev, the director of police, in *Witnesses to the Russian Revolution*, ed. Roger Pethybridge (London, 1964), 102.

64. GARF, f. 111, op. 5, ed. khr., 669, ll. 289, 325; GARF, f. 7952, op. 4, d. 82(1), l. 25;

"Iz doneseniia nachal'nika Petrogradskogo okhrannogo otdeleniia direktoru departmenta politsii generalu Vasil'ievu o sobytiiakh v stolitse," in *Fevral'skaia revoliutsiia 1917: Sbornik dokumentov i materialov*, ed. O. A. Shahshkov (Moscow, 1996), 29; S. N. Valk et al., eds., *Oktiabr'skoe vooruzhënnoe vosstanie* (Leningrad, 1967), 2:52; Hasegawa, *The February Revolution*, 236; M. Mitel'man et al., eds., *Istoriia putilovskogo zavoda 1801–1917* (Moscow, 1961), 550.

65. "For Kerensky, see *Stenograficheskii otchet gosudarstvennoi dumy*, chetverty sozyv, sessia V, zasedaniie 23, 23/II (1917), 1650. On empress, see M. N. Pokrovskii, ed., *Perepiska Nikolaia i Aleksandry Romanovykh, 1916–1917gg*, (Moscow, 1927), 5:218; for reference to banners see Richard Pipes, *The Russian Revolution*, 275. Pitirim Sorokin, *Leaves From a Russian Diary* (New York, 1924), 1–2. Sergei Mstislavsky, *Five Days Which Transformed Russia*, trans. Elizabeth Kristofovich Zelensky (Bloomington, Ind., 1988), 23.

66. I. I. Mints, *Istoriia velikogo oktiabria* (Moscow, 1967), 1:498.

67. M. N. Pokrovskii, *Oktiabr'skaia revoliutsiia: Sbornik statei, 1917–1927* (Moscow, 1929), 82–83; E. V. Genkina, *Fevral'skii perevorot*, in *Ocherki po istorii oktiabr'skoi revoliutsii*, ed. M. N. Pokrovskii (Moscow, 1927) 2; K. Shelavin, *Rabochii klass i VKP(b) v fevral'skoi revoliutsii* (Leningrad, 1927); K. Samoilova, *Rabotnitsy v rossiiskoi revoliutsii* (Moscow, 1920), wrote that, "Although the demonstrations of the Petrograd women workers on International Women's Day, 23 February 1917, was to a considerable degree elemental and disorganized. . . . it was the spark that lit the flame of the February Revolution" (3). Similarly, a short piece in the *Krasnaia gazeta*, March 12, 1918, described the February Revolution thus: "it began with the disorganized movements of hungry men and women who were joined by the army, and the slavery of the ages disappeared into oblivion" (2); S. Smidovich, *Rabotnitsa i krest'ianka v oktiabr'skoi revoliutsii* (Moscow, Leningrad, 1927), 13.

68. GARF, f. 7952, op. 10, d. 38, l. 7, 9; f. 7952, op. 4, d. 82(1), l. 22; f. 7952, op. 4, d. 170(1), l. 1; E. M. Iaroslavskii, *Istoriia VKP(b)*, vol. 2 (Moscow, 1933); *V dni velikoi proletarskoi revoliutsii* (Moscow, 1937); M. Mitel'man, "Zhenskii miting," in *Povesti minuvshego*, (USSR, 1937), 137–47; *History of the Communist Party of the Soviet Union (Bolsheviks): Short Course* (Moscow, 1939), 175–76.

69. See, for example, *Vyborgskaia storona. Sbornik statei i vospominaniia* (Leningrad, 1957); N. Popova, *Women in the Land of Socialism* (Moscow, 1949), 38; *Bol'shaia sovetskaia entsiklopediia*, (USSR, 1954), 54: 36; *Ocherki istorii SSSR, 1907–mart 1917* (Moscow, 1954), 328; M. Mitel'man et al., eds., *Istoriia putilovskogo zavoda, 1801–1917* (Moscow, 1961), 546; S. Serditova, *Bol'sheviki v bor'be proletarskie massy* (Moscow, 1959), 124–29.

70. E. N. Burdzhalov, *Russia's Second Revolution*, trans. and ed. Donald J. Raleigh (Bloomington, Ind., 1987); I. P. Lieberov, "Petrogradskii proletariat v bor'be za pobedu fevral'skoi burzhuazno-demokraticheskoi revoliutsii v Rossii," *Istoriia SSSR*, no. 1 (1957): 41–73.

71. *Partiia bol'shevikov v fevral'skoi revoliutsii 1917 goda* (Moscow, 1971), 142.

72. Leiberov, *Na shturm samoderzhaviia*, 120.

### Chapter 3

1. A. V. Lunacharsky, "O narodnykh prazdnestvakh," in *Organizatsiia massovykh narodnykh prazdnestv*, ed. S. Kogan (Moscow, 1921), 3–6. There is extensive Soviet literature

on revolutionary holidays and a small, but growing number, of publications in English. See E. Riumin, *Massovye prazdnestva* (Moscow, Leningrad), 1927; *Massovye prazdnestva: Sbornik komiteta sotsiologicheskogo izucheniia iskusstv* (Leningrad, 1926); *Agitatsionno-massovoe iskusstvo pervykh let' okt'iabria* (Moscow, 1971); O. V. Nemiro, *V gorod prishel prazdnik: Iz istorii khudozhestvennogo oformleniia sovetskikh massovykh prazdnestv* (Leningrad, 1978); A. I. Mazaev, *Prazdnik kak sotsial'no-khudozhestvennoe iavlenie* (Moscow, 1978). Christel Lane, *The Rites of Rulers: Ritual in Industrial Society—The Soviet Case* (Cambridge, England, 1981); Christopher Binns, "The Changing Face of Power: Revolution and Accommodation in the Development of the Soviet Ceremonial System," *Man*, no. 14 (Dec. 1979): 585–606; Richard Stites, *Revolutionary Dreams: Utopian Vision and Experimental Life in the Russian Revolution* (New York, 1989), 79–100; V. P. Tolstoi, I. M. Bibkova, and Catherine Cooke, ed., *Street Art of the Revolution: Festivals and Celebrations in Russia, 1918–1933* (London, 1990); James von Geldern, *Bolshevik Festivals, 1917–1920* (Berkeley, 1993); Karen Petrone, *Life Has Become More Joyous, Comrades: Celebrations in the Time of Stalin* (Bloomington, Ind., 2000).

2. Victoria Bonnell, "The Representation of Women in Early Soviet Political Art," *The Russian Review* 50 (1991): 267–68; Elizabeth Waters, "The Female Form in Soviet Political Iconography, 1917–1932," in *Russia's Women: Accommodation, Resistance, Transformation*, ed. Barbara Evans Clements, Barbara Alpern Engel, and Christine Worobec (Berkeley, 1991), 225–42.

3. On January 23 (February 5) 1918, at a meeting of the Sovnarkom, Lunacharsky proposed the creation of a Red Calendar, then a list of revolutionary holidays was created. The decree was passed by the Sovnarkom the next day. Although the list was amended several times, May Day, anniversary of the October Revolution, and International Women's Day held their place in the years to come. Mazaev, *Prazdnik*, 274.

4. K. N. Samoilova, one of the main organizers of the Bolshevik women's movement, was fiercely opposed to any concessions to what she deemed as feminism, as was Kollontai. A. Kollontai, "Tvorcheskoe v rabote tovarishcha Samoilovoi," *Revoliutsionnania deiatel'nost Konkordii Nikolaevny Samoilovoi. Sbornik vospominanii* (Moscow, 1922), 9; Carol Hayden Eubanks, "Feminism and Bolshevism: The Zhenotdel and the Politics of Women's Emancipation in Russia, 1917–1930" (Ph.D. diss., University of California, Berkeley, 1979), 84–157.

5. G. E. Zinoviev, "Zadacha rabotnits i krest'ianok v nynesheii period revoliutsii," in *Mezhdunarodnyi den' rabotnitsy* (Moscow, 1925), 71.

6. Many Bolsheviks viewed the publication of *Rabotnitsa* as a "deviation towards feminism." See A. Kollontai, "Zhenshchiny v semnadtsatom godu," *Iz moei zhizni i raboty* (Moscow, 1974), 270. On Zhenotdel, see V. Moirova, "Piat' let raboty partii sredi rabotnits i krest'ianok," *Kommunistka*, no. 11 (Nov. 1923): 9; A. Unskova, "Za tri goda," *Tri goda diktatury proletariata* (Moscow, 1921), 19–20.

7. For an overview of Zhenotdel politics, see Elizabeth Wood, *The Baba and the Comrade: Gender and Politics in Revolutionary Russia* (Bloomington, Ind., 1997). A couple of Women's Day meetings were held in Petrograd in 1918 and were addressed by well-known Bolshevik women such as Kollontai, Samoilova, Lilina, Stal', and Kudelli; see *Krasnaia gazeta*, March 3, 1918, 3.

8. Barbara Evans Clements, "The Effects of the Civil War on Women and Family Relations," in *Party, State, and Society in the Russian Civil War*, ed. Diane P. Koenkar, William G. Rosenberg, and Ronald Grigor Suny (Bloomington, Ind., 1989), 51–57.

9. A. Kollontai, "K mezhdunarodnomu zhenskomu dniu: Mezhdunarodnyi den' rabotnits v 1921," *Kommunistka*, no. 8–9 (Jan.–Feb. 1921): 1–4.

10. In another article, Kollontai reaffirmed the close interdependence of the transformation of *byt* and the reconstruction of the national economy. See "Proizvodstvo i byt," *Kommunistka*, no. 10–11 (March–Apr. 1921): 6–9. On special care of women, see RGASPI, f. 134, op. 1, d. 179, l. 1.

11. RGASPI, f. 17, op. 10, d. 25, ll. 4–5.

12. KPSS, *Trinadtsatyi s"ezd RKP(b). Stenograficheskii otchet* (Moscow, 1973), 290–300, 574–77, 678–80.

13. E. Riumin, *Massovye prazdnestva* (Moscow, Leningrad), 1927; *Massovye prazdnestva: Sbornik komiteta sotsiologicheskogo izucheniia iskusstv* (Leningrad, 1926); *Krest'ianka*, no. 6 (Apr. 1922): 30. In the survey of young workers in the agricultural sector, respondents were asked to provide data on daily activities and how they celebrated Soviet holidays; see GARF, f. 5466, op. 1, d. 785, ll. 16–220. For Zhenotdel reports, see RGASPI, f. 17, op. 10, d. 104, l. 28.

14. *Krest'ianka*, no. 4 (Feb. 1925): 4.

15. See O. Sokolova, "Chto sdelano v den' rabotnits v proshlye gody," *Krest'ianka*, no. 4 (Feb. 1924): 21.

16. In 1928 Krupskaia, *8 marta, mezhdunarodnyi zhenskii den'* (Moscow, 1928), described the situation in villages as terrible. It appeared that only in 1927 did the state start building a few nurseries and crèches. And as for laundries and dining rooms, they simply did not exist.

17. Rakhil Kovnator, *Pervye gody* (Moscow, 1964): 157; RGASPI, f. 17, op. 12, d. 317, l. 4; Unskova, "Za tri goda," in *Tri goda diktatury proletariata*, 23; *Rabotnitsa*, no. 3 (March 1923): 2; GARF, f. 5457, op. 10, d. 250, ll. 13, 55.

18. Marguerite Harrison, *Marooned in Moscow: The Story of an American Woman Imprisoned in Russia* (New York, 1921), 80–82. Balabanova explained the apathetic response by using a class analysis: "It is hard to make women appreciate ideals when they are cold and hungry," she said, "especially women of this type—unskilled workers, former servants and members of the small bourgeoises. You will see a different attitude among industrial workers" (81).

19. TsGAKFD, "Goskino Kalendar'," 1924, no. 1–544; TsAODM, f. 369, op. 1, d. 1, l. 16; RGASPI, f. 17, op. 10, d. 576, l. 13; RGASPI, f. 17, op. 60, d. 42, l. 13.

20. RGASPI, f. 17, op. 10. d. 56, l. 13; G. Kochenova, "Rabota sredi zhenshchin," *Klub*, no. 3 (March 1923): 68; A. Fogel, *8 marta v gorode i derevne* (Moscow, 1928), 10.

21. N. K. Krupskaia, ed., *Revoliutsionnye prazdniki v biblioteke* (Moscow, 1923), 41; M. Mekhonoshina, "Kak provesti mezhdunarodnyi zhenskii kommunisticheskii den' v izbechital'ne," in *8 marta v izbe-chital'ne. Instruktivnyi sbornik* (Moscow, 1926), 48, 50.

22. L. Stal', "Obzor 'stranichek rabotnitsy' i gazet, posvoiashchennikh mezhdunarodnomu zhenskomu dniu," *Kommunistka*, no. 5 (May 1923): 47–51; F. Niurina, "8 marta 1927 goda," *Kommunistka*, no. 2 (Feb. 1927): 39–43; G. Mastiukova, "8 marta v derevne," *Kommunistka*, no. 2 (Feb. 1927): 44–50.

23. Fogel, *8 marta v gorode i v derevne*, 27, 35.

24. *Krest'ianka*, no. 4 (Feb. 1923): 31.

25. "Babii den'," *Krest'ianka*, no. 4 (1923): 31–33.

26. RGASPI, f. 17, op. 32, d. 115, l. 3.

27. Soviet publications such as *Klub* carried articles in almost every issue during the

1920s decrying the hooliganism of young males, making it impossible for more sedate workers to frequent the club. See also John Hatch, "Hangouts and Hangovers: State, Class and Culture in Moscow's Workers' Club Movement, 1925–1928," *Russian Review*, no. 1 (Jan. 1994): 97–117.

28. For an overview of Bolshevik policies toward women in Central Asia, see Gregory J. Massell, *The Surrogate Proletariat: Moslem Women and Revolutionary Strategies in Soviet Central Asia, 1919–1929* (Princeton, N.J., 1974); Douglas Northrop, "Uzbek Women and the Veil: Gender and Power in Stalinist Central Asia" (Ph.D. diss., Stanford University, 1999); idem; Northrup, "Languages of Loyalty: Gender, Politics, and Party Supervision in Uzbekistan, 1927–1941," *Russian Review* no. 2 (Apr. 2000): 179–200.

29. See for example, Tinieva, "Vostok i 8-e marta," *Kommunistka*, no. 5–6 (May–June 1924): 48–49; A. Nelli, "8-oe marta y musul'manok," *Rabotnitsa*, no. 5 (May 1923): 21; *Za piat' let. Sbornik po voprosam raboty kommunisticheskoi partii sredi zhenshchin Srednei Azii* (Moscow, 1925); "Zhenshchiny Vostoka," *Pravda*, March 8, 1924, 4.

30. In 1928 on Women's Day, 1,896 Muslim women in and around Tashkent, Samarkhand, Khokand, and Andizhan, publicly unveiled themselves. See GARF, f. 5466, op. 2, d. 1322, l. 147.

31. *Kommunistka*, no. 6 (1923): 33; E. Tarasova, *Pod znamenem bol'shevikov. Zhenshchiny i revoliutsii* (Moscow, 1959), 356.

32. GARF, f. 5466, op. 1, d. 1350, l. 51.

33. E. D. Emel'ianova, *Revoliutsiia, partiia, zhenshchina* (Smolensk, 1971), 174.

34. A. Kalygina, *Krest'ianka i vosmoe marta* (Moscow, 1926), 7.

35. Jessica Smith, *Women in Soviet Russia* (New York, 1928), 37.

36. L. A. Tul'tseva, *Sovremennye prazdniki i obriady narodov SSSR* (Moscow, 1985), 34; RGASPI, f. 17, op. 32, d. 115, l. 3.

37. Ella Winter, *Red Virtue: Human Relationships in the New Russia* (New York, 1933), 51.

38. Fogel', *8 Marta v gorode i v derevne*, 29; S. Gopner, *Nash boevoi prazdnik* (Moscow, 1926), 1; Kalygina, *Krest'ianka i vosmoe marta*, 7.

39. Kalygina, *Krest'ianka i vosmoe marta*, 29; *Ogonëk*, March 4, 1928, front cover.

40. VtsSPS, in instructions to trade unions about Women's Day celebrations, strongly urged them to open social service institutions as part of the March 8 ceremonies. See, for example, the 1924 circular from the director of VtsSPS, Dogadov, GARF, f. 5451, op. 8, d. 90, l. 43. For similar Women's Day instructions from Glavsotsvos, department of Narkompros in 1927, see TsGA RSFSR, f.1575, op. 10, d. 39, ll. 50, 50b, 51 and TsGA, f. 1575, op. 10, d. 31, ll. 47, 48. Newspapers such as *Pravda, Leningradskaia pravda, Trud, Izvestiia*, and other regional and local papers, every year published detailed lists of social service institutions opened in honor of Women's Day, and film clips usually featured the opening of such institutions. A short documentary film shot in Ivanovo-Voznesensk on March 8 showed a very clean nursery, with unnaturally clean children. They washed their hands before eating, took naps on clean beds, and wore hygienic clothes. See TsGAKFD, I-1591, no. 12, 1928.

41. RGASPI, f. 134, op. 1, d. 179, ll. 3–6.

42. RGASPI, f. 17, op. 10, d. 83, l. 7. G. Mel'nichanskii, "Profsouizy i 8 marta," *Kommunistka*, no. 2 (Feb. 1925): 14–15; V. Moirova, "Den' rabotnits," *Kommunistka*, no. 1–2 (Jan.–Feb., 1923): 3–4.

43. Although Soviet heroines became a major focus of Stalinist propaganda, the practice of singling out women for public praise started in the 1920s. See *Pravda*, March 8, 1924, 3, 4, 5; *Izvestiia*, March 7, 1926, 3, 4; *Izvestiia*, March 7, 1927, 4, 5, 6; L. Sosnovskii, "Sovetskaia zhenshchina," in *Mezhdunarodnyi den' rabotnitsy* (Proletarii, 1925), 125–34; "Rabotnitsy i krest'ianki v revoliutsii," in *Mezhdunarodnyi den' rabotnits* (Moscow, 1925), 52–75. Instructions on the celebration of March 8 in libraries highlighted the need to display portraits of famous leaders of the Russian women's movement together with brief biographical sketches. Krupskaia, ed., *Revoliutsionnye prazdniki v biblioteke*, 42. See chapter 6 of this book for an elaboration on the theme of Soviet heroines.

44. *Krest'ianka*, no. 4 (February 1925): 4.

45. The women featured in the film stepped out of the prison led by male guards. But the solemnity of the occasion was marred by the fact that when two of the amnestied prisoners received their document of liberation, they started giggling. TsGAKFD, "Goskino Kalendar'," 1924, no. I-544. For accounts of similar ceremonies, see RGASPI, f. 17, op. 15, d. 1. 4; *Krest'ianka*, no. 6 (March 1924): 31, for the text of the TsIK resolution granting amnesty to women prisoners on Women's Day.

46. A. Rozanova, "Mezhdunarodnyi den' rabotnits v Rossii," *Kommunistka*, no. 12–13 (May–June, 1921): 25.

47. I-176, Goskino kalendar', TsGAKFD, I-76. (Moscow, 1924).

48. R. Kovnator, "Budem pomnit' o Lenine–druge rabotnits i krest'ianok," *Kommunistka*, no. 3 (March 1924): 5–7; E. Iaroslavskii, "Sem'ia Lenina," *Kommunistka*, no. 4 (Apr. 1924): 1–3; I. Stalin, "Rabotnitsy i krest'ianki, pomnite i vypolniaite zavety Il'icha," *Kommunistka*, no. 1 (Jan. 1925): 3; N. K. Krupskaia, "Lenin i narodnoe prosveshchenie," *Kommunistka*, no. 1 (Jan. 1925): 12–16; Klavdiia Nikolaeva, "Tov: Lenin i raskreposhchenie zhenshchin," *Leningradskaia pravda*, March 8, 1924, 1.

49. Nina Tumarkin, *Lenin Lives: The Lenin Cult in Soviet Russia* (Cambridge, Mass., 1983); See also O. V. Velikanova, "Obraz Lenina v massovom soznanii," *Otechestvennaia istoriia*, no. 2 (March–Apr. 1994): 177–85. It was crucial for the Party to step up the circulation of propaganda, for as late as 1923 there were reports that peasants in some of the provinces did not even recognize the name Lenin. See M. Vener, "Litsom k derevne: sovetskaia vlast' i krest'ianskii vopros," *Otechestvennaia istoriia*, no. 5 (Sept. 1992): 87.

50. *Leningradskaia pravda*, March 8, 1924, 1.

51. The following Women's Day publications contain articles by Lenin and about his work for women's liberation: *Mezhdunarodnyi den' rabotnitsy* (Moscow, 1924); Moirova, "8-go Marta v 1924 godu," *Krest'ianka*, no. 4 (Feb. 1924): 20; G. S. Maliuchenko, ed., *Mezhdunarodnyi den' rabotnits* (Rostov-Don, 1925); *Mezhdunarodnyi den' rabotnits* (Moscow, 1925); *8 marta i rabotnitsa* (Moscow, 1925); *8-e marta i krest'ianka* (Moscow, 1925); *8-e Marta: Materialy k provedeniiu mezhdunarodnogo dnia rabotnits k krest'ianok k derevne* (Omsk, 1925); *Mezhdunarodnyi den' rabotnitsy* (Proletarii, 1925); F. Niurina, *Zare navstrechu. 8-e marta mezhdunarodnyi zhenskii den'* (Moscow, 1926); *Mezhdunarodnyi zhenskii den'* (Proletarii, 1927). For a translation of the writings of Lenin on the "woman question" and the articles written by Lenin on Women's Day, see *Women and Communism: Selected Writings from the Works of Marx, Engels, Lenin, and Stalin* (Westport, Conn., 1973); *The Emancipation of Women: From the Writings of V. I. Lenin* (New York, 1966).

52. R. Kovnator, "Zhenskii vopros v svete leninizma," *Kommunistka*, no. 1 (Jan.

1925): 16; S. Smidovich, "K XIII s"ezdu RKP," *Kommunistka*, no. 5-6 (May-June 1924): 3.

53. Vera Lebedeva, "Tov. Lenin i nashe kul'turnoe stroitel'stvo," *Kommunistka*, no. 4 (Apr. 1924): 4. The underfunding of OMM was legend and Lebedeva complained about it at various times. For a similar story detailing Lenin's kindness and contrasting it with the rigorous strictness of the party, see Mavshovich, "Moia vstrecha s Il'ichem," in *Mezhdunarodnyi den' rabotnitsy* (USSR, 1925), 134-35.

54. "Torzhestvennoe zasedanie v teatre Zimina po povodu piatiletiia raboty RKP sredi zhenshchin, 26 November, 1923," in *Mezhdunarodnyi den' rabotnitsy* (Moscow, 1924), 61.

55. L. Stal', "Rabotnitsy i krest'ianki o Lenine," *Kommunistka*, no. 1 (Jan. 1925): 35.

56. Ibid., 35.

57. Ibid., 33. In Nina Chertova's short story, "New Galoshes," a frivolous woman, who buys footwear on the black market, undergoes a total transformation when she hears of Lenin's death. See N. Chertova, "Novye Galoshi," *Pereval* 1 (1925): 176-87; qtd. in Catriona Kelly, *A History of Women's Writing, 1820-1992* (Oxford, 1994), 240.

58. RGASPI, f. 17, op. 10, d. 56, l. 14.

59. At the First Congress of the Comintern in March 1919, delegates promised to educate women in the spirit of communism and recruit them to communist parties. In 1920, an international conference of communist women was called in Moscow at which the delegates decided to form the International Women's Secretariat (MZHK). This committee was to oversee the work of all women's sections of the Comintern. The MZHK and the Comintern subsequently sent detailed instructions on Women's Day celebrations to their international counterparts. Iu. Shtaerman, "Mezhdunarodnyi zhenskii den': K istorii ego voznikoveniia i prazdnovaniia," in *Mezhdunarodnyi den' rabotnits: Sbornik* (USSR, 1928), 98-99; "Komintern i rabotnitsa," in *8 marta i rabotnitsa* (Moscow, 1925). Needless to say, all the slogans, photographs, and placards sent abroad for the holiday emphasized the privileged status of women in the Soviet Union and called for close cooperation between the Soviet Union and other countries of the world.

60. "Mezhdunarodnyi zhenskii den' v Germanii," *Kommunistka*, no. 5 (May 1923): 42; "Bor'ba germanskikh proletarok," *Pravda*, March 8, 1924, 3; "Rabotnitsa na zapade," *Izvestiia*, March 8, 1927, 5.

61. L. Stal', "Itogi prazdnovaniia mezhdunarodnogo dnia rabotnits 1921 g. Mezhdunarodnyi zhenskii den' v Zapadnoi Evrope," *Kommunistka*, nos. 11-12 (May-June 1921): 20-23.

62. G. Shturm, "Mezhdunarodnyi zhenskii den' na zapade," *Kommunistka*, no. 6 (June 1925): 96-101.

63. Klara Zetkin, "Mezhdunarodnyi kommunisticheskii den'—shag k mirovoi revoliutsii," *Kommunistka*, no. 2 (Feb. 1927): 1-7; A. Artiukhina, "Rabota partii sredi rabotnits v Germanii," *Kommunistka*, no. 2 (Feb., 1927): 16-22.

64. L. Heifetz, "Mezhdunarodnoe dvizhenie rabotnits: Kak razvivaetsia v germanskoi kommunisticheskoi partii rabota sredi zhenshchin," *Kommunistka*, nos. 10-11 (March-Apr. 1921), 11-16; RGASPI, f. 507, op. 2, d. 104, l. 130-31. For criticisms by German colleagues, see RGASPI, f. 507, d. 87, op. 2, ll. 323-25; "Komintern i rabotnitsa," in *8 marta i rabotnitsa* (Moscow, 1925), 30, 31.

65. According to Adam Ulam, *Expansion and Coexistence: Soviet Foreign Policy*,

*1917–1973* (New York, 1974), 156, the Russians were deeply hostile to liberals and parliamentarianism. They believed that fascists were more desirable as allies than middle-class parties, like the Social Democrats, as they would facilitate the communist rise to power.

66. L. Stal', "Pochemu perestali prazdnovat' zhenskii den' vo Frantsii," *Kommunistka*, nos. 8–9 (Jan.–Feb. 1921): 7–8.

67. Z. Boiarskaia, "Mezhdunarodnoe dvizhenie rabotnits," *Kommunistka*, no. 2 (Feb. 1922): 6–7.

68. See for example, "O rabote germanskikh kommunistok," *Kommunistka*, nos. 8–9 (Jan.–Feb. 1921): 6–7.

69. Steinhard, "Zhenskoe dvizhenie v nemetskoi Avstrii," *Kommunistka*, nos. 8–9 (Jan.–Feb. 1921): 9; Iza Strasser, "Zhenskii trud i sotsial-demokrataiia v Avstrii," *Kommunistka*, nos. 1–2 (Jan.–Feb. 1923): 19–21.

70. Jeffrey Brooks, "The Press and Its Message: Images of America in the 1920s and 1930s," in *Russia in the Era of NEP*, ed. Sheila Fitzpatrick, Alexander Rabinowitch, and Richard Stites (Bloomington, Ind., 1991), 231–52.

71. For a blatant reiteration of this theme, see the MZHK article written in English for Women's Day in 1927, RGASPI, f. 507, op. 2, d. 113, ll. 125–33.

72. "Kak frantsuzkie kapitalisty eksploatiruiut rabotnits," *Rabotnitsa*, no. 6 (June 1923): 37; "Bor'ba nemetskikh rabotnits protiv dorogovizny," *Kommunistka*, no. 2 (Feb. 1923): 25; "Iz zhizni i byta rabotnits Zapada," in *8-oe marta–mezhdunarodnyi den' rabotnits: Sbornik materialov* (Leningrad, 1926), 39–46. As the decade progressed, Soviet propaganda about the status of women in the West became more critical and dire. See, for example, Augusta Derks, "Iz byta germanskikh rabotnits," *Kommunistka*, no. 1 (Jan. 1927): 79–80; V. Gutman, "Rabotnitsa i selianka v mirovom revoliutsionnom dvizhenii," *Mezhdunarodnyi zhenskii den': Sbornik* (USSR, 1927), 31–60; Margarita Bergweiler, "Zhilishchinyi krizis v Germanii," *Kommunistka*, no. 1 (Jan. 1927): 81–82; F. Niurina, "Polozhenie rabotnitsy v zapadnikh stranakh," *Kommunistka*, no. 2 (Feb. 1927): 23–27; E. Kent, "Rabotnitsa v Anglii," ibid., 27–30; M. Karagodskaia, "Trudiaschiesia zhenshchiny v burzhuaznikh stranakh," in *Mezhdunarodnyi den' rabotnitsy*, (USSR, 1928), 17–25.

73. See, for example, Iza Strasser, "Okhrana materinstva v Zapadnoi Evrope," *Kommunistka*, no. 3 (March 1925): 80–83.

74. "Angliiskii sud," *Rabotnitsa*, no. 7 (July 1923): 39.

75. L. Stal', "Kak zhivut frantsuzkie rabotnitsy," *Kommunistka*, no. 7 (July 1923): 38. It appeared that similar conditions prevailed in Czechoslovakia; see, for example, "Kak okhraniaetsia materinstvo i mladenchestvo v Chekhoslovakii," *Rabotnitsa*, no. 5 (May 1923): 22.

76. *Krest'ianka*, no. 4 (Feb. 1926): 16.

77. RGASPI, f. 507, op. 2, d. 63, l. 29.

78. T. Kasparova, "Trudiaschiesiia zhenshchiny stran vostoka," *Kommunistka*, nos. 1–2 (Jan.–Feb. 1923): 25–26; "Rabotnitsy v Iaponii," *Rabotnitsa*, no. 5 (May 1923): 23; Al'-muhamedov, "Iz zhizni rabotnits Turtsii," *Rabotnitsa*, no. 6 (June 1923): 38; V. Kasparova, "8-oe marta v stranakh zarubezhnogo Vostoka," *Kommunistka*, no. 2 (Feb. 1926): 22–27; "Tekstil'schitsa Iaponii," *Kommunistka*, no. 2 (Feb. 1927): 32–37.

79. V. Kasparova, "Zhenskoe dvizhenie na vostoke," in *Mezhdunarodnyi den' rabotnitsy* (USSR 1925): 54–56.

## Chapter 4

1. For state policies toward women and their experiences during this period, see Wendy Goldman, *Women, the State and Revolution: Soviet Family Policy and Social Life, 1917–1936* (New York, 1993); Richard Stites, *The Women's Liberation Movement in Russia: Feminism, Nihilism, and Bolshevism, 1860–1930* (Princeton, N.J., 1978).

2. The Glavpolitprosvet (Chief Committee for Political Enlightenment) was a political organization that functioned under the aegis of Narkompros. It disseminated propaganda and political education among the masses. Peter Kenez, *Birth of the Propaganda State: Soviet Methods of Mass Mobilization, 1917–29* (Cambridge, 1985); Sheila Fitzpatrick, *Education and Social Mobility in the Soviet Union, 1921–1934* (Cambridge, 1979).

3. The Proletkult drama circles and the Sinnaia Bluza were amateur dramatic organizations. These circles very popular among the workers and soldiers in towns and countryside. For literature on amateur dramatics in the 1920s, see A. I. Piotrovskii, *Za sovetskii teatr* (Leningrad, 1925); A. I. Piotrovskii, *Krasnoarmeiskii teatr* (Petrograd, 1921); A. A. Gvozdev, "Samodeiatel'nyi teatr," *Molodaia gvardiia*, no. 8 (August 1925): 189–97; *Istoriia sovetskogo teatra* (Leningrad, 1933), vols. 1, 2; H. O. Carter, *The Theater and Cinema of Soviet Russia* (London, 1924); T. A. Remizova, *Kul'turno-prosvetitel'naia rabota v RSFSR. 1921–1925* (Moscow, 1962); A. I. Piotrovskii, *Teatr, kino, zhizn* (Leningrad, 1969); V. Mirnova, *TRAM, agitatsionnyi molodezhnyi teatr 1920–1930-x godov* (Leningrad, 1977); V. K. Aizenshtadt, *Sovetskii samodeiatel'nyi teatr* (Kharkov, 1983); Richard Stites, *Russian Popular Culture* (Cambridge, 1992), 49–53; Lynn Mally, "The Rise and Fall of the Soviet Youth Theater TRAM'" *Slavic Review* 51 (Fall 1992): 411–30; idem, *Revolutionary Acts: Amateur Theater and the Soviet State* (Ithaca, 2000).

4. D. Nikolai, "Rabochii klub i revoliutsionnaia intsenirovka," *Leningradskaia Pravda*, March 23, 1924, 5–6.

5. *Virineya* was originally written as a *povest'* or a long tale and adapted for the theater in 1925. For an extended analysis of the plays, see Xenia Gasiorowska, *Women in Soviet Fiction, 1917–1965* (Madison, Wis., 1968); R. Russell, "First Soviet Plays," in *Russian Theater in the Age of Modernism*, ed. R. Russell and A. Barratt (New York, 1990).

6. On Stalin viewing *Liubov Yarovaya*, see Svetlana Alliluyeva, *Twenty Letters to a Friend*, trans. Priscilla Johnson McMillan (New York, 1967), 144; on *Vireneya*, see *Zhizn iskusstva*, no. 12 (March 24, 1925): 19.

7. *Soviet Scene: Six Plays of Russian Life*, trans. Alexander Bakshy (New Haven, 1946), 23–100.

8. *October Storm and After: Stories and Reminiscences* (Moscow, 1974), 175–235.

9. Bertold Brecht, *Brecht on Theater* (New York, 1964), 73. For a good analysis of agitprop theater, see Hassan Tehranchian, *Agitprop Theater: Germany and the Soviet Union* (Ph.D. diss., New York University, 1982).

10. Helen Keyssar, *Feminist Theatre: An Introduction to the Plays of Contemporary British and American Women* (Basingstoke, England, 1984), 13.

11. See Barbara Evans Clements, "The Utopianism of the Zhenotdel," *Russian Review*, no. 3 (fall 1992), 485–96, on the depth of Zhenotdel commitment to the role of popular initiative in communalizing daily life.

12. N. Bukharin and E. Preobrazhenskii, *The ABC of Communism*, trans. Eden and Cedar Paul (Ann Arbor, Mich., 1966), 74; *Kommunisticheskaia Partiia i organizatsiia rabotnits: Posobie dlia propagandistok* (Moscow, 1919), 26–34.

13. See, for example, V. Golubeva, "Trud zhenotdelov v novykh usloviakh," *Pravda*,

April 13, 1923; V. Molotov and V. Golubeva, "Metody raboty sredi zhenshchin pri novykh usloviiakh," *Kommunistka*, 18 (Jan. 1922); P. Smilga, "Zadachi zhenotdelov v oblasti kooperatsii," *Kommunistka*, nos. 16–17, (Sept.–Oct. 1921). Golubeva was the deputy head of Zhenotdel. In a similar trend, the marriage law reform of 1926 stated that parents, rather than the state, should be primarily responsible for the care of the children.

14. L. Trotsky, "Pis'mo tov. Trotskogo," in *Mezhdunarodnyi den' rabotnits: Sbornik materialov dlia chtenia i prorabotka v klubakh, izbakh chital'niakh, narodnykh domakh i shkolakh*, ed. G. S. Maliuchenko (Rostov-Don, 1925), 20–21; GARF f. 5451, op. 9, d. 526, l. 1, 2, and f. 5451, op. 14, d. 603, l. 1, 2. Central Trade Union reports in GARF from 1921 to 1939 have extensive references to the necessity of involving women in the improvement of the condition of daily life and the creation of communal facilities.

15. V. I. Lenin, "Rech tov. Lenina na konferentsii moskovskikh rabotnits," in *Mezhdunarodnyi den' rabotnits: Materialy dlia Komsomolskogo i Pionerskogo kluba* (Moscow, 1925), 9. This viewpoint is echoed in numerous articles; see, for example, "Nash prazdnik, mezhdunarodnyi kommunisticheskii den'," *Krest'ianka*, no. 4 (Feb. 1926): 2–4; "Meropriatii po usileniiu raboty sredi krest'ianok (Postanovlenie Orgburo TsK ot 22 iiunia 1925g)," rpt. in *Vos'moe marta v derevne* (Leningrad, 1926).

16. Similarly, Abram Room's controversial, 1927 film, *No. 3 Meshchanskaya Street*, was criticized as being insufficiently revolutionary. As it dealt with the awakening of a woman's consciousness by exploring the complicated sexual and emotional relationships of a menage á trois of which she was a part, critics felt that it was concerned more with social misfits than with new citizens of Soviet society. For an analysis, see Lynne Attwood, ed. *Red Women on the Silver Screen* (London, 1993), 46–48.

17. *8-oe marta–mezhdunarodnyi den' rabotnits: Sbornik materialov* (Leningrad, 1926), 144–48.

18. See also Cheremnykh's cartoon of the "parasitical doll," whose outstanding quality was her *prazdnost'* or inactivity. This woman disdained both her maternal and domestic functions. See *Kommunistka*, nos. 10–11 (Oct.–Nov., 1920), 57.

19. *8 marta v izbe chital'ne* (Leningrad, 1925), 57–59.

20. *Six Soviet Plays*, trans. Charles Malamuth (Cambridge, Mass., 1934) 85–154.

21. For negative references to priests, see *"Bab'i pobedy*, in *Mezhdunarodnyi zhenskii den'* (Proletarii, 1926), 143–54; *Prosnis' krest'ianka*, in *Mezhdunarodnyi den' rabotnits*, 78–90.

22. "Materialy dlia zhivoi gazety ko dniu rabotnitsy 8 marta 1926," in *8-oe marta–mezhdunarodnyi den' rabotnits: Sbornik materialov* (Leningrad, 1926), 132.

23. *Den' rabotnitsy*, in *Mezhdunarodnyi zhenskii den': Sbornik pod redaktsiei i predisloviem tsentral'nogo otdela rabotnits TsK KP(B)U* (Proletarii, 1927), 116–31.

24. D. Dmitrievich, *Prosnis' krest'ianka*, in *Mezhdunarodnyi den' rabotnits*, 78–90. In Sasha Krasnyi's *intsenirovka*, *Litsom k derevne*, a peasant woman proclaims to the audience that her husband has an "iron fist." Maria Rozen, ed., *Den' rabotnitsy v klube* (Moscow, 1925), 99. Diatribes against wife beating were a prominent theme in Women's Day articles and lectures. See, for example, Z. I. Lilina, ed., *Krest'ianki ukreplaiite sovetskuiu vlast': Sbornik k mezhdunarodnomy zhenskomu dniu* (Leningrad-Moscow, 1925), 8.

25. Printed in *8 marta i rabotnitsa* (Moscow, 1925), 49–75.

26. Ibid., 75.

27. *8-oe marta–mezhdunarodnyi den' rabotnits: Sbornik materialov* (Leningrad, 1926), 139–43.

28. According to the American observer Ella Winter, this story was part of the repertoire of jokes and anecdotes on the Soviet alimony laws. See *Red Virtue* (New York, 1933), 144–45.

29. *Mezhdunarodnyi zhenskii den'* (Proletarii, 1927), 131–44.

30. For other examples of wicked mothers-in-law, see *Politsud nad krest'ianskoi delegatkoi*, in *Mezhdunarodnyi den' rabotnits*, 31–51; *V staryi byt dolzhen kol byt' vbit*, in *Mezhdunarodnyi zhenskii den': Sbornik* (Proletarii, 1927), 144–50.

31. G. S. Maliuchenko, "Pervye teatralnye sezony novoi epokhi," in *U istokov. Sbornik statei* (Moscow, 1960), 281.

32. Reproduced in Stephen White, *The Bolshevik Poster* (New Haven, 1988), 71, fig. 4.7.

33. V. P. Tolstoi, I. M. Bibkova, and Catherine Cooke, ed., *Street Art of the Revolution: Festivals and Celebrations in Russia 1918–1933* (London, 1990), doc. 19, 129.

34. *8-oe marta–mezhdunarodnyi den' rabotnits: Sbornik materialov*, 107–55. A 1928 report of the Textile Workers' Union characterized the play *Leninka* as very primitive and naive in its propaganda content. Nonetheless, it was recommended for performance on Women's Day as the language was accessible and the content easy for adaptation by amateur drama circles. GARF, f. 5457, op. 12, d. 200, l. 59.

35. For other negative references to the counter-revolutionary tendencies of old women, see the play *Vos'moe marta prezhde i teper'*, in *Mezhdunarodnyi den' rabotnits* (Moscow, 1924). In this play, older women counsel the workers to refrain from going on strike and threaten to inform the factory management. In *8-e Marta*, the mother tries to prevent her daughter from joining the Bolsheviks in celebrating Women's Day in 1914 and defending the tsarist order. See *8-e marta: Materialy k provedeniiu mezhdunarodnogo dnia rabotnits i krest'ianok v derevne* (Omsk, 1925).

36. *Vos'moe marta i krest'ianka* (Moscow, 1925).

37. Ibid., 33.

38. The negligible representation of peasant women in rural cooperative institutions was a matter of concern to the Bolsheviks. As late as October 1925, women made up a scant 3 percent of the membership in all agrarian cooperatives in the Soviet Republic. This was explained by the fact that the male membership of the village households tended to form cooperatives. The party advocated the involvement of poor women peasants in cooperatives both as a means of promoting socialism in the countryside and as a means of convincing women of their economic independence and capability. Agrarian cooperatives were instructed to ceremoniously induct women members on Women's Day. *8 marta v derevne* (Leningrad, 1926), 20; *8 marta v izbe-chital'ne* (Moscow-Leningrad, 1926), 32–33; Z. Shamurina, ed., *8-oe marta–Mezhdunarodnyi zhenskii den'* (Moscow-Leningrad, 1926).

39. Male peasant hostility to Zhenotdel workers was legion and men would go to any extreme, including murder, to prevent these workers from influencing their wives. E. Blonina, "Volostnoe delegatskoe sobranie krest'ianok," *Kommunistka*, nos. 1–2 (June–July 1920): 34–35; E. Kogan-Pismanik, "Soldatki revoliutsii," in *Zhenshchiny v revoliutsii*, ed. A. V. Artiukhina (Moscow, 1959), 195–96. And V. Talachova, "Na mirnom rabote," in ibid., 300; A. M. Bol'shakov, *Derevnia 1917–1927* (Moscow, 1927), 352. Rakhil Kovnator, a Zhenotdel organizer, recalled that in a delegate meeting Vichuga in Ivanovo-Voznesensk, men came armed with bayonets to protest against the liberation of women. See Rakhil Kovnator, *Pervye gody* (Moscow, 1964), 120.

40. *Samokritika*, which literally means self-criticism, was notoriously abused by the Stalinist state in the 1930s when party members and state bureaucrats were urged to own up to imagined and real acts of omission and commission. Often prominent members of the Soviet elite would engage in displays of public penitence in the hopes of warding off arrest and incarceration in the camps.

41. Social criticism of old-fashioned attitudes toward women often inhibited men from taking drastic action against female activism. Ella Winter in *Red Virtue* describes the following incident: "In 1927, at the Thirteenth Soviet Congress, a group of women delegates were discussing the nomination of a woman president of a village Soviet to the All-Russian Executive committee. The woman's husband, a social worker in his village, declared: "I'll have to divorce my wife." "Why?" "What if I have to teach my wife reason (the Russian phrase for "beat") and she is in the government?" One of the woman delegates proposed that the anxious peasant challenge his wife's candidature. "What! Do you want me to expose myself to general mockery? I should be called an advocate of serfdom, I, a social worker? How could I ever go back to my village?" (112).

42. The fact that the inclusion of women would improve the quality of goods available in a cooperative was a common propaganda theme. See Z. Shamurina, ed., *8-oe marta–Mezhdunarodnyi zhenskii den'* (Moscow, Leningrad, 1926), 23–25.

43. According to Lynn Attwood, readers' letters to *Krest'ianka* reinforced the message that men could be reeducated to accept women's equality and activism. See *Creating the New Soviet Woman* (New York, 1999), 63–64.

44. *Mezhdunarodnyi den' rabotnits. Vos'moe marta* (Rostov-Don, 1925).

45. Ibid., 72.

46. Reprinted in *8-oe marta–mezhdunarodnyi den' rabotnits: Sbornik materialov* (Leningrad, 1926), 83–106. For a play constructed on a similar theme of kulak corruption and oppression of women in the countryside, see *Lavrik*, by I. V. Leonov, in *8 marta v izbe-chital'ne: Instruktivnyi sbornik* (Moscow-Leningrad, 1926), 51–65.

47. *Russian Literature Since the Revolution*, ed. Joshua Kunitz (New York, 1948), 402–08.

48. S. Svirnovskaia, a director of the statistical department of the TsIk, later recounted that male peasants were fiercely opposed to women attending elections to the soviets. And any attempts to nominate women as candidates were met with abusive laughter and mockery. S. Svirinovskaia, "Zhenshchiny v sovetakh," in *Zhenshchiny v revoliutsii*, 290.

49. For other analyses of female iconography in the early Soviet era, see Barbara E. Clements, "The Birth of the New Soviet Women," in *Bolshevik Culture: Experiment and Order in the Russian Revolution*, ed. Abbott Gleason, Peter Kenez, and Richard Stites (Bloomington, Ind., 1989); Victoria E. Bonnell, "The Representation of Women in Early Soviet Political Art," *Russian Review* 50 (1991): 267–88; Elizabeth Waters, "The Female Form in Soviet Political Iconography, 1917–1932," in *Russia's Women: Accommodation, Resistance, Transformation*, ed. Barbara Evans Clements, Barbara Alpern Engels, and Christine D. Worobec (Berkeley, 1991), 225–42.

50. *8-e Marta: materialy dlia provedeniia mezhdunarodnogo zhenskogo kommunisticheskogo dnia v gorode* (Moscow, 1927).

51. *Six Soviet Plays*, trans. Charles Malamuth (Cambridge, Mass., 1934), 313–87.

52. Ibid., 386.

## Chapter 5

1. Roger Pethybridge, *The Social Prelude to Stalinism* (New York, 1974); Lynne Viola, *Best Sons of the Fatherland: Workers in the Vanguard of Soviet Collectivization* (New York, 1987); William Chase, *Workers, Society and the Soviet State: Life and Labor in Moscow, 1918-1929* (Chicago, 1989); Sheila Fitzpatrick, ed., *Cultural Revolution in Russia, 1928-1931* (Bloomington, Ind., 1978).

2. Wendy Z. Goldman, *Women, the State and Revolution: Soviet Family Policy and Social Life, 1917-1936* (Cambridge, 1993), 310-317; Gail W. Lapidus, "Sexual Equality in Soviet Policy: A Developmental Perspective," in *Women in Russia*, ed. Dorothy Atkinson, Alexander Dallin and Gail W. Lapidus (Stanford, 1977), 116-138; Solomon M. Schwarz, *Labor in the Soviet Union* (New York, 1951), 64-76.

3. The sole exception to this rule that focuses on the cultural and social aspect of mobilization of women, is Heather Jean Coleman, *Mobilizing Urban Women For the First Five-Year Plan: The Zhenotdel and the Rapid Industrialization of the USSR 1928-1932* (Master's thesis, Queen's University, Canada, 1992).

4. See O. Biriukov, *Bor'ba za novyi byt: K stroitel'stvu sotsialisticheskikh gorodov* (Moscow, 1931); A. Grigorovich, *Zhivem* (Moscow, 1930). For an overview of this subject, see E. M. Zuikova, *Byt pri sotsializme* (Moscow, 1977).

5. See "O rabote po pereustroiistvu byta, Postanovlenie TsK VKP(b) ot 16 May 1930," in *Spravochnik partiinogo rabotnika* (Moscow, 1934), 8:733.

6. For a similar viewpoint, see V. Moirova, "Rabota sredi zhenshchin v perelomnyi period," *Partiinoe stroitel'stvo*, nos. 13-14 (July 1930).

7. *Leningradskaia pravda*, March 8, 1929, 3.

8. *Izvestiia*, March 8, 1929, 1.

9. *Komsomol'skaia pravda*, March 8, 1929, 1.

10. Artiukhina reported that as late as 1929, large industries such as Treugolnik, Proletarka, Osvobozhdennyi Trud, and Trekhgorka had not promoted a single woman to an administrative post. Nor had a single *batrachka* (landless laborer) been promoted to the administration of a cooperative. And as for young girls and female Komsomol members, the issue of *vydvizhenie* had not even been addressed. See A. Artiukhina, "8 marta vse na proverku," *Kommunistka*, no. 3 (1929): 13. For similar criticism, see A. Artiukhina, *Pravda*, March 8, 1929, 3.

11. GARF, f. 5457, op. 12, d. 200, l. 6. For similar reports, see also GARF, f. 5457, op. 10, d. 250, l. 128; *Trud*, Jan 29, 1928, 4; *Golos tekstil'nitsa*, February 25, 1928, 5, reported the case of a woman worker in the Reutovskii factory, who before her promotion earned fifty-three rubles, and after being promoted to the post of supervisor only made forty-five rubles.

12. *Trud*, March 9, 1929, 1; another cartoon, *Kommunistka*, no. 5 (May 1929): 19, shows foremen brandishing bayonets at newly promoted women.

13. *Komsomol'skaia pravda*, April 5, 1929, 1.

14. "Prestuplenie Marusi Kozlovoi," *Komsomol'skaia pravda*, April 5, 1929, 1.

15. *Trud*, Jan. 29, 1928, 4; A. Artiukhina, "Likvidatsionnyi zud nuzhno uniat," *Kommunistka*, no. 6 (June 1928): 6-7, reported that in a factory in Ukraine, due to the viciousness of the foreman and a member of the party, three women workers tried to commit suicide.

16. Rose L. Glickman, *Russian Factory Women. Workplace and Society, 1880-1914*

(Berkeley, 1984), 141–143. See also E. A. Oliunina, "The Tailoring Trade in Moscow and the Villages of Moscow and Riazan Provinces: Material on the History of the Domestic Industry in Russia," in *The Russian Worker. Life and Labor under the Tsarist Regime* ed. Victoria Bonnell (Berkeley, 1983), 181.

17. *Piatnadtsatyi S"ezd VKP(b)*, Stenograficheskii otchet (Moscow, 1962), 2:875–76, 1452.

18. L. Sabsovich, in "Problemy rabochego byta v piatiletke," *Torgovo-promyshlennaia gazeta*, March 8, 1929, 3, drew a direct connection between the success of industrialization, increased labor participation of women, and the socialization of daily life. For similar views, see G. Lebedev and B. Fridman, "Za kul'turno-bytovuiu kooperatsiiu," *Pravda*, March 8, 1929, 4.

19. M. Tunik, "Ocherednye zadachi," *Trud*, March 7, 1929, 1.

20. S. Smidovich, "8 Marta i novyi byt," *Kommunistka*, no. 2 (Feb. 1928): 52.

21. Varvara Moirova, "Bytovoi pokhod," *Izvestiia*, March 8, 1929, 3, underlined the various shortcomings of Soviet institutions and called for improvement of their services.

22. Anikseeva, "Ne tol'ko proverim, no i ispravim," *Kommunistka*, no. 2 (Feb. 1929): 43–45.

23. Aleksandra Artiukhina, "8 marta–den' general'noi proverki," *Pravda*, March 8, 1929, 3.

24. It was envisaged that these commissions would ultimately take over the work of Zhenotdel, as proposals for its liquidation were already in the air. See Carol Eubanks Hayden, *Feminism and Bolshevism: The Zhenotdel and the Politics of Women's Emancipation in Russia, 1917–1930* (Ph.D. diss., University of California, Berkeley, 1979), 351–74.

25. At a party meeting in the Trekhgorniaia textile combine, a woman delegate reported that the factory administration refused to give the delegates a room in the workers' barracks for literacy classes. This happened despite the widely advertised antiilliteracy campaigns popular during this period. TsAODM, f. 369, op. 1, d. 72, l. 41.

26. As late as 1928, the Ukrainian Zhenotdel publicly admitted that the government lacked the resources for the socialization of daily life and women had to rely on their own voluntarism and initiative. See *Mezhdunarodnyi den' rabotnitsy: Sbornik pod redaktsiei tsentral'nogo otdela rabotnits i selianok, TsK KP(b)U* (Proletarii, 1928).

27. *Komsomol'skaia pravda*, March 7, 1929, 2; *Klub i revoliutsiia*, "Kak ustroit' vystavki ko dniu rabotnitsy," (Jan. 1929): 1. A decree of the Second All Union conference of the Commissions for the Improvement of the Life and Labor of Women advised all TsIK (Central Executive Committees) of the Soviet republics to attract funds and labor from the local population itself for the construction of cultural and social service institutions. GARF, f. 5451, op. 13, d. 347, l. 19. See also my chapter 4 for an elaboration of this theme.

28. *Piatnadtsatyi S"ezd VKP(b), stenograficheskii otchet* (Moscow, 1962), 2:203–06. For Lebedeva quote, see *Vsesoiuznyi s"ezd rabotnits i krest'ianok: Stenograficheskii otchet. 10–16 oktiabr'ia 1927 goda* (Moscow, 1927), 448, 450.

29. Ibid., 204.

30. J. Arch Getty, *Origins of the Great Purges: The Soviet Communist Party Reconsidered, 1933–1938* (Cambridge, 1985); David L. Hoffman, *Peasant Metropolis: Social Identities in Moscow, 1929–1941* (Ithaca, N.Y., 1994); Gabor Rittersporn, *Stalinist Simplifications and Soviet Complications: Social Tensions and Soviet Complications in the USSR, 1933–1953* (Chur, Switzerland, 1991).

31. For example, in a factory in Kharkov that employed 279 women, the administration congratulated itself with a 100 percent increase in promotions of women, when the number of *vydvizhenki* jumped from five to nine in 1928. See *Komsomol'skaia pravda*, March 8, 1929, 2.

32. TsAODM, f. 369, op. 1, d. 88.

33. *Komsomol'skaia pravda*, March 8, 1929, 1.

34. *Leningradskaia pravda*, 8 March 1929, 4.

35. See, for example, M. Dimitrieva, "V nastuplenie na staryi byt," *Kommunistka*, no. 6 (1929), 39–44; idem, "S fronta kul'turno-bytovogo pokhoda," *Kommunistka*, no. 7 (1929): 42–44; M. Zagumennykh, "V nastuplenie na fronte kul'turnoi' revoliutsii," *Kommunistka*, no. 8 (1929): 18–20.

36. GARF, f. 5451, op. 13, d. 532, l. 1.

37. GARF, f. 5451, op. 13, d. 532, ll. 2–3.

38. According to some estimates, there were 56,000 crèche beds serving more than a million female industrial workers. See Susan M. Kingsbury and Mildred Fairchild, *Factory, Family and Woman in the Soviet Union* (New York, 1935), 39, 149; *Women and Children in the USSR* (Moscow, 1963), 98. On crèches in Leningrad, see GARF, f. 5451, op. 13, d. 400, l. 8; on dining halls, see ibid., l. 7.

39. N. Alekseeva, "Na put massovogo obshchestvennogo pitaniia," *Kommunistka*, no. 1 (1929): 15.

40. Alan M. Ball, *And Now My Soul Is Hardened: Abandoned Children in Soviet Russia, 1918–1930* (Berkeley, 1994).

41. Anikeeva, "Ne tol'ko proverim, no i ispravim," *Kommunistka*, no. 4 (1929): 45–46; D. Suchkov, "V nastuplenie na staryi byt," *Kommunistka*, no. 7 (1929): 32.

42. N. Alekseeva, "Rabochaia kazarma eshchë vo t'me," *Kommunistka*, no. 7 (1929): 34.

43. Ibid., p. 34; I. Shuman, "O ratsionalizatsii domovodstva," *Kommunistka*, no. 2 (1929): 27–29.

44. Petro, "Grimasy sovetskogo byta," *Kommunistka*, no. 7 (1929): 39.

45. During this time, Zhenotdel was increasing efforts to prevent peasant women, newly arrived in cities, from falling into the clutches of pimps. But the liberal policies of the NEP era, when women prostitutes were seen as victims requiring rehabilitation, were being replaced in 1929 by those who advocated redeeming the prostitute through labor and punishment. See Elizabeth Waters, "Victim or Villain: Prostitution in Post-Revolutionary Russia," in *Women and Society in Russia and the Soviet Union*, ed. Linda Edmondson (Cambridge, 1992), 160–77; Elizabeth Woods, "Prostitution Unbound: Representation of Sexual and Political Anxiety in Postrevolutionary Russia," in *Sexuality and the Body in Russian Culture*, ed. Jane T. Costlow, Stephanie Sandler, and Judith Vowles (Stanford, 1993), 124–35.

46. Ibid., 40; D. Zaslavskii, "Tryzhki starogo byta," *Kommunistka*, no. 16 (1929): 17–20.

47. "Postanovlenie TsK VKP(b) ob ocherednikh zadachakh partii po rabote sredi rabotnits i krest'ianok" (June 15, 1929), in *Kommunisticheskaia Partiia Sovetskogo Soiuza v rezoliutsiiakh i resheniiakh s"ezdov konferentsii i plenumov TsK* (Moscow, 1970), 4:271–80.

48. "U nas i u nikh. Vovlechenie zhenshchin v proizvodstvo-krupnyi shag v bor'be s prostitutsei," *Kul'tura i byt*, no. 6 (Feb. 1936): 16–17.

49. Ibid., 271.
50. Ibid., 280.
51. Judith Grunfeld, "Women's Work in Russia's Planned Economy," *Social Research* 9 (1942): 32; *Izvestiia*, Feb. 28, 1930, 5.
52. *Five-Year Plan of Economic Construction of the USSR* (Moscow, 1929), 2:80; G. N. Serebrennikov, *Zhenskii trud v SSSR* (Moscow, 1934), 60; B. Marsheva, "Problema zhenskogo truda v sovremennikh usloviakh," *Voprosy truda*, no. 2 (1929): 40.
53. S. Kheinman, "Zhenshchina-na proizdvostvo! Za korenniu rekonstrutsiiu zhenskogo truda," *Za industrilizatsii*, March 8, 1930, 3. See also "Ob itogakh 2-go vsesoiuznogo soveschaniia komissii po uluchsheniiu truda i byta zhenshchin," *Izvestiia*, February 28, 1930, 5.
54. GARF, f. 3316, op. 22, d. 941, l. 78.
55. B. Khaskin, "Vovlechenie zhenshchin v tsenzovuiu promyshlennost' SSSR v 1931g," *Voprosy truda*, no. 2 (1932): 47; "Nachat' podgotovku k dniu rabotnits (Postanovlenie VTsSPS)," *Trud*, Feb. 3, 1931, 1. See also *Trud*, March 6, 1931, 4. Here, the estimated number of women to be mobilized is given as 1,527,000, rather than the 1,600,000 used in VTsSPS sources.
56. G. N. Serebrennikov, *Zhenskii trud v SSSR* (Moscow, 1934), 62–63. See also *Sovetskie zhenshchiny i profsoiuzy* (Moscow, 1984), 48.
57. See, for example, A. Aluf, "Rabotnitsa na peredovikh postakh revoliutsionnoi bor'by," *Voprosy truda*, nos. 3–4 (1931): 3–6; *Za industrilizatsiiu*, March 8, 1931, 2; *Leningradskaia pravda*, March 8, 1931, 3; Anna Razumova, *Russian Women in the Building of Socialism* (New York, 1930?); *K mezhdunarodnomu zhenskomu kommunisticheskomu dniu 8 marta 1931g: Materialy dlia dokladchikov i gruppovykh agitatorov* (Moscow, 1931).
58. GARF, f. 5451, op. 15, d. 367, ll. 26–28.
59. GARF, f. 5451, op. 15, d. 364, l. 219; f. 5451, op. 15 d. 364(1), ll. 14–15; f. 5451, op. 15, d. 364(2), ll. 93–94.
60. *Za industrilizatsiiu*, 8 March 1931, 3; For a similar story see *Trud*, 6 March 1931, 4.
61. See V. Sibiriak, *Rabotnitsa v sovetskom souize* (Moscow, 1932), for similar stories.
62. GARF, f. 5451, op. 15, d. 367, l. 33; GARF, f. 5451, op. 15, d. 366, l. 17, 34.
63. GARF, f. 5451, op. 15, d. 361, ll. 15–16; GARF, f. 5451, op. 15, d. 362 (1), l. 80.
64. B. Marsheva, "Zhenskii trud v 1931 gody," *Voprosy truda*, no 1. (1931): 32–41; for similar criticisms of trade unions and factory administrations, see "Nam nekogda schitat'," *Kul'tura i byt*, no. 6 (Feb. 1931): 10, and "Oshibka dolzhna byt' ispravlena," idem., 11.
65. S. Morozov, "Stranitsy novoi istorii," *Kul'tura i byt*, no. 6 (Feb. 1931): 5–6.
66. GARF, f. 5451, op. 15, d. 362(1), l. 94. An article in *Trud*, Feb. 4, 1931, 4, entitled "Udarnye brigady rabotnits derutsia za promfinplan ne khuze brigad rabochikh," made a similar point.
67. On dining room costs, see GARF, f. 5451, op. 15, d. 362(1), l. 49. On kindergarten statistics, see A. Popov, "K itogam shestnadtsatoi vse-soiuznoi Partkonferentsii: Piatiletkii plan velikoi stroiki," *Kommunistka*, no. 11 (1929): 9–10. On new construction projects, see *Trud*, Feb. 5, 1931, 4.
68. An investigation by the VTsSPS in 1931 revealed these figures. GARF, f. 5451, op. 15, d. 363(2), l. 188.

69. Ibid., l. 188.

70. GARF, f. 5451, op. 15, d. 364, l. 224–25.

71. See, for example, Linda Gordon, ed., *Women, the State and Welfare* (Madison, Wis., 1990); Carole Pateman, *The Patriarchal Welfare State: Women and Democracy* (Center for European Studies Working Paper Series, Cambridge, 1987); Seth Koven and Sonya Michel, eds., *Mothers of a New World: Maternalist Politics and the Origins of Welfare States* (New York, 1993).

72. On long-term loans, see Ia. Perel and A. A. Liubimova, eds., *Okhrana materinstva i mladenchestva* (Moscow, 1932), 24, 25, 27, 31–32; on mandatory enrollment, see GARF, f. 5451, op. 16, d. 854, l. 4. On appropriation of funds, see "Rezoliutsii i postanovleniia XVI s'ezda VKP(b)," in the *Shestnadtsatyi S'ezd VKP(B)*, Stenograficheskii otchet (Moscow, 1935), 738.

73. TsGA, RSFSR, f. 482, op. 24, d. 43, l. 7, 22; op. 21, d. 57, l. 8.

74. *Zhenshchina v SSSR* (Moscow, 1936) 124, 127.

75. GARF, f. 5451, op. 21, d. 133, l. 16.

76. GARF, 5451 op. 17, d. 385, ll. 73–74.

77. G. N. Serebrennikov, *Zhenskii Trud v SSSR*, 63, 64.

78. Schwarz, *Labor in the Soviet Union*, 160–66; Goldman, *Women, the State and Revolution*, 316–17.

79. See the testimony of Pogrebenkina, a woman worker at the Mechanical Factory in Zlatoust, who said that although her husband opposed her working, she liked being independent and wanted to participate in the Five-Year Plan; GARF, f. 5451, op. 15, d. 362(1), l. 87; A. Aluf, "Rabotnitsa na peredovikh postakh revoliutsionnoi bor'be," *Voprosy truda*, nos. 3–4, (1931): 5–6. Subsequent Soviet literature on women in the first Five-Year Plan stressed the voluntary participation of women in socialist construction rather than the party efforts to recruit women to compensate for labor shortages. The Five-Year Plan was represented as the first concrete step toward emancipation of women from domesticity, and as an era of burgeoning opportunities and rapid promotion of women in all sectors of the economy and administration. See, for example, *Zhenshchiny Urala v revoliutsii i trude*, (Sverdlovsk, 1963); L. Stishova, ed., *V budniakh velikikh stroek. Zhenshchiny-kommunistki, geroini pervykh piatiletok* (Moscow, 1986); *Uchastnitsy velikogo sozidaniia* (Moscow, 1962); *V edinom stroiu* (Moscow, 1960).

80. "Vypolnit' plan vovlecheniia zhenshchin v promyshlennost'," *Kul'tura i byt*, no. 6 (Feb. 1931): 4; A. Smirnova, "Byt na sluzhbu piatiletke," *Kul'tura i byt*, no. 6, (Feb. 1931): 5; "Mezhdunarodnyi zhenskii den': Vosmoe marta," *Kul'tura i byt*, no. 4, (March 1932): 4–5.

81. Between 1926 and 1939, the number of city-dwelling literate women between the ages of 9 and 49 grew from 73.9 percent to 90.7 percent, and in the villages from 35.4 percent to 76.8 percent. See *Zhenshchiny strany sovetov* (Moscow, 1977), 171.

82. E. Lishchina, "Podgotovka spetsialistov," *V edinom stroiu* (Moscow, 1960), 317. For details on women's educational achievements in various fields of industry and professions, see Dodge, *Women in the Soviet Economy*, 100–59.

83. According to VTsSPS calculations, by 1932 the percentage of female *udarniki* by industry tended to be roughly the same as men, and slightly lower in areas like machine construction. See G. Serebrennikov, "Zhenskii trud v SSSR za 15 let," *Voprosy Truda*, nos. 11–12 (1932): 66.

84. See, for example, the film clip *8-go marta, Moscow. Vecher v klube tekstil'noi fabrike im. Kalinina*, TsGAKFD, I-2120, 1930; *Trud*, March 8, 1932, 1; *Leningradskaia pravda*, March 8, 1932, 3; "Itogi piatiletki i polozhenie trudiaschikhsia zhenshchin v SSSR," in *K mezhdunarodnomu zhenskomu kommunisticheskomu dniu* (Moscow, 1933), 8–12.

85. GARF, f. 5451, op. 16, d. 845, l. 68.

## Chapter 6

1. Another version of this chapter was published as "Soviet Heroines and Public Identity, 1930–1939," *The Carl Beck Papers in Russian and East European Studies*, no. 1402 (October 1999).

2. According to Sheila Fitzpatrick, "there was a discourse in which women (like peasants and members of ethnic minorities) represented backwardness, and another in which their achievements were cited as evidence of modernity. The latter did not really replace the former" (private communication from Fitzpatrick, 1996). However, for the purposes of this chapter, I am going to concentrate overwhelmingly on the constructions of modernity of the New Soviet Woman.

3. A survey of speeches given by famous Soviet women at the Kremlin, in *Geroini sotsialisticheskogo truda* (Partizdat, 1936), shows that protestations of love, gratitude, and devotion formed an essential component of public addresses in the Stalinist era.

4. John Gray, *Post-Liberalism: Studies in Political Thought* (New York, 1993), 158.

5. Since the literature on what constitutes modernization and the experience of modernity is vast, I will only cite a few works that I found particularly useful: Liah Greenfeld, *Nationalism: Five Roads to Modernity* (Cambridge, Mass., 1992); Marshall Berman, *All That Is Solid Melts Into Air: The Experience of Modernity* (New York, 1982); Leszak Kolakowski, *Modernity on Endless Trial* (Chicago, 1990); Cyril E. Black, ed., *The Modernization of Russia and Japan: A Comparative Study* (New York, 1975).

6. Jurgen Habermas, *The Structural Transformation of the Public Sphere: An Inquiry Into a Category of Bourgeois Society*, trans. Thomas Burger (Cambridge, Mass., 1989); *Habermas and the Public Sphere*, ed. Craig Calhoun (Cambridge, Mass., 1992); Benedict R. Anderson, *Imagined Communities: Reflections on the Origins and the Spread of Nationalism* (London, 1982).

7. Habermas, echoing the critique of the Frankfurt school, claimed that by the twentieth century mass democracy and the commodification of culture would lead to the replacement of a contentious and informed public by an audience of passive and uncritical consumers. This cultural despair was reflected in the works of Foucault, who claimed that the scientific metanarratives of the nineteenth century, far from emancipating the individual, helped create a candidate for a disciplinary society based on surveillance. See Michel Foucault, *The Order of Things: An Archaeology of the Human Sciences* (New York, 1970), *Power/Knowledge: Selected Interviews and Other Writings, 1972–1977*, trans. Colin Gordon (New York, 1980).

8. See Seyla Benhabib and Drucilla Cornell, eds., *Feminism as Critique: The Politics of Gender* (Minneapolis, 1987); Carole Pateman, *The Sexual Contract* (Stanford, 1988); Joan Landes, *Woman and the Public Sphere in the Age of the French Revolution* (Ithaca, N.Y., 1988); Lynn Hunt, *The Family Romance of the French Revolution* (Berkeley, 1992).

9. Barbara Evans Clements, "The Birth of the New Soviet Woman," in *Bolshevik Cul-*

ture: *Experiment and Order in the Russian Revolution,* ed. Abbott Gleason, Peter Kenez, and Richard Stites (Bloomington, Ind., 1985); Thea Margaret Durfee, "Cement and How the Steel was Tempered: Variations on the New Soviet Woman," in *A Plot of Her Own: The Female Protagonist in Russian Literature,* ed. Sona Stephan Hoisington (Evanston, Ill., 1995), 89–101.

10. Despite this numerical increase, women filled the ranks of lowest skilled and the worst paid workers. See Donald Filtzer, *Soviet Workers and Stalinist Industrialization* (New York, 1986), 63–67.

11. Roberta Manning, "Women in the Soviet Countryside on the Eve of World War II, 1935–1940," in *Russian Peasant Women,* ed. Beatrice Farnsworth and Lynn Viola (New York, 1992), 206–35, has calculated that from the mid to late 1930s there were 2,500 rural Soviet chairwomen, and 7,000 to 10,000 collective farm chairwomen. Also, nearly 80 percent of the agricultural *stakhanovites* were female. Dorothy Atkinson, *The End of the Russian Land Commune, 1905–1930,* (Stanford, 1983), 367–68; Sue Bridger, *Women in the Soviet Countryside: Women's Roles in Rural Development in the Soviet Union* (Cambridge, 1987), 10–16.

12. In 1933 there were only 305 women who served as directors of factories in the Soviet Union, and a total of 26,264 women were employed by Narkomtiazhprom (Commissariat of Heavy Industry) as specialists, managers, and research scientists. See M. A. Shaburova, *Zhenshchina-bol'shaia sila* (Partizdat, 1935), 51. Stalin, in his speech to the Seventeenth Party Congress, said that there were 6,000 *kolkhoz* chairwomen who, distributed among the large numbers of collective farms, were statistically insignificant. See *Voprosy Leninizma* (Moscow, 1939), 449, 453, 460.

13. Such are the types of sources I selected to review. See, for example, *Naidionnaia doroga: Sbornik ocherkov o rabote zhenshchin v kolkhoze* (OGIZ, 1935); *Geroini sotsialisticheskogo truda* (Partizdat, 1936); *Povesti minuvshego* (Moscow, 1938); *Sovetskie zhenshchiny* (Moscow, 1938); I. S. Akopian, ed., *Zhenshchiny strany sotsializma* (OGIZ, 1939).

14. Ilya Ehrenburg, *Out of Chaos,* trans. Alexandr Bakshy (New York, 1934), 49; Boris Pilniak, *The Volga Falls to the Caspian Sea,* trans. Charles Malamuth (New York, 1931), 240–41; Maksim Gorkii, ed., *White Sea Canal: Being an Account of the Construction of the New Canal Between the White Sea and the Baltic Sea,* trans. Amabel Williams-Ellis (London, 1935), 328. See also Nikolai Pogodin's play, *Aristocrats* (London, 1937).

15. See February and March issues of *Sputnik agitatora* from 1933 through 1938 for biographical sketches; see also "O mezhdunarodnom kommunisticheskom zhenskom dne 8 marta," Postanovlenie TsK VKP (b). *Partiinoe stroitel'stvo,* no. 2 (March 1936): 25; *Sputnik agitatora,* no. 4 (Feb. 1937): 9; *8 Marta. Mezhdunarodnyi kommunisticheskii zhenskii den'. Materialy dlia dokladov i besed* (Rostov, 1938), 3.

16. See *K mezhdunarodnomy zhenskomu kommunisticheskomu dniu, Material dlia dokladchikov i gruppovykh agitatorov,* (Moscow, 1931), 15; GARF, f. 5451, op. 17, d. 525, ll. 1–2; f. 5451, op. 15, d. 364(1), l. 14; f. 5451, op. 16, d. 845, l. 7; f. 5457, op. 19, d. 196, ll. 33, 44; f. 5451, op. 18, d. 553, ll. 4–6; f. 5457, op. 22, d. 80, l. 31; on *stakhanovites,* see GARF, f. 5451, op. 20, d. 191, ll. 44–45.

17. Stalin said this in a speech to a meeting of outstanding male and female combine operators on December 1, 1935. See Robert McNeal, ed., *I. V. Stalin: Works* (XIV) (Stanford, 1967), 106.

18. For an analysis of the strange coexistence of Stalinist terror and carnival, see Ros-

alind Sartorti, "Stalinism and Carnival: Organization and Aesthetics of Political Holidays," in *The Culture of the Stalin Period*, ed. Hans Gunther (London, 1990), 41–77; Karen Petrone, *Life Has Become More Joyous, Comrades: Celebrations in the Time of Stalin* (Bloomington, Ind., 2000); Malte Rolf, "Constructing a Soviet Time: Bolshevik Festivals and Their Rivals During the First Five-Year Plan. A Study of the Central Black Earth Region," *Kritika* 1 (2000): 447–73.

19. *Vecherniaia Moskva*, March 10, 1935, 2. The tango was very popular at such events. In 1933, the trade union cultural departments of the city of Moscow and Moscow province published lists of officially approved dances. These included the waltz, folk dances, mazurka, and other square ballroom dances, and expressly forbade the dancing of the rhumba, tango, Charleston, and fox-trot because of the eroticism implicit in them. However, city youth continued to flout orders and engage in American dances at dance halls and clubs. The decision then to allow the tango at Women's Day festivities may have been a tacit submission to popular pressure. See discussion on dancing in issues of *Klub*, no. 3 (Feb. 1933), and no. 7 (May 1933).

20. Nina Markovna, *Nina's Journey: A Memoir of Stalin's Russia and the Second World War* (Washington D.C., 1989), 13–22.

21. *Vecherniaia Moskva*, March 9, 1936, 1.

22. A photograph of the reception depicts much conviviality. There is confetti floating in the air, and one of the guests is wearing a frivolous paper hat. See TsGAKFD, photo no. 015577.

23. *Vecherniaia Moskva*, March 7, 1935, 2.

24. For a complete transcript of the meetings from 1934 to 1939, see TsMAM, f. 150, op. 25, d. 77, 78, 83; f. 150, op. 5, d. 91, 94, 150. See also *Pravda*, March 9, 1935, 3; March 9, 1936, 1; March 8, 1937, 1; March 9, 1938, 1; March 9, 1939, 1; and *Vecherniaia Moskva*, March 9, 1936, 1.

25. For example, in 1934 Sergei Kirov presided at a Women's Day meeting of notable women held at the Opera Theater in Leningrad.

26. Soviet publications from the 1930s almost always included a section on the terrible conditions for women in capitalist countries, including unemployment, repressive legal codes, male oppression, lack of health care and welfare institutions, sexual exploitation, and prostitution. The public identity of Soviet women was thus inextricably linked with that of women in both European and non-Western countries. See, for example, Shaburova, *Zhenshchina bol'shaia sila*, 8–30.

27. Having women narrate their life stories was a popular event at Women's Day celebrations in factory clubs and collective farms across the nation in the 1930s. GARF, f. 5457, op. 22, d. 80, l. 33.

28. Examining the major characteristics of the "New Soviet Woman," a journalist wrote, "Her distinguishing features lie in the fact that her interest in socialist production engages all her attention, labor for her is a matter of honor, valor and heroism, and that she has mastered technology." See "Boevoe pokolenie stroiteleii kommunizma," *Obshchestvennitsa*, no. 11 (November 1939): 2; N. Labkovsky, "The Story of a Heroine of Labor," *Soviet Cultural Review*, nos. 2–3 (1932): 40.

29. GARF, f. 5451, op. 19, d. 401, l. 40. For similar data on the high living standards of women *stakhanovites*, see ll. 42, 50, 51, 62. Also see Mary Buckley, "Why Be a Shock-Worker or a Stakhanovite," in *Women in Russia and the Ukraine*, ed. Rosalind Marsh

(New York, 1996), 199–213. Of course, women workers were substantially underrepresented among the *stakhanovites* in industry primarily due to their low level of technical skills and protective legislation that prevented women from working in certain branches of the industry. See Lewis Siegelbaum, *Stakhanovism and the Politics of Productivity in the USSR, 1935–1941* (New York, 1988), 170–72.

30. Pasha Angelina, a tractor driver, actually divorced her husband when he demanded that she spend more time with her family. See Arkadii Slavutskii, *Praskov'ia Angelina* (Moscow, 1960), 20–30, 178–79.

31. At this point, women were in charge of 7000 kolkhozes in the Soviet Union. *Vecherniaia Moskva*, 8 March 1935, 1. In 1936, 170,000 women served as members of the collective farm-boards, 19,000 as managers of dairies, 200,000 as field brigade leaders, and 329,726 women were members of rural Soviets. *Pravda*, 22 December 1936, 1. But as Sheila Fitzpatrick's work shows, it was very difficult for women to retain positions of authority in the countryside. *Stalin's Peasants: Resistance and Survival in the Russian Village after Collectivization* (New York, 1994), 181–183. While Fitzpatrick believes that the Party was committed to the upward mobility of women and was frustrated in its intentions by the activities of misogynous rural officials and peasants, I see this oppositional tension of the good central party and bad local representatives as a central plank of the Soviet discourse on women issues and thus representative of a "reality" that Soviet propaganda tried to perpetuate.

32. *Izvestiia*, March 9, 1936, 1.

33. Smirnova and others like her became a recognizable social type and were satirized by the Soviet novelist Vladimir Voinovich in the character of Lyushka in *The Life and Extraordinary Adventures of Private Chonkin*, trans. Richard Lourie (New York, 1977). See Xenia Gasiorowska, *Women in Soviet Fiction, 1917–1964* (Madison, Wis., 1968), 75–89, for a sketch of the *kolkhoz* maidens in Soviet prose.

34. TsMAM, f. 150, op. 25, d. 83, l. 19; for similar stories, see *Naidionnaia doroga. Sbornik ocherkov o rabote zhenshchin v kolkhoze* (OGIZ, 1935).

35. TsMAM, f. 150, op. 25, d. 83, l. 26.

36. Sheila Fitzpatrick, "Middle-Class Values and Soviet Life in the 1930s," in *Soviet History and Culture*, ed. Terry L. Thompson and Richard Sheldon (Boulder, Colo., 1988), 20–38, advanced a class analysis of the propaganda aimed at women. According to her, while Stalinist propaganda stressed that it was important for the wives of administrators and engineers to be supportive helpmeets to their husbands, in the countryside, the liberation of women from patriarchal domination continued to be an important theme. For further elaboration on this theme, see Manning, "Women in the Soviet Countryside." Manning finds that the party was consistent in supporting the enrollment of women in nontraditional pursuits and as a result they faced great hostility from their villages and families. As she says, "no Great Retreat from emancipatory goals can be discerned in the Soviet government's policies towards rural women in the mid- to late 1930s" (226). Siegelbaum, *Stakhanovism*, 236–38.

37. See Victoria E. Bonnell, "The Peasant Woman in Stalinist Political Art of the 1930s," *American Historical Review* 98, (1993): 55–82, on the changing image of the *kolkhoznitsa* in the 1930s.

38. On "Cinderella stories," see *Zhenshchina v kolkhoze–bol'shaia sila* (Moscow, 1934), 26–32. *Member of the Government* cited in Lynne Attwood, *Red Women on the Sil-*

*ver Screen* (London, 1993), 65. For a discussion of Eisenstein, see Denise J. Youngblood, *Soviet Cinema in the Silent Era, 1918–1935* (Ann Arbor, Mich., 1985), 204–06.

39. For women's resistance to collectivization, see Lynne Viola, *Peasant Rebels Under Stalin: Collectivization and the Culture of Peasant Resistance* (New York, 1996); Robert Conquest, *Harvest of Sorrow: Soviet Collectivization and the Terror Famine* (New York, 1986), 152, 154–55, 166; A. A. Novosel'skii, ed., *Materialy po istorii SSSR: Dokumenty po istorii sovetskogo obshchestva* (Moscow, 1955), 327–67; M. Shaburova, *Zhenshchina bol'shaia sila* (USSR, 1935), 61–67. *Zhenshchiny v sel'sovetakh* (Moscow, 1934), 16; E. Bushmanova, "O tekh, kto pervymi shagali v stroiu," in *Zhenshchiny Urala v revoliutsii i trude*, ed., V. E. Buzunov and Z. S. Popova (Sverdlovsk, 1963), 304–09. Rather than attribute agency to women themselves, in public propaganda the influence of kulaks and priests and the political immaturity of women themselves were cited as reasons for this counter-revolutionary behavior, as not wanting to join the *kolkhoz* was considered. On polling in Northern Caucasus, see "Pochemu my idem v kolkhoze," *Krest'ianka*, no. 5 (March 1931): 14.

40. RGASPI, f. 78, op. 1, d. 483, l. 29. For similar stories, see *Izvestiia*, March 8, 1930, 5; *Krest'ianka*, no. 4 (Feb. 1932): 11; V. Sidorova, *Rabota sredi zhenshchin v kolkhozakh i sovkhozakh* (Moscow, 1932), 25; Praskovya Angelina, *My Answer to an American Questionnaire* (Moscow, 1951), 22. On Khitrikova, see *Zhenshchiny v sotsialisticheskom stroitel'stve SSSR* (Leningrad, 1932), 27.

41. M. Iur'eva, "Oktiabr'skaia revoliutsiia i raskreposchenie zhenshchiny," *Obshchestvennitsa*, no. 19 (Oct. 1937), 10–13, explains that following the October Revolution, women received legal rights and privileges, and attempts were made by Zhenotdel to raise their political consciousness. However, only after the inception of the first Five-Year Plan in industry and agriculture did women become free of economic dependence on men and assume the status of full-fledged citizens of the Soviet Union. For a repetition of the theme, see *Krest'ianka*, no. 4 (March 1930): 5; no. 4 (Feb. 1931): 3; no. 5 (March 1934): 6; no. 5 (March 1935): 1; and *Mezhdunarodnyi zhenskii den'* (Magnitostroi, 1934), 3–4.

42. *Pravda*, March 8, 1933, 3.

43. For a cinematic treatment of the same theme, see I. Pyrev's film, *The Party Card*, in which the wife unmasks her husband as the enemy *kulak*. Cited in Peter Kenez, *Cinema and Soviet Society, 1917–1953* (New York, 1992), 145–46. For accounts of women activists singled out for retaliation, see Viola, *Peasant Rebels*, 126.

44. *Pravda*, March 8, 1937, 3. Mashalkina, chairman of the Orshanskii district mutual aid fund, in a conversation with Kalinin in 1934, said that her primary objective was to acquire an automobile so that they could convey medical help quickly to women in labor. (RGASPI, f. 78, d. 483, op. 1, l. 5). Female solidarity was also crucial as a means of survival for victims of the Stalinist terror. For examples, see Evgeniia Ginzburg, *Journey into the Whirlwind*, trans. Paul Stevenson and Max Hayward (New York, 1967), and *Within the Whirlwind*, trans. Ian Boland (New York, 1981); Nadezhda Mandelshtam, *Hope Against Hope*, trans. Max Hayward (New York, 1970), and *Hope Abandoned*, trans. Max Hayward (New York, 1974).

45. For an elaboration of this concept, see Katerina Clark, *The Soviet Novel: History as Ritual* (Chicago, 1985).

46. *Vecherniaia Moskva*, March 10, 1936, 1.

47. *Vecherniaia Moskva*, March 7, 1935, 3; see also E. V. Vinogradova, "Speech Deliv-

ered at the Tenth Congress of the Young Communist League," April 4, 1936, in *Soviet Union 1936* (Moscow, 1936), 723; Biography of Klavdiia Sakharova, Deputy to the Supreme Soviet, in *Sovetskie zhenshchiny* (Moscow, 1938), 44–45.

48. *Vecherniaia Moskva*, March 8, 1938, 3. Often, women workers were forced to form female work brigades on the shop floor because of the hostility of the men, but of course this reason was not advertised in the propaganda. See David Hoffman, *Peasant Metropolis: Social Identities in Moscow, 1929–1941* (Ithaca, 1994), 119.

49. *Vecherniaia Moskva*, March 7, 1937, 2; *Vecherniaia Moskva*, March 8, 1937, 3. The theme of international solidarity of proletarian women was repeatedly cited in Women's Day propaganda. See "8 Marta—mezhdunarodnyi kommunisticheskii zhenskii den'. Materialy dlia dokladov i besed." *Sputnik agitatora*, no. 4 (Feb. 1938): 11; "Primernye plany dokladov i besed. 8 Marta—mezhdunarodnyi kommunisticheskii den'," *Sputnik agitatora*, no. 4 (Feb. 1938): 24.

50. As Sheila Fitzpatrick pointed out to me, there was a difference between reactionary male family members and wise male Communist mentors who guided and helped the heroines. (Private communication, Aug. 1997.)

51. For a representative sample see N. K. Samoilova, *K mezhdunarodnomu sotsialisticheskomu dniu rabotnits* (Petrograd, 1918); N. K. Samoilova, *V ob'edinenii zalog pobedi. K mezhdunarodnomu sotsialisticheskomu dniu rabotnits, 8 marta* (Moscow, 1921); *Tri goda diktatury proletariata*, MK RKP(b) (Moscow, 1920). See chapter 1 on the issue of female backwardness.

52. A. F. Smirnova, deputy to the Supreme Soviet, was forced to divorce her husband as he constantly interfered with her political and social engagements and criticized her for coming home late. See M. Mikhailov, "Zhenshchiny-deputaty ver'khovnogo soveta," *Obshchestvennitsa*, no. 21 (Oct. 1937): 27; Sh. Khadzhimirova, chairwoman of a *kolkhoz* in Kazakhstan, left her husband for similar reasons; see *Sputnik agitatora*, no. 3 (Feb. 1935): 73–74; *Vecherniaia Moskva*, 8 March 1938, 3.

53. TsMAM, f., 150, op. 25, d. 83, l. 15.

54. *Pravda*, March 8, 1936, 5. Maria Osipenko faced similar problems with her first fiancé when she wanted to become a pilot. Her second fiancé was undisciplined and at the point of being demobilized, but she took him in hand and together with the party and the Red Army turned him into an exemplary citizen. See "Maria Osipenko letchik," *Sovetskie zhenshchiny* (Moscow, 1938), 122. For similar stories, see N. Lur'i, "Mat'," *Obshchestvennitsa*, no. 12 (June 1937): 12–13.

55. *Pravda*, March 8, 1935, 2.

56. T. Slovachevskaia, "Agitator Agafiia Karpovna Durniashova," in *Sputnik agitatora*, no. 4 (Feb. 1936): 32–35.

57. Natal'ia Fedorova, chairman of the *kolkhoz* "Revolution" in the Leningrad *oblast*, recounted that when the *kulaks* in their village waged a violent campaign against collectivization, her husband was so afraid that he ran away. He only returned when the *kolkhoz* started producing results. See "Dva delegata," *Leningradskaia pravda*, March 8, 1933, 3. According to one source, about 18.7 million people, mostly men, migrated to urban areas from the countryside between 1927 and 1938. *Bol'shaia sovetskaia entsiklopediia*, 3rd ed. (Moscow, 1977), vol. 24, bk. 2, 16. If, to this number, we add the many millions who were killed and deported during collectivization, we can get some sense of the huge shortages of able-bodied men in the Soviet countryside in the 1930s.

58. TsMAM, f. 150, op. 25, d. 83, l. 26. We find an identical sentiment expressed by Seligeeva, a secretary of a party cell in a *kolkhoz* in the Black Earth region. She was obviously resentful of the fact that men from the village ran away during collectivization. When they returned the women refused to feed them or pay them despite the fact that they had worked the equivalent of forty-five workdays. See RGASPI, f. 78, op. 1, d. 483, l. 21.

59. Joan Wilson, "Domesticity as the Dangerous Supplement of Liberalism," *Journal of Women's History* 2 (1991): 60–80; Linda Kerber, *Women of the Republic: Intellect and Ideology in Revolutionary America* (Chapel Hill, N.C., 1980); Bonnie Smith, *Ladies of the Leisure Class: The Bourgeoises of Northern France in the Nineteenth Century* (Princeton, 1981).

60. Jessica Tovrov, *The Russian Noble Family: Structure and Change* (New York, 1987); David L. Ransel, ed., *The Family in Imperial Russia: New Lines of Historical Research* (Urbana, Ill., 1978); Samuel C. Ramer, "Childbirth and Culture: Midwifery in the Russian Countryside," in *Russian Peasant Women*, ed. Farnsworth and Viola, 107–20; David L. Ransel, "Infant Care Cultures in the Russian Empire," in *Russia's Women: Accommodation, Resistance, Transformation*, ed. Barbara Evans Clements (Berkeley and Los Angeles, 1991), 113–34.

61. For early Soviet efforts to instruct the population in scientific notions of obstetrics and child rearing, see E. D. Emelianova, *Revoliutsiia, partiia, zhenshchina* (Smolensk, 1971), 151–58; Elizabeth Waters, "The Modernization of Russian Motherhood," *Soviet Studies* 44 (1992): 123–35; Fanina Halle, *Women in Soviet Russia* (London, 1934), 148–52; Susan M. Kingsbury and Mildred Fairchild, *Factory Family and Woman in the Soviet Union* (New York, 1935), 145–56; A. Kollontai, "'Pervye shagi po okhrane materinstva,'" in *Iz moei zhizni i raboty* (Moscow, 1974), 336–40.

62. F. Niurina, "O slave zhenskoi, o radosti materinskoi, o gordosti sovetskoi. (Materialy dlia doklada i besed o 8 marta)," in *Materialy k mezhdunarodnomu kommunisticheskomu zhenskomu dniu. 8 marta, 1936* (Rostov-Don, 1936), 28–53.

63. Cited in Irina Korovushkina, "Gender Equality under Real Socialism: Women and Their Careers in the USSR, 1930s–1960s," in *Women in History–Women's History: Central and East European Perspectives*, ed. Andrea Peto and Mark Pittaway (Budapest, 1994), 101.

64. Chiara Saraceno, "Redefining Maternity and Paternity: Gender, Pronatalism, and Social Policies in Fascist Italy," and Gisela Bock, "Antinatalism, Maternity and Paternity in National Socialist Racism," in *Women and the Rise of the European Welfare States, 1880s–1950s*, ed. Gisela Bock and Pat Thane (London, 1991), 233–55; Claudia Koonz, *Mothers in the Fatherland: Women, the Family, and Nazi Policies* (New York, 1987); Victoria de Grazia, *How Fascism Ruled Women: Italy, 1922–1945* (Berkeley, 1992).

65. In reality, the Soviet birth rate had declined considerably between 1928 and 1934. See Wendy Goldman, "Women, Abortion, and the State, 1917–1936," in Clements, ed., *Russia's Women*, 263.

66. *Sputnik agitatora*, no. 4 (Feb. 1937): 18–23; no. 4 (Feb. 1938): 10–11; no. 3 (Feb. 1939): 33; F. Zborskaia, "Sovetskaia mat'," *Obshchestvennitsa*, no. 1 (Aug. 1936): 14–15; "Schastliveiishaia v mire mat'," *Obshchestvennitsa*, no. 6 (June 1938): 3–5; "8 marta—mezhdunarodnyi kommunisticheskii zhenskii den'" *Sputnik dlia agitatora*, no. 4 (Feb. 1938): 10–11; F. E. Niurina, *Patriotki sovetskoi strany* (SSSR, 1937), 55; K. Nikolaeva,

*Zhenshchina za boiakh za kommunizm* (SSSR, 1940), 11. The theme of differential birth rates was also highlighted in Women's Day articles published by the International Women's Secretariat of the Comintern in the 1930s; see RGASPI, f. 507, op. 2, d. 243, l. 18 and f. 507, op. 2, d. 242, ll. 24, 25.

67. On the situation in Germany, see Dr. E. Konius, "Strana schastlivogo materinstva," *Obshchestvennitsa*, no. 5 (1937): 16; Women's Day articles such as "8 marta—mezhdunarodnyi kommunisticheskii zhenskii den'. Materialy dlia dokladov i besed," *Sputnik agitatora*, no. 4 (Feb. 1938): 10, pointed to the complete lack of governmental concern for pregnant women in fascist countries. On number of suicides, see RGASPI, f. 507, op. 2, d. 235, l. 254.

68. On Maria Il'inichna, see *Pravda*, March 12, 1936, 4. For typical Soviet hyperbole on children's care, see V. Zorin, "Vospitanie novogo pokolenie," *Obshchestvennitsa*, no. 4 (1936): 3-4; M. Amshinskii, "Schastlivye deti schastlivoi strany," *Obshchestvennitsa*, no. 5 (1936): 24-26; A. S. Berliand, *Okhrana materinstva i mladenchestva* (Moscow, 1935); V. Papernova, "Woman in Socialist Construction: On Equal Terms with Man," *Soviet Cultural Review*, no. 2 (1933): 30.

69. M. Shaburova, "Rabotnitsa i kolkhoznitsa v peredovye riady," *Pravda*, March 8, 1933, 2. See Krupskaia, *Vtoroi vsesoiuznyi s"ezd kolkhoznikov-udarnikov. 11-17 fev. 1935g.* (Moscow, 1935), 116-17; *Sputnik agitatora*, no. 3 (Feb. 1935), 55; no. 4 (Feb. 1937): 171-18. In "Zakon schastlivogo materinstvo," *Obshchestvennitsa*, no. 7 (July 1939).

70. There were comparable organizations such as the Wives of Leaders of Light Industry, and the Wives of the Commanders and Leaders of the Red Army. For a good survey, see Mary Buckley, "The Untold Story of Obshchestvennitsa in the 1930s," *Europe-Asia Studies* 48, (1996): 569-86.

71. M. Sokolova, "V pomosch' materiam i detiam," *Obshchestvennitsa*, no. 1 (1938): 36; *Zheny inzhenerov i tekhnikov*, Profizdat, 1936; V. Shveitzer and A. Ul'rikh, *Zheny komandirov tiazheloi promyshlennosti* (Moscow-Leningrad, 1936).

72. On Agafiia Karpovna, see N. Lur'i, "Mat'," *Obshchestvennitsa*, 12-13. On film clip, see I. Setkina, director, *Mart' 1937*, Soiuz Kinozhurnal, T-I 2190, TsGAKFD.

73. See for example A. Kollontai's article, "Mezhdunarodnyi zhenskii den'," RGASPI, f. 134, op. 1, d. 238, ll. 96-100.

74. "Diary of Galina Vladimirovna Shtange," in *Intimacy and Terror: Soviet Diaries of the 1930s*, ed. Veronique Garros, Natalia Korenevskaya, and Thomas Lahusen (New York, 1995), 167-217.

75. *Pravda*, May 26, 1936, 1; "Schastliveiishaia v mire mat'," *Obshchestvennitsa*, no. 6 (June 1938): 3; G. N. Serebrennikov, *The Position of Women in the U.S.S.R.* (London, 1937), 261-77.

76. See *Sbornik instruktsii otdela TsK. RKP po rabote sredi zhenshchin* (Moscow, 1920), 76-77; Wendy Goldman, "Women, Abortion, and the State, 1917-1936," in Clements, ed., *Russia's Women*, 243-66.

77. For letters from women criticizing the 1936 restrictions on abortion, see RGASPI, f. 78, op. 1, d. 588, l. 55; *Pravda*, June 6, 1936, 4; June 1, 1936, 4; June 4, 1936, 3; June 30, 1936, 4. On illegal abortion statistics and Sovnarkom's assessment of the situation, see TsGA, RSFSR, f. 482, op. 29, d. 5, ll. 9-11, 17-19, 28-29.

78. See *Rabotnitsa*, no. 17 (July 1936): 4-6; no. 18 (July 1936): 12-13; *Pravda*, March 12, 1936, 4, 10; Dr. V. Iushkova, "Kakoi vred prinosit zhenshchine abort," *Obshchestven-*

*nitsa*, no. 20 (1937): 38–39; Janet Evans, "The Communist Party of the Soviet Union and the Women's Question: The Case in the 1936 Decree 'In Defence of Mother and Child,'" *Journal of Contemporary History* 16 (1981): 757–75.

79. *Izvestiia*, March 8, 1938, 1.

80. See, for example, a letter from a woman worker to *Rabotnitsa*, no. 16 (July 1936): 6, where she castigates men who take advantage of their wives' illiteracy to force them to have abortions. S. Kapelianskaia, "Zashchita prav materi i rebënka," *Obshchestvennitsa*, no. 5 (1937): 18, makes the same point. Blaming men for abortions while celebrating the maternal instincts of women was an old Bolshevik line, popular among social conservatives in the 1920s such as Sofia Smidovich, former head of the Zhenotdel. See Beatrice Farnsworth, *Aleksandra Kollontai: Socialism, Feminism and the Bolshevik Question* (Stanford, 1980), 336–67. On men forcing women to have abortions, see A. Agranovskii, "Materinstvo," in *Molodaia gvardiia* (Jan. 1936): 178. On alimony and child support, see Wendy Goldman, *Women, the State and Revolution*, (Cambridge, 1993), 327–31.

81. *Soviet Stories of the Last Decade*, trans. Elisaveta Fen, (London, 1945), 60–70.

82. Pearl S. Buck, *Talk About Russia with Masha Scott* (New York, 1945), 37. But this system was not foolproof. In many collective farms the work days completed by women were usually registered in their husbands' tables. In some *kolkhozes* in Uzbekistan, husbands actually confiscated their wives' workbooks. See E. K. Kravchenko, *Krest'ianka pri sovetskoi vlasti* (Moscow, 1932), 39.

83. Stalin, "Rech na prieme kol'khoznits-udarnits sveklovichnykh polei rukovoditeliami partii i pravitel'stva," Nov. 10, 1935, in *I. V. Stalin: Works*, vol. 1, ed. Robert H. McNeal (XIV) 74–77.

84. *Vecherniaia Moskva*, March 7, 1937, 3.

85. See Kollontai's articles and speeches written for Women's Day in 1933, 1934, and 1937, RGASPI, f. 134, op. 1, d. 238, ll. 2, 4, 34, 35, 99.

86. *Obshchestvennitsa*, no. 6 (June 1939): 46; Aleksandra Kuznetsova, caught in a similar situation with her husband, had little trouble in telling him that he could either live with her on her terms or leave. See *Zhenshchina v strane sovetov: V pomoshche besedchikam I agitatoram* (OGIZ, 1938), 30. On party's "modern notions," see "Zhenshchiny nashei rodiny," *Pravda*, March 11, 1936, 1, in which men are upbraided for not doing their fair share in parenting. See also D. Bakhshiev, "O liubvi, sem'e i brake," in *Obshchestvennitsa*, no. 10 (Oct. 1939): 33–34; Klavdiia Nikolaeva, *Zhenshchiny v boiakh za kommunizm* (Moscow, 1940), 21–22.

87. "Schast'ie rabochei sem'i," *Sputnik agitatora*, no. 19 (Oct. 1938): 27. See E. Iaroslavskii's strictures to irresponsible men in "Kommunisticheskaia moral," *Komsomol'skaia pravda*, May 30, 1936; "Otets," *Pravda*, June 9, 1936.

88. Stalin, *Socialism Victorious* (New York, 1936), 53.

89. Other pictures of women from this period showed them typing, using the bank services, playing the gramophone, driving tractors, working in factories, listening to the radio, and reading books. See, for example, the issues of *Krest'ianka*, *Pravda*, *Leningradskaia pravda*, *Sputnik dlia agitatora* March 8 in the 1930s; L. G. Evseeva, director of the factory, *Osvobozhdennyi trud*, mentioned in her Women's Day interview that she traveled by car to work. See *Sputnik agitatora*, no. 3 (Feb. 1935): 71.

90. Stalin, *Pravda*, March 8, 1933, 1. See also "Mezhdunarodnyi kommunisticheskii zhenskii den'. Materialy dlia dokladov i besed," *Sputnik agitatora*, no. 3 (Feb. 1939): 32.

91. For examples of such letters, see *Pravda*, March 11, 1936, 1; March 10, 1938, 1; March 10, 1939, 4; and *Rabotnitsa i krest'ianka*, no. 14 (1936): 14. Stalin's personal contribution to women's liberation and their public gratitude was acknowledged in every biographical sketch of Soviet heroines.

92. An article in *Pravda*, March 8, 1937, 3, uses the phrase "miraculous transformation" regarding a *stakhanovite* worker, Tamra Vladimirova, who went from being an unskilled laborer to the leader of a labor team with twenty workers under her command.

**Epilogue**

1. RGASPI, f. 78, op. 1, d. 588, l. 55. For similar letters from women criticizing the 1936 law against abortion, see *Pravda*, June 1, 1936, 4; June 4, 1936, 4; June 6, 1936, 3; June 30, 1936, 4.

2. GARF, f. 5451, op. 19, d. 453, l. 81.

3. For a new publication that problematizes the notion of Soviet modernity, see *Russian Modernity: Politics, Knowledge, Practices*, ed. David L. Hoffman and Yanni Kotsonis (New York, 2000).

4. In a recently published series of interviews conducted with women who lived through the period 1917–1939, the subjects told their stories through the grid of official Soviet history, without exception. See *A Revolution of Their Own: Voices of Women in Soviet History*, ed. Barbara Alpern Engel and Anastasia Posadskaya-Vanderbeck, trans. Sona Hoisington (Boulder, Colo., 1998).

5. *Karl Marx: Selected Writings*, ed. David McLellan (New York, 1977), 224.

# Selected Bibliography

### Archival Sources
Citations of archival materials are by *fond, opis', delo, listy* and abbreviated: f., op., d., l.

A. GARF (Gosudarstvennyi arkhiv Rossiiskoi Federatsii)
    Fond 93. Chancellory for Police Work
    Fond 102. St. Petersburg Department of Police
    Fond 111. Department of the Petrograd Okhrana
    Fond 1167. Material Evidence (Department of Police)
    Fond 5451. The Central Council of Trade Unions of the USSR (VTsSPS)
    Fond 5515. National Commissariat of Labor
    Fond 5457. Central Committee of Trade Union of Workers in Textile and Light Industries
    Fond 5466. Central Committee of Trade Union of Agricultural and Forestry Workers of USSR
    Fond 7952. History of Plants and Factories
    Fond 9601. Personal Papers of A. V. Artiukhina
B. RGASPI (Rossiiskii gosudarstvennyi arkhiv sotsial'noi politicheskoi istorii)
    Fond 17. Central Committee of the TsK KPSS
    Fond 70. History of the Party (Istpart)
    Fond 78. Personal papers of Mikhail I. Kalinin
    Fond 134. Personal papers of Aleksandra Kollontai
    Fond 456. Papers of the journal *Rabotnitsa*
    Fond 507. International Women's Secretariat of the Comintern
C. TSAODM (Tsentral'nyi arkhiv obshchestvennykh dvizhenii Moskvy)
    Fond 369. Factory Party Cell VKP (b) of the Trekhgorniaia Manufaktura im. Dzerzhinskogo
D. TsGA RSFSR (Tsentral'nyi Gosudarstvennyi Arkhiv, RSFSR)
    Fond 259. Council of National Commissariats
    Fond 482. National Commissariat of Health
    Fond 2306. National Commissariat of Enlightenment
E. TsMAM, (Tsentral'nyi munitsipal'nyi arkhiv Moskvy)
    Fond 150. Protocols of the Moscow City Soviet
    Fond 718. Moscow City Soviet of Trade Unions (MGsPS)

F. TSGAKFD (Tsentral'nyi gosudarstvennyi arkhiv kinofoto dokumentov). I have used various photographs and film clips from this archive that are identified in the text.

## II. Periodicals and Journals

Izvestiia
Klub
Kommunistka
Komsomol'skaia Pravda
Krasnaia gazeta
Krasnaia letopis'
Krasnyi arkhiv
Krest'ianka

Obshchestvennitsa
Ogonëk
Partiinoe stroitel'stvo
Pravda
Proletarskaia revo-
    liutsiia
Rabotnitsa
Rech'

Sputnik agitatora
Trud
Vecherniaia Moskva
Voprosy truda
Za industrilizatsiiu
Zhenskii vestnik
Zhenskoe delo

## III. International Women's Day Brochures

Den' vosmogo marta: Mezhdunarodnyi den' rabotnits i krest'ianok. Artemovsk, 1925.
Fogel', A. *8 marta v gorode i derevne.* Moscow-Leningrad, 1928.
Gopner, S. *Nash boevoi prazdnik.* Moscow-Leningrad, 1926.
*K mezhdunarodnomu zhenskomu kommunisticheskomu dniu: Materialy dlia dokladchikov.* Moscow, 1933.
*K mezhdunarodnomu zhenskomu kommunisticheskomu dniu: Materialy dlia dokladchikov i gruppovikh agitatorov.* Moscow, 1931.
Kalygina, A. *Krest'ianka i vosmoe marta.* Moscow, 1926.
*Kolkhoznitsa: Sbornik, posvoiashchennyi mezhdunarodnomu dniu 8 marta.* Saratov, 1930.
Kollontai, A. M. *Mezhdunarodnyi den' rabotnits.* Moscow, 1920.
Kudelli, P. F. *Bor'ba za zhenskii den'.* Leningrad, 1928.
Lilina, Z. I., ed. *Krest'ianki, ukreplaite sovetskuiu vlast': Sbornik k mezhdunarodnomu zhenskomu dniu.* Moscow-Leningrad, 1925.
*Materialy k provedeniiu mezhdunarodnogo kommunisticheskogo zhenskogo dnia.* Krasnoiarsk, 1925.
*Materialy zhenskomu dniu—8 marta 1936.* Rostov-Don, 1936.
*Mezhdunarodnyi den' rabotnits: Materialy dlia komsomol'skogo i pionerskogo kluba.* Moscow, 1925.
*Mezhdunarodnyi den' rabotnits: Sbornik materialov dlia chteniia i prorabotki v klubakh, izbakh-chital'niakh, narodnikh-domakh, i shkolakh.* Rostov-Don, 1925.
*Mezhdunarodnyi den' rabotnitsy.* Proletarii, 1925.
*Mezhdunarodnyi den' rabotnitsy: Sbornik materialov k 8-mu marta.* Moscow, 1924.
*Mezhdunarodnyi den' rabotnitsy: Sbornik.* Proletarii, 1929.
*Mezhdunarodnyi zhenskii den': Sbornik.* Proletarii, 1927.
*Mezhdunarodnyi zhenskii kommunisticheskii den'-8 marta. Materialy dlia besedchikov i delegatskikh sobranii.* Leningrad, 1933.
Niurina, F. *Zare navstrechu: 8 marta mezhdunarodnyi zhenskii den'.* Moscow-Leningrad, 1926.
Rozen, Maria, ed. *Den' rabotnitsy v klube: Sbornik materialov dlia provedeniia mezhdunarodnogo dnia rabotnitsy.* Moscow, 1925.
Samoilova, K. N. *K mezhdunarodnomu sotsialisticheskomu dniu rabotnits (23 fevralia–3 marta): Rabotnitsy i revoliutsiia (k godovschine fevral'skoi revoliutsii).* Petrograd, 1918.

———. *V ob'edinenii-zalog pobedy. (K mezhdunarodnomu sotsialisticheskomu dniu rabotnits, 8 marta 1921)*. Moscow, 1921.
Shamurina, Z., ed. *8-e marta mezhdunarodnyi zhenskii den'*. Moscow-Leningrad, 1926.
*8-e marta i rabotnitsa*. Moscow, 1925.
*8-e marta 1927 goda*. Moscow, 1927.
*8 marta v izbe-chital'ne*. Leningrad, 1925.
*8-e marta: Materialy dlia dokladchikov i rabotnikov sredi rabotnits i selianok*. Ukraine, 1925.
*8-e marta: Materialy dlia provedeniia mezhdunarodnogo zhenskogo kommunisticheskogo dnia*. Moscow, 1926.
*8-e marta: Materialy dlia provedeniia mezhdunarodnogo zhenskogo kommunisticheskogo dnia*. Moscow, 1927.
*8-e marta: Materialy dlia provedeniia mezhdunarodnogo zhenskogo kommunisticheskogo dnia v gorode*. Moscow, 1927.
*8-e marta: Mezhdunarodnyi den' rabotnits. Sbornik materialov*. Leningrad, 1926.
*8-e marta i krest'ianka*. Moscow, 1925.
*8 marta v derevne*. Leningrad, 1926.
*8 marta v izbe-chital'ne: Instruktivnyi sbornik*. Moscow-Leningrad, 1926.

## IV. Other Primary Sources

Alliluyeva, Anna. *The Alliluev Memoirs*. Trans. and ed. David Tutaev. New York, 1968.
Alliluyeva, Svetlana. *Twenty Letters to a Friend*. Trans. Priscilla Johnson. New York, 1967.
Armand, Inessa. *Stat'i, rechi, pis'ma*. Moscow, 1975.
Artiukhina, A. V., ed. *Zhenshchiny v revoliutsii*. Moscow, 1959.
Artiukhina, A. V. et al., eds. *Oktiabriem rozhdennye*. Moscow, 1967.
Avdeev, N. *Revoliutsii 1917 goda*. Moscow, 1923.
Bakhrina, F., and V. Efimov. *Rabotnitsa v zabastovochnom dvizhenii: Zhizn i bor'ba rabotnitsy pri tsarizme*. Moscow-Leningrad, 1931.
Bebel, Auguste. *Women under Socialism*. Trans. Daniel De Leon. New York, 1904.
*Bez nikh my ne pobedili by: Vospominaniia zhenshchin-uchastnits Oktiabr'skoi revoliutsii, grazhdanskoi voiny, i sotsialisticheskogo stroitel'stva*. Moscow, 1975.
*Bol'sheviki v gody imperialisticheskoi voiny: 1914–fevral' 1917. Sbornik dokumentov bol'shevistkikh organizatsii*. Moscow, 1939.
Bryant, Louise. *Mirrors of Moscow*. New York, 1923.
Bukharin N., and E. Preobrazhensky. *The ABC of Communism*. Ann Arbor, 1966.
Buzunov, V. E., and Z. S. Popova, eds. *Zhenshchiny Urala v revoliutsii i trude*. Sverdlovsk, 1963.
Cole, Margaret, I., ed. *Twelve Studies in Soviet Russia*. London, 1933.
Engel, Barbara Alpern, and Anastasia Posadskaya, eds. *A Revolution of Their Own: Voices of Women in Soviet History*. Boulder, 1998.
Engels, Friedrich. *The Condition of the Working Class in England*. Trans. W. O. Henderson and W. H. Challoner. Oxford, 1958.
———. *The Origin of the Family, Private Property and the State*. New York, 1942.
Garros, Veronique, Natalia Korenevskaya, and Thomas Lahusen, eds. *Intimacy and Terror: Soviet Diaries of the 1930s*. New York, 1995.
*Geroi Oktiabria*. Vols 1 and 2. Leningrad, 1967.

Giliarova, E. A., et al., eds. *Zhenshchiny goroda Lenina*. Leningrad, 1963.
Ginzburg, Evgeniia Semenova. *Journey into the Whirlwind*. New York, 1967.
Golder, Frank A., ed. *Documents of Russian History*. Trans. Emanuel Aronsberg. New York and London, 1927.
Grekov, A., and P. Borko. *Rabotnitsa v bor'be za uluchshenie sovetskogo apparata*. Moscow, 1932.
Halle, Fanina. *Women in Soviet Russia*. New York, 1935.
Kabo, E. O. *Ocherki rabochego byta*. Moscow, 1928.
Kingsbury, Susan M., and Mildred Fairchild. *Factory, Family and Woman in the Soviet Union*. New York, 1935.
Kogan, Sofiia, ed. *Organizatsiia massovykh narodnykh prazdnestv*. RSFSR, 1921.
Kollontai, Aleksandra. *Izbrannye stat'i i rechi*. Moscow, 1972.
———. *Iz moei zhizni i raboty*. Moscow, 1974.
———. *K istorii dvizheniia rabotnits v Rossii*. Kharkov, 1920.
———. *Rabotnitsa i krest'ianka v Sovetskoi Rossii*. Petrograd, 1921.
———. *Rabotnitsy za god revoliutsii*. Moscow, Petrograd, 1918.
———. *Selected Writings of Alexandra Kollontai*. Trans. and ed. Alix Holt. New York, 1977.
———. *Sotsial'nye osnovy zhenskogo voprosa*. St. Petersburg, 1909.
———. *Trud zhenshchiny v evoliutsii khoziaistva*. Moscow, 1922.
Kommunisticheskaia Partiia Sovetskogo Soiuza. *Chetyrnadtsatyi s"ezd VKP(b). Stenograficheskii otchet*. Moscow-Leningrad, 1926.
———. *Desiatyi s"ezd RKP(b). Stenograficheskii otchet*. Moscow, 1963.
———. *Deviatyi s"ezd RKP(b). Protokoly*. Moscow, 1960.
———. *Dvenadtsatyi s"ezd RKP(b). Stenograficheskii otchet*. Moscow, 1968.
———. *KPSS v rezoliutsiiakh i resheniiakh s"ezdov, konferentsii i plenumov TsK*. 2 vols., 7th ed., Moscow, 1954.
———. *Odinnadtsatyi s"ezd RKP(b). Stenografichskii otchet*. Moscow, 1966.
———. *Piatnadtsataia konferentsiia VKP(b). Stenograficheskii otchet*. Moscow, 1927.
———. *Shestnadtsatyi s"ezd VKP(b). Stenograficheskii otchet*. Moscow-Leningrad, 1930.
———. *Trinadtsatyi s"ezd RKP(b). Stenograficheskii otchet*. Moscow, 1963.
———. Ts.K. Otdel po rabote sredi zhenschin. *Kommunisticheskaia Partiia i organizatsiia rabotnits. Sbornik statei, rezoliutsii i instruktsii*. Posobie dlia propagandistok. Moscow, 1919.
———. Ts.K. Otdel po rabote sredi zhenschin. *Otchet otdela Ts.K. RKP(b) po rabote sredi zhenschin za god raboty*. Moscow, 1921.
———. Ts.K. Otdel po rabote sredi zhenschin. *Sbornik instruktsii otdela TsK RKP(b) po rabote sredi zhenschin*. Moscow, 1920.
Kozhanyi, P. *Rabotnitsa i byt*. Moscow, 1926.
Krupskaia, N. K. *Reminiscences of Lenin*. Trans. Bernard Isaacs. New York, 1970.
———. *Zhenshchina-rabotnitsa*, 2nd ed. Moscow-Leningrad, 1926.
———. *Zhenshchina strany sovetov ravnopraynyi grazhdanin*. Soviet Union, 1937.
Kudelli, P. I. *K. N. Samoilova-Gromova. ("Natasha")*. Leningrad, 1925.
Lenin, V. I. *The Emancipation of Women: From the Writings of V. I. Lenin*. New York, 1966.
*Leningradki: Vospominaniia, ocherki, dokumenty*. Leningrad, 1968.
*Listovki Petrogradskikh bol'shevikov*. Vols. 2–3. Leningrad, 1957.

*Massovye prazdnestva.* Leningrad, 1926.
*Peterburgskii komitet RSDRP: Protokoly-i materialy zasedanii' iul' 1902–fevral' 1917.* Leningrad, 1986.
Pethybridge, Roger, ed. *Witnesses to the Russian Revolution.* London, 1964.
Pokrovskii. M. N., ed. *Perepiska Nikolaia i Aleksandry Romanovikh.* Vol. 5. Moscow, Leningrad, 1927.
Rashin, A. G. *Zhenskii trud v SSSR.* Moscow, 1928.
*Reports to the First International Conference of Socialist Women, 1907.* Stuttgart, 1907.
*Revoliutsionnaia deiatel'nost Konkordii Nikolaevny Samoilovoi: Sbornik vospominanii.* Moscow, 1922.
Riazanova, A. *Zhenskii trud.* Moscow, 1923.
Riumin, E. *Massovye prazdnestva.* Moscow, 1927.
Schegolev, P. E., ed. *Padenie Tsarskogo rezhima.* Vol. 1. Moscow-Leningrad, 1924.
Schlesinger, Rudolph, ed. *The Family in the U.S.S.R. Documents and Readings.* London, 1949.
Serebrennikov, G. N. *The Position of Women in the USSR.* London, 1937.
*Skvoz gody i buri.* Moscow, 1969.
Smith, Jessica. *Women in Soviet Russia.* New York, 1928.
Stasova, E. D. *Stranitsy zhizni i bor'by.* Moscow, 1957.
Sukhanov, M. N. *Zapiski o revoliutsii.* Vol. 1. St. Petersburg, 1922.
Tarasov-Rodionov, Alexei. *February 1917.* Trans. William A. Drake. New York, 1931.
Trotsky, Leon. *Problems of Everyday Life.* New York, 1973.
———. *Women and the Family.* New York, 1970.
*V ogne revoliutsionikh boev.* Moscow, 1967.
Winter, Ella. *Red Virtue: Human Relationships in the New Russia.* New York, 1933.
*Woman and Communism: Selections from the Writings of Marx, Engels, Lenin, and Stalin.* London, 1950.
Zetkin, Clara. *Lenin on the Woman Question.* New York, 1934.
Zhak, L. P., and A. M. Itkina, eds. *Zhenshchiny russkoi revoliutsii.* Moscow, 1968.
*Zhenshchiny goroda Lenina.* Leningrad, 1963.
*Zhenshchiny strany Sovetov,* Moscow, 1937.
*Zhenshchiny v SSSR,* Moscow, 1937.

## V. Secondary Sources in English

Agulhon, Maurice. *Marianne into Battle: Republican Imagery and Symbolism in France, 1789–1880.* Trans. Janet Lloyd. Cambridge, 1981.
Atkinson, Dorothy, Alexander Dallin, and Gail W. Lapidus, eds. *Women in Russia.* Stanford, Conn., 1977.
Attwood, Lynne. *Creating the New Soviet Woman: Women's Magazines as Engineers of Female Identity, 1922–1953.* New York, 1999.
Bakhtin, M. M. *Rabelais and His World.* Trans. Helene Iswolsky. Cambridge, 1968.
Barthes, Roland. *Mythologies.* Trans. Annette Lavers. New York, 1972.
Bell, Catherine. *Ritual Theory, Ritual Practice.* Oxford, 1992.
Ben-David, Joseph, and Terry Clark, eds. *Culture and Its Creators: Essays in Honor of Edward Shils.* Chicago, 1977.

Binns, Christopher A. P. "The Changing Face of Power: Revolution and Accommodation in the Development of the Soviet Ceremonial System." Part 1: *Man* 14 (Dec. 1979), 585–606. Part 2, *Man* 15 (1980): 170–87.

Bobroff, Anne. "The Bolsheviks and Working Women, 1905–1920," *Soviet Studies* 26 (1974): 540–67.

Bonnell, Victoria E. *The Iconography of Power: Soviet Political Posters Under Lenin and Stalin.* Berkeley, 1997.

Boym, Svetlana. *Common Places: Mythologies of Everyday Life in Russia.* Cambridge, 1994.

Boxer, Marilyn J. and Jean H. Quartaert. *Socialist Women: European Socialist Feminism in the Nineteenth and Early Twentieth Centuries.* New York, 1978.

Brooks, Jeffrey. *Thank You Comrade Stalin!: Soviet Public Culture from Revolution to Cold War.* Princeton, 2000.

Buckley, Mary. *Perestroika and Soviet Women.* Cambridge, 1992.

———. "The Untold Story of Obshchestvennitsa in the 1930s." *Europe-Asia Studies* 48 (1996): 569–86.

———. *Women and Ideology in the Soviet Union.* Ann Arbor, 1989.

Cannadine, David. *Rituals of Royalty: Power and Ceremonial in Traditional Societies.* Cambridge, Mass., 1987.

Carter, Ellwood R. *Inessa Amand: Revolutionary Feminist.* Cambridge, 1992.

Clark, Katerina. *Petersburg: Crucible of Cultural Revolution.* Cambridge, Mass., 1995.

———. *The Soviet Novel: History as Ritual.* Chicago, 1985.

Clements, Barbara Evans. *Bolshevik Feminist: The Life of Aleksandra Kollontai.* Bloomington, 1979.

———. *Bolshevik Women.* Cambridge, 1997.

Clements, Barbara Evans, Barbara Alpern Engels, and Christine D. Worobec, eds. *Russia's Women: Accommodation, Resistance, Transformation.* Berkeley, 1991.

Costlow, Jane, Stephanie Sandles, and Judith Vowles, eds. *Sexuality and the Body in Russian Culture.* Stanford, 1993.

Davies, Sarah. *Popular Opinion in Stalin's Russia: Terror, Propaganda, and Dissent, 1934–1941.* Cambridge, 1997.

De Grazia, Victoria. *How Fascism Ruled Women: Italy, 1922–1945.* Berkeley, 1992.

Dodge, Norton, T. *Women in the Soviet Economy.* Baltimore, 1966.

Dunham, Vera S. *In Stalin's Time: Middle-Class Values in Soviet Fiction.* New York, 1976.

Durkheim, Emile. *The Elementary Forms of Religious Life.* London, 1976.

Edmondson, Linda. *Feminism in Russia, 1900–1917.* Stanford, Calif., 1984.

Edmondson, Linda, ed. *Women and Society in Russia and the Soviet Union.* Cambridge, 1992.

Eliade, Mircea. *Cosmos and History: The Myth of the Eternal Return.* Trans. Willard R. Trask. New York, 1959.

Engel, Barbara Alpern. *Mothers and Daughters: Women of the Intelligentsia in Nineteenth-Century Russia.* Cambridge, 1983.

Engelstein, Laura. *The Keys to Happiness: Sex and the Search for Happiness in Fin-de-Siecle Russia.* Ithaca, N.Y., 1992.

Eubanks, Carol H. *Feminism and Bolshevism: Zhenotdel and the Politics of Women's Emancipation in Russia, 1917–1930.* Ph.D. thesis, University of California, Berkeley, 1979.

Farnsworth, Beatrice. *Aleksandra Kollontai: Socialism, Feminism and the Bolshevik Revolution.* Stanford, Calif., 1980.
Farnsworth, Beatrice, and Lynne Viola, eds. *Russian Peasant Women.* New York, 1992.
Figes, Orlando, and Boris Kolonitskii. *Interpreting the Russian Revolution: The Language and Symbols of 1917.* New Haven, Conn., 1999.
Fitzpatrick, Sheila. *The Cultural Front: Power and Culture in Revolutionary Russia.* Ithaca, N.Y., 1992.
——. *Everyday Stalinism: Ordinary Lives in Extraordinary Times: Soviet Russia in the 1930s.* New York, 1999.
——. *Stalin's Peasants: Resistance and Survival in the Russian Village After Collectivization.* New York, 1994.
Fitzpatrick, Sheila, ed. *Cultural Revolution in Russia, 1928–1931.* Bloomington, Ind., 1978.
Fort, Bernadette, ed. *Fictions of the French Revolution,* Evanston, Ill., 1991.
Foucault, Michel. *The Archaeology of Knowledge.* Trans. A. M. Sheridan. New York, 1972.
Frierson, Cathy. *Peasant Icons: Representations of Rural People in Late Nineteenth Century Russia.* Oxford, 1993.
Fulop-Miller, René. *The Mind and Face of Bolshevism: An Examination of Cultural Life in the Soviet Union.* London, 1927.
Gasirowska, Xenia. *Women in Soviet Fiction, 1917–1964.* Madison, 1968.
Geertz, Clifford. *The Interpretation of Cultures: Selected Essays.* New York, 1973.
——. *Local Knowledge: Further Essays in Interpretive Anthropology.* New York, 1983.
——. *Negara: The Theater State in Nineteenth Century Bali.* Princeton, 1980.
Gleason, Abbott, Peter Kenez, and Richard Stites, eds. *Bolshevik Culture: Experiment and Order in the Russian Revolution.* Bloomington, Ind., 1985.
Glickman, Rose L. *Russian Factory Women: Workplace and Society, 1880–1914.* Berkeley, 1984.
Goldman, Wendy Z. *Women, the State and Revolution: Soviet Family Policy and Social Life, 1917–1936.* Cambridge, 1993.
Golub, Spencer. *The Recurrence of Fate: Theater and Memory in Twentieth-Century Russia.* Iowa City, 1994.
Groys, Boris. *The Total Art of Stalinism: Avant-Garde, Aesthetic Dictatorship, and Beyond.* Trans. Charles Rougle. Princeton, 1992.
Gunther, Hans, ed. *The Culture of the Stalin Period.* London, 1990.
Hayden, Carol Eubanks. "Feminism and Bolshevism: The Zhenotdel and the Politics of Women's Emancipation in Russia, 1917–1930." Ph.D. diss., University of California, Berkeley, 1979.
Heitlinger, Alena. *Women and State Socialism.* Montreal, 1979.
Heldt, Barbara. *Terrible Perfection: Women and Russian Literature.* Bloomington, Ind., 1987.
Hellbeck, Jochen. "Fashioning the Stalinist Soul: The Diary of Stepan Podlubnyi (1931–1939)." *Jahrbücher für Geschichte Osteuropas* 44 (1996): 344–73.
Hobsbawm, Eric, and Terence Ranger, eds. *The Invention of Tradition.* Cambridge, 1982.
Hoffman, David L. *Peasant Metropolis: Social Identities in Moscow, 1929–1941.* Ithaca, N.Y., 1994.

Hoffman, David L., and Yanni Kotsonis, eds. *Russian Modernity: Politics, Knowledge, Practices.* New York, 2000.
Holmgren, Beth. *Women's Works in Stalin's Time.* Bloomington, Ind., 1993.
Hubbs, Joanna. *The Feminine Myth in Russian Culture.* Bloomington, Ind., 1988.
Huizinga, Johann. *Homo Ludens: A Study of the Play-Element in Culture.* Trans. R. F. C. Hull. Boston, 1949.
Hunt, Lynn. *The Family Romance of the French Revolution.* Berkeley, 1992.
———. *Politics, Culture and Class in the French Revolution.* Berkeley, 1984.
Ilic, Melanie. *Women Workers in the Soviet Interwar Economy: From "Protection" to "Equality."* New York, 1999.
Kenez, Peter. *The Birth of the Propaganda State: Soviet Methods of Mass Mobilization, 1917-1929.* Cambridge, 1985.
Kent, Geiger, H. *The Family in Soviet Russia.* Cambridge, Mass., 1968.
Koenker, Diane P. "Men Against Women on the Shop Floor in Early Soviet Russia: Gender and Class in the Socialist Workplace." *American Historical Review* 100 (Dec. 1995): 1438-64.
Kotkin, Stephen. *Magnetic Mountain: Stalinism as a Civilization.* Berkeley, 1995.
Lahusen, Thomas. *How Life Writes the Book: Real Socialism and Socialist Realism in Stalin's Russia.* Ithaca, N.Y., 1997.
Lane, Christel. *The Rites of Rulers: Ritual in Industrial Society—The Soviet Case.* Cambridge, 1981.
Lapidus, Gail. *Women in Soviet Society: Equality, Development and Social Change.* Berkeley, 1978.
Lewin, Moshe. *The Making of the Soviet System: Essays on the Social History of Interwar Russia.* New York, 1985.
MacAloon, John J., ed. *Rite, Drama, Festival, Spectacle: Rehearsals Towards a Theory of Cultural Performances.* Philadelphia, 1984.
Madison, Bernice. *Social Welfare in the Soviet Union.* Stanford, Calif., 1968.
Mally, Lynn. *Revolutionary Acts: Amateur Theater and the Soviet Stage, 1917-1938.* Ithaca, N.Y., 2000.
Marsh, Rosalind, ed. *Women in Russia and the Ukraine.* New York, 1996.
Massell, Gregory. *The Surrogate Proletariat: Moslem Women and Revolutionary Strategies in Soviet Central Asia.* Princeton, 1974.
McDermid, Jane, and Anna Hillyar. *Midwives of the Revolution: Female Bolsheviks and Women Workers in 1917.* Athens, Ohio, 1999.
McNeal, Robert. *Bride of Revolution: Krupskaya and Lenin.* Ann Arbor, 1972.
Melzer, Sara E., and Leslie W. Rabine. *Rebel Daughters: Women and the French Revolution.* New York, Oxford, 1992.
Merquior, J. G. *The Veil and the Mask.* London, 1979.
Meyer, Alfred G. *The Feminism and Socialism of Lily Braun.* Bloomington, Ind., 1985.
Naiman, Eric. *Sex in Public: The Incarnation of Early Soviet Ideology.* Princeton, 1997.
Nakhimovsky, Alexander D., and Alice Stone Nakhimovsky. *The Semiotics of Russian Cultural History.* Ithaca, N.Y., 1985.
Ozouf, Mona. *Festivals and the French Revolution.* Trans. Alan Sheridan. Cambridge, Mass., 1988.
Petrone, Karen. *Life Has Become More Joyous Comrades: Celebrations in the Time of Stalin.* Bloomington, Ind., 2000.

Poovey, Mary. *Uneven Developments: The Ideological Work of Gender in Mid-Victorian England.* Chicago, 1988.

Ransel, David, ed. *The Family in Imperial Russia: New Lines of Historical Research.* Urbana-Champaign, Ill., 1978.

Reid, Susan. "All Stalin's Women: Gender and Power in Soviet Art of the 1930s," *Slavic Review* 57 (1998): 133–73.

Robin, Regine. *Socialist Realism: An Impossible Aesthetic.* Stanford, 1992.

Rolf, Malte. "Constructing a Soviet Time: Bolshevik Festivals and Their Rivals During the First Five-Year Plan: A Study of the Central Black Earth Region." *Kritika* 1 (2000): 447–73.

Sahlins, Marshall. *Islands of History.* Chicago, 1985.

Schwarz, Solomon M. *Labor in the Soviet Union.* New York, 1952.

Scott, Joan Wallach. *Gender and the Politics of History.* New York, 1988.

Slaughter, Jane, and Robert Kern, eds. *European Women on the Left: Socialism, Feminism and the Problems Faced by Political Women, 1880 to the Present.* Westport, Conn., 1981.

Stites, Richard. *Revolutionary Dreams: Utopian Vision and Experimental Life in the Russian Revolution.* New York, 1989.

———. *The Women's Liberation Movement in Russia: Feminism, Nihilism, and Bolshevism, 1860–1930.* Princeton, 1990.

Thompson, Terry L., and Richard Sheldon, eds. *Soviet History and Culture: Essays in Honor of Vera S. Dunham.* Boulder, 1988.

Timasheff, Nicholas S. *The Great Retreat: The Growth and Decline of Communism in Russia.* New York, 1946.

Tolstoy, Vladimir, Irina Bibikova, and Catherine Cooke, eds. *Street Art of the Revolution: Festivals and Celebrations in Russia 1918–1933.* London, 1990.

Tumarkin, Nina. *Lenin Lives! The Lenin Cult in Soviet Russia.* Cambridge, Mass., 1983.

Turner, Victor. *The Anthropology of Performance.* New York, 1986.

———. *The Ritual Process.* Chicago, 1969.

Turner, Victor, ed. *Celebration: Studies in Festivity and Ritual.* Washington, D.C., 1982.

Viola, Lynne. *Peasant Rebels Under Stalin: Collectivization and the Culture of Peasant Resistance.* New York, 1996.

Vogel, Lise. *Marxism and the Oppression of Women: Toward a Unitary Theory.* New Brunswick, N.J., 1983.

Von Geldern, James. *Bolshevik Festivals, 1917–1920.* Berkeley, 1993.

Wagner, Roy. *The Invention of Culture.* Chicago, 1981.

Walkowitz, Judith R. *City of Dreadful Delight: Narratives of Sexual Danger in Late-Victorian London.* London, 1992.

Weber, Max. *Max Weber on Charisma and Institution Building.* Ed. S. N. Eisenstadt. Chicago, 1968.

White, Hayden. *The Content of the Form: Narrative Discourse and Historical Representation.* Baltimore, 1987.

———. *Metahistory: The Historical Imagination in Nineteenth Century Europe.* Baltimore, 1978.

Wilentz, Sean, ed. *Rites of Power: Symbolism, Ritual, and Politics Since the Middle Ages.* Philadelphia, 1985.

Wortman, Richard S. *Scenarios of Power: Myth and Ceremony in Russian Monarchy.*
Vol. 1. Princeton, 1995.

## VI. Secondary Sources in Russian

Aizenshtadt, V., ed. *Rezhissura i organizatsii massovykh zrelishch.* Kharkov, 1973.
Artiukhina, A. V., ed. *Vsegda s vami: Sbornik, posviashchennyi piatidesiatiletiiu zhurnal "Rabotnitsa."* Moscow, 1964.
Avrekh, Aron I. *Tsarizm nakanune sverzheniia.* Moscow, 1989.
*Bestuzhevki v riadakh stroitelie sotsializma.* Moscow, 1958.
Bil'shai, V. *Reshenie zhenskogo voprosa v SSSR.* Moscow, 1959.
Bochkareva, E., and S. Liubimova, eds. *Svetlyi put'.* Moscow, 1967.
Brudnyi, V. I. *Obriady vchera i segodnia.* Moscow, 1968.
Chirkov, P. M. *Reshenie zhenskogo voprosa v SSSR (1917–1937gg).* Moscow, 1978.
Emel'ianova, E. D. *Revoliutsiia, partiia, zhenshchina.* Smolensk, 1971.
*Fevral'skaia burzhuazno-demokraticheskaia revoliutsiia 1917g v Rossi: Sovetskaia istoriografiia 70-80-x godov: Nauchno-analiticheskii obzor.* Moscow, 1987.
Genkin, D. M. *Massovye prazdniki.* Moscow, 1975.
Igumnova, Zoia. *Zhenshchiny Moskva v gody grazhdanskoi voiny.* Moscow, 1958.
Ionov, A. *Bor'ba bol'shevistskoi Partii za soldatskie massy Petrogradskogo Garizona.* Moscow, 1954.
Isaev, V. I. *Byt' rabochikh Sibiri, 1926–1937gg.* Novosibirsk, 1988.
*Istoriia sovetskogo teatra.* Leningrad, 1933.
Karpetskaia, N. D. *Rabotnitsy i velikii Oktiabr'.* Leningrad, 1974.
Leiberov, I. P. *Na shturm samoderzhaviia.* Moscow, 1979.
Leiberov, I. P., and S. D. Rudachenko. *Revoliutsiia i khleb.* Moscow, 1990.
Liubimova, S. T. *Okt'iabrskaia revoliutsiia i polozhenie zhenshchin v SSSR.* Moscow, 1967.
*Massovye prazdniki i zrelishcha.* Moscow, 1961.
Mazaev, A. I. *Prazdnik kak sotsial'no-khudozhestvennoe iavlenie: Opyt istoriko-teoreticheskogo issledovannia.* Moscow, 1978.
Nemiro, Oleg. *V gorod prishël prazdnik. Iz istorii khudozhestvennogo oformleniia sovetskikh massovykh prazdnestv.* Leningrad, 1973.
Novikova, E. E., T. N. Sidorova, and S. Ia. Turchaninova, eds. *Sovetskie zhenshchiny i profsouizy.* Moscow, 1984.
*Oktiabriem mobilizovannye: Zhenshchiny-kommunistki v bor'be za pobedu sotsialisticheskoi revoliutsii.* Moscow, 1987.
*Opyt KPSS v reshenii zhenskogo voprosa.* Moscow, 1981.
Piotorovskii, A. I. *Za sovetskii teatr.* Leningrad, 1925.
Podliashuk, Pavel. *Tovarisch Inessa.* Moscow, 1973.
*Rabochii klass–vedushchaia sila v stroitel'stve sotsialisticheskogo obshchestva 1921–1937gg.* Moscow, 1984.
*Revoliutsionerki Rossii,* Moscow, 1983.
*Sankt-Petersburgskie Vysshie Zhenskie (Bestuzhevskie) Kursy.* Leningrad, 1973.
Serditova, S. *Bol'sheviki v bor'be za zhenskie proletarskie massy 1903g–1917 fevral'.* Moscow, 1959.
Speranskaia, E., ed. *Agitatsionno-massovoe iskusstvo pervykh let oktiabria.* Moscow, 1971.

Stishova, L. I., ed. *V budniakh velikikh stroek: Zhenshchiny kommunistki, geroini-pervykh piatiletok*. Moscow, 1986.
Suliaeva, Nadezhda. *Revoliutsionnyi prazdnichnyi plakat*. Leningrad, 1982.
*Sverzhenie samoderzhaviia*. Moscow, 1970.
Tolstoi, V. P., ed. *Agitatsionno-massovoe iskusstvo: Oformlenie prazdnestv, 1917–1932*. Moscow, 1984.
Tarasov, E. *Pod znamenem bol'shevikov: Zhenshchiny i revoliutsii*. Moscow, 1959.
Zaorskaia, Irina I. *Ot-podpol'ia do pobedy Oktiabria: Ocherki istorii stroitel'stva RSDRP(b), fevral'-oktiabr, 1917 goda*. Moscow, 1987.
Zuikova, E. M. *Byt pri sotsializme*. Moscow, 1977.

# Index

abortion, 153–55, 159–60, 201n80
activism and activists, 87–88, 89, 95, 113, 114, 146, 153
Agadzhanova, N. F., 49–50, 174n24
Agitprop, 8, 65
*agitsudy* (dramatized mock trials), 84, 117
Alekseeva, N., 119
Alekseeva, Shura, 21, 24–26
alimony, 153, 155
America, 80, 129, 149
Angelina, Pasha, 140
Armand, Inessa, 18, 30, 42
arrests, 34, 35, 51; of revolutionaries, 26, 31–32, 52, 54, 176n62
artels, 101, 106
Artiukhina, Aleksandra, 109, 115–16, 143
*Autobiography of a Sexually Emancipated Communist Woman* (Kollontai), 14
autocracy, movement against, 29, 38, 41, 44

*baba* (old woman), 93, 101, 157, 158
"Babii den'" (short story), 67
*Babii' vyigrysh* (Goriachhi), 95–98
*Baby ne raby* (Ilinskii), 93
backwardness of women, 15, 39, 41, 73, 74, 145, 193n2; cultural, 112, 131; as motif, 14, 17, 29, 35, 146; in plays, 94; political, 20, 112; Russian, 5, 135, 144, 158
Balabanova, Angelica, 66, 179n18
Bebel, August, 12, 112
Benderskii family, 120
*Blokha* (play), 95, 100–102
Bolshevik ideology, 2, 5–6, 11, 16, 85–86, 91, 98
Bolshevik propaganda, 7, 17, 35–36, 45; for women, 16, 61, 68, 71, 74, 88, 102
Bolshevik revolution, 10–11, 17, 23, 49–50
Bolsheviks, 3, 8, 18, 121–23, 150; and February Revolution, 38–43, 44–45, 47, 49–50, 52, 54, 56–58; and International Women's Day, 20–23, 25, 27–32, 35–36, 60–61, 65, 83–84; and "woman question," 10–17, 22, 28, 86; and women, 12, 38, 41, 81–83, 121, 169n42
Bolshevik women, 15–16, 50, 52, 75, 77–78, 163n3, 174n23; and International Women's Day, 36, 40, 72, 178n7; and struggles in Party, 23, 61. *See also* Armand, Inessa; Krupskaia, Nadezhda; Samoilova, Konkordiia; Zetkin, Clara
Bolshevik women's movement, 17, 18, 36
bourgeois groups, 22, 36, 61. *See also* feminists, bourgeoisie
bourgeois ideas, 5, 16, 80, 118–19, 150, 151, 156
bourgeoisie, 12, 51, 81, 90, 123; in literature, 13, 139
bread riots, 38, 44, 47–48, 57
Brecht, Bertold, 86
Britain, 80–81
brochures, 71, 75, 84, 204–5
Brooks, Jeffrey, 80
Buck, Pearl, 155
Bukharin, N., 88
Burdzhalov, E. N., 57–58

capitalism, 15, 27, 94, 124; movement against, 29, 41, 42; oppression by, 2, 11–12, 36, 45, 82, 195n26
carnivals, 141–42
cartoons, 67, 107–8, 110–11
*Cement* (Gladkov), 139
Central Asia, 68–69, 125
Central Committee, 106, 114, 116, 130, 154, 157; and International Women's Day, 20, 63, 117
Cheremnykh, Mikhail, 93

215

child care, 106, 113, 119, 147, 150, 152, 156; deficiencies in facilities for, 160, 179n16, 190n38; facilities for, 66, 88, 113–14, 116, 128, 129–30, 152–54
child support, 92–93, 155
Chugurin, I. D., 40
civil society, 136, 137–38
civil war, 5, 8, 61, 76, 85, 145–46
class bias, 34, 196n36
class conflict, 51, 121–22
class consciousness, 15, 36, 44–45, 61
class enemies, 145–46
class ties, 53–55
collective consciousness, 18, 27, 29
collectivization, 5, 9, 102, 105, 139, 144–46, 157. See also kolkhozes
communal institutions, 88, 101, 106, 113–14, 117, 118. See also child care, facilities for; kolkhozes
communalization, 120, 121
communes, 64, 106
communism, 12, 13, 62–63, 82
*Communist Manifesto* (Marx), 161
communist movement, international, 78–79
Communist Party, 78, 79; and motherhood, 150, 154, 156; and women, 3, 72, 76, 102–3, 114–16, 142, 148–49. See also Central Committee; Zhenotdel
conscious citizens, 13, 68, 73, 78, 95, 103–4, 159
cooperatives, 64, 96–97, 114, 122, 129, 186n38. See also kolkhozes
Cossacks, 53–55, 58, 100
cost of living, 42–43
counter-revolutionary behavior, 157, 186n35, 197n39
cultural revolution, 8, 112, 117, 121

daily life, 8, 113–21; and family relationships, 120–21; and lack of cleanliness, 113, 114, 119–20, 160. See also kul'turno-bytovoi pokhod; living conditions
Demchenko, Maria, 140
demonstrations, 19, 34, 40, 51, 56; state-sponsored, 59, 65, 83, 117. See also marches
*Den' rabotnitsy* (skit), 91
deportations, 149, 198n57
discourse, 8, 9, 103, 135, 161
divorce, 80–81, 153, 196n30, 198n52
domesticity, 112, 156
domestic work, 12, 75–76, 106, 139, 153; Bolshevik views of, 86, 87–88; facilities for, 113–39; liberation from, 2, 62, 72, 95, 109, 115, 123–24; in plays, 96–97. See also child care
Doroshenko, Iosif, 145
Doroshenko, Matrena, 145–46
Drabkina (revolutionary), 31
Duma, 28, 32, 50, 56
Durniasheva, Agafiia, 148–49

East, the, 81–82
economic crisis, 61–62, 72, 83, 124
economic reconstruction, 62–63, 111
education, 112, 113, 133, 160; for women, 28, 35, 114, 119–20, 123–25, 139, 148–49. See also literacy
Efimovna, Praskov'ia, 147
Eisenstein, Sergei, 144
Elizarova, Anna I., 29–30, 32–33, 39, 42, 171n72
employment, 103, 121, 123, 126, 128, 160. See also unemployment
Engels, Friedrich, 11, 13
*Eulogy to the Revolution* (play), 93
Europe, 19, 78–81, 129, 138, 149–50, 151
exile, 35, 42, 74
exploitation, 30, 36, 45, 76

factory women, 26, 30, 81, 111, 147, 150; and February Revolution, 40, 43–49; and International Women's Day, 3, 33–34, 63–64, 66; in plays, 103–4; and social services, 128, 160. See also textile workers
family, 84, 88, 95, 97–98, 102, 104, 143; and kul'turno-bytovoi pokhod, 112, 118–19; nuclear, 12, 21, 93, 144, 147, 152–53, 155–56. See also husband-wife relationships
famine, 61, 63, 66. See also food shortages
fascism, 151, 182–83n65
fathers, 144, 147, 155–56
February Revolution (1917), 5, 7–8, 36, 59; and Bolsheviks, 7, 38–43, 44–45, 47, 49–50, 52, 54, 56–58; and food riots, 43–48, 51, 56; gendered representation of, 56–58; and International Women's Day, 38–43, 45–47, 52–53, 57–58; and marches, 46–50; and soldiers, 37–38, 45, 52–56, 175n43; and strikes, 39, 41, 43, 47–50, 52; and symbols, 50–53; and transport disruption, 49–50, 58, 62

216  Index

femininity, 14, 15, 56, 59, 72, 108. *See also* gender
feminism, 18, 86, 103, 160, 178nn4, 6; socialist, 18, 36. *See also* women's movements
feminists, 21, 28, 103–4, 170n58; bourgeois, 22–23, 27, 28, 34–35, 41, 61
*Fenia Travina* (Yarovoi), 95, 98–100
films, 66, 73, 74, 144, 153, 186n16
Five-Year Plan, 8–9, 113, 115, 121–25, 157, 192n79; first, 5, 75, 102–3, 105–7, 131, 139, 145; goals of, 112, 117, 123, 128, 197n41; second, 130
food riots, 43–48, 51, 56
food shortages, 7, 42, 50, 58, 124, 130, 174–75n27
*Forty First, The* (Lavreynov), 86
France, 79, 81, 151
French Revolution, 3, 10–11

Gasikhanova (woman), 68–69
gender, 2, 8–9, 11; and revolutions, 38, 56–58; Soviet construction of, 6, 84, 107
gender equality, rhetoric of, 6, 135, 138
gender hierarchy, 10–11, 26
gender relations, 70, 109, 135, 140, 149
gender roles, 98, 149
general strikes, 40, 47–50, 57
Genkina, E. V., 57
Germany, 79, 151
Gladkov (novelist), 139
Glavpolitprosvet (Chief Committee for Political Enlightenment), 84, 184n2
Glebov, Anatole, 103
Glickman, Rose, 111
Golubeva, Maria, 50
Goriachhi, A., 95–98
Gosplan, 122, 130
Gray, John, 136

Habermas, Jurgen, 137–38, 193n7
heroines: in plays, 85, 87, 88–89, 94, 95–102
heroines, Soviet, 4, 9, 14, 72, 103, 134–35, 139–49; life histories of, 140–41, 143, 145; in private sphere, 149–55; in public sphere, 143–49, 160; and Stalin, 155–58
*History of the Revolution* (Trotsky), 37
holiday discourse, 5–6
holiday rituals, Soviet, 1, 70–71. *See also* International Women's Day, rituals for; May Day; October Revolution, anniversary of

Honeycut, Karen, 16
housewives, 50, 87, 111, 123, 145, 176n61
husband-wife relationships, 67–69, 80–81, 127, 145–48, 154–56, 187n41, 201nn82, 86; in plays, 89–93, 95–100, 102

identity, 11; female, 9, 52–53, 88, 146; of heroines, 134, 144; public, 2, 7, 138; Soviet, 80, 138
Il'inichna, Maria, 152
Ilinskii, F., 93
illiteracy, 105, 113, 123, 156, 189n25
illustrations, 93, 107–8, 110–11
individualism, 2, 61, 87, 95, 99
industrialization, 9, 105, 112, 123, 124, 131, 189n18
*Inga* (Glebov), 103–4
Inotdel (Information Department of the Central Committee of the Party), 67–68
*Intsenirovka Prosnis' krest'ianka* (skit), 91
International Women's Day, 1–9, 18, 73, 133, 142, 153, 173n15; celebrations of, 35, 70, 74, 83, 97, 117, 125; deficiencies of, 107–8, 110–11, 114, 116; and February Revolution, 38–43, 45–47, 52–53, 57–58; and food riots, 45–48; and internationalism, 78–82, 143; and Kollontai, 24, 29, 62; meetings for, 33, 34, 43, 65–66, 69, 83, 142; and men, 65, 67, 70, 174n22; opposition to, 8, 60–61, 63, 65, 68; plays for (*See* propaganda plays); and police, 25–28, 31, 34, 36; and *Pravda*, 21, 23, 24, 28, 34, 117; rallies for, 68, 117, 125, 132, 141; and recruitment of women to industry, 106–7; and revolution, chronology of, 39–43; rituals for, 84, 87, 107, 129, 132, 157; and St. Petersburg, 20–22, 25, 28–29, 31–35; and Samoilova, 21, 23, 25–26, 29; slogans for, 112, 124; and Social Democrats, 25, 28, 35; speeches for, 24–27, 65–66, 111, 125, 141, 149, 150; stories for, 146–47; and strikes, 39, 43, 47–50, 52, 53; support for, 8, 17, 36, 65; and trade unions, 21, 33, 66, 117, 118, 132, 141; and women's liberation, 17, 73, 108–9, 111–12; and women workers, 23, 25, 29, 36, 39–43, 45–50, 52–53; and Zhenotdel, 62–68, 71–72, 78, 83–84, 106, 112–13, 116
International Women's Day propaganda, 8, 71–73, 75, 84, 87, 124; and state goals, 131–32; and the West, 79–80; and women's rights, 67–68, 109, 126

International Women's Secretariat, 81, 182*n59*
Isaakovna, Maria, 143
Islam and Muslims, 68–69
*Izvestiia* (newspaper), 117, 123

journals, 4, 71, 115, 141. *See also Kommunistka*; *Rabotnitsa*

Kaiurov, V. N., 40
Kalinin, Mikhail, 145, 159
Karpovna, Agafiia, 152–53
Kartacheva (worker), 24
Kasakova, Halima Apa, 146
Kataev, Valentin, 90
Kempe (worker), 160
Kerensky, Alexander, 56
Keyssar, Helen, 87
Kheifits, I., 144
Khitrikova (worker), 145
Kiev (city), 28, 35
kindergartens, 128, 130, 160
kinship ties, 53–55
*kolkhoz* chairwomen, *12*, 144–46, 147, 149, 155–56, 157, 194*nn11*
*kolkhozes* (collective farms), 124, 144–46, 147, 149, 155–56, 198*n57*, 201*n82*
Kollontai, Aleksandra, 12–16, 18–19, 42, 71, 76, 78, 166*n16*; and International Women's Day, 24, 29, 62; and women's liberation, 87–88, 165*n4*
*Kommunistka* (journal), 62, 71–72, 76, 113, 115, 117, 119
Komsomol (Communist Youth League), 67–68, 70, 76, 90, 106, 156, 159
*Komsomol'skaia pravda* (periodical), 106, 109, 111
Kondratiev, Taras, 50
Kosareva, P., 77–78
Kovnator, Rakhil, 76, 176*n49*
Kozlova, Marusia, 111
*Krest'ianka* (magazine), 64, 81, 115, 145, 150, 157
Krokhotkina, Masha, 147
Kruglova, A. I., 52–53, 176*n52*
Krupskaia, Nadezheda, 14, 30, 42, 74, 143
Kudelli, Praskov'ia F., 22, 35, 167*n28*; and International Women's Day, 21–22, 27, 29; and *Rabotnitsa*, 31–32
*kulaks* (rich peasants), 100, 101, 116, 145–46, 198*n57*
*kul'turno-bytovoi pokhod* (campaign for the cultural reconstruction of daily life), 8, 106, 112–17, 119–20, 125, 128, 189*n18*
*kul'turnost'* (cultural level), 112, 141, 157
Kuskova, Ekaterina, 28

labor: shortage of, 123, 127, 139. *See also* domestic work
labor movement, 18, 61, 78, 82. *See also* trade unions
language, 6, 7
Larin, Iu., 106
Lavreynov, Boris, 86
law, 14, 80–81, 93, 101. *See also* women's rights, legal
League of Equal Righters, 34–35
Lebedeva, Sara, 93
Lebedeva, Vera, 76, 115
Lemeshova (woman), 120–21
Lenin, V. I., 14, 16, 30, 44, 112; cult of, 8, 74–75, 77; and "woman question," 73–78, 87–88, 165*n6*
Leningrad, 65, 117, 118, 125, 154
Leninist theory, 39, 57
*Leninka* (play), 93–94
liberals and liberalism, 28, 33, 160
Lieberov, I. P., 57–58
literacy, 118, 131, 192*n81*
literature, 4, 11, 33, 37, 100, 139, 161; novels, 13–14, 54–55, 139; short stories, 15, 67, 86, 155
*Liubov Yarovaya* (Trenev), 85
living conditions, 106, 115, 117–20, 121, 124
Longley, David, 40–41
Lunacharsky, Anatoly, 59

magazines, 64, 81, 115, 145, 150, 157
marches, 46–50
Margulies-Aitova, Margarita Nikolaevna, 27
Marsheva, B., 123, 127
Marx, Karl, 161
Marxism, 4, 11–13, 18, 22, 166*n18*
Marxist theory, 6, 7, 17, 112, 131, 143
*Mar'yana* (Serafimovich), 85
*Marya the Bolshevik* (Neverov), 100
masculinity, 97. *See also* gender
maternalism, 149–50, 152. *See also* motherhood
maternity leave, 28, 29. *See also* pregnancy
May Day, 3, 59, 61, 63, 64
*Member of the Government* (film), 144

men, 34, 65, 67, 147, 154–56, 198n57; symbolic erasure of, 4, 13, 14. *See also* husband-wife relationships
Mensheviks, 18, 29, 41
Menzhinskaia, L., 31–32
Menzhinskaia, V. P., 33
Meyer, Alfred, 13
Mezhraiontsy, 41–42, 45
Mikhailovna, Barbara, 148
Mikoian, Anastas, 63
Mints, I. I., 57
misogyny, 2, 5–6, 23, 91, 116, 127, 148; efforts to erode, 91, 109, 138. *See also* gender hierarchy; sexism; violence against women
modernity, 16, 133–34, 135–39, 151–53, 155, 157–58, 160–61
modernization, 131, 135–37
morality, 27, 112, 118, 121, 135; in plays, 87, 88, 93, 99, 101, 103
Moscow, 113, 117, 118, 128, 141, 147, 154; and International Women's Day, 28, 34, 65, 125, 142, 144, 148
motherhood, 12, 16, 139, 149–54, 156. *See also* maternalism; pregnancy
mothers, 24, 62, 71, 81
mothers-in-law, 84, 94
Mstislavsky (socialist), 57

Narkompros (Commissariat of Enlightenment), 63, 66, 113, 122, 154
Narkomtrud (Commissariat of Labor), 114, 122, 123, 127, 129
Narkomzdrav (Commissariat for Public Health), 113, 122, 130, 154
Narkomzem (Commissariat of Land Affairs), 122, 154
Narpit (company responsible for dining facilities), 66, 113, 118
narrative and women, 1, 4, 18, 135, 161
"Natasha's Dreams" (short story), 15
NEP (New Economic Policy) era, 13, 86, 90, 102, 105; early years of, 8, 66; and women's needs, 83, 88, 112, 115, 124
Neverov, Alexander, 100
New Soviet Man, 92, 98, 105
New Soviet Woman, 1, 5, 8, 73, 105, 138–39, 159; characteristics of, 11, 60, 82, 103, 133, 157–58, 195n28; discourses about, 161; in plays, 88, 98, 100, 102, 104
newspapers, 4, 29, 67, 84, 91, 117, 123. *See also Pravda*; press

Nikiferova (worker), 21
novels, 13–14, 54–55, 139

*obshchestvennitsy* (Wives of Industrialists and Engineering-Technical Personnel), 152–53
October Revolution, 38–39, 57, 81–82, 120, 145, 153; achievements of, 5, 90; anniversary of, 3, 59, 61, 63, 64; goals of, 73, 127, 129, 160
Okhrana (police agency), 25, 28, 29
Ollennikova (worker), 148
OMM (Section for Maternity Protection), 63, 76, 113, 115, 150, 153, 182n53
Ordzhonikidze, Sergo, 144, 152
*Origin of the Family, Private Property and the State* (Engels), 11, 13
Osipenko, Polina, 140

Panova (worker), 33
parent-child relationships, 120–21. *See also* fathers; motherhood
paternalism, 71, 154
patriarchal state, 13, 27
patriarchy, 2, 6, 9, 11, 69, 85, 129; socialist, 14, 68
Pavlova, Maria, 51
peasant rebellions, 54, 62
peasants, 60, 111, 121, 145, 150, 159–60, 186n39; and International Women's Day, 24, 64, 67, 87; plays about, 95–102; upward mobility of, 144, 156–57
periodicals, 25, 123, 126, 154. *See also Komsomol'skaia pravda*; *Zhenskii vestnik*
Petrograd, 42, 52; and February Revolution, 36, 41, 43–46, 48–53, 58; and strikes, 39, 43, 47–50
Platonova, Masha, 28
plays, 85. *See also* propaganda plays
Pokrovskaia, Maria, 22–23, 168n37, 170n58
Pokrovskii, M. N., 57
police, 32–33, 45–46; and February Revolution, 49, 51, 53, 55–56; and food riots, 44, 48; and International Women's Day, 25–28, 31, 34, 36; repression by, 34, 35–36, 42, 56
popular culture, 84, 102
popular participation, 88, 114, 115
poverty, 83, 87. *See also* economic crisis; wages
*Pravda* (newspaper): and February Revolution,

**Index** 219

(*Pravda* [newspaper] *continued*)
　39–40; and International Women's Day,
　21, 23, 24, 28, 34, 117
pregnancy, 81, 92–93, 120, 152, 153–54, 159
press, 80, 117, 121, 123, 144, 152, 161; and International Women's Day, 33–34, 72. See also newspapers; *Pravda*
*Priatali kontsy, popali v otsy* (play), 92–93
prisoners, women, 42, 51–52, 73, 176*n*52
private lives of workers, 119–21
private sphere, 11, 71, 109, 112; politicization of, 87, 102, 104; reconstruction of, 122, 124; Soviet heroines in, 149–55
productivity, 112, 117, 132. See also shock work; *stakhanovism* and *stakhanovites*
Prokof'eva (worker), 160
proletarian women, 17–19, 64. See also women workers
proletariat, 22, 27, 36, 45, 81, 121
Proletkult, 84, 184*n*3
propaganda, 53, 79; Soviet, 81, 95, 129, 131, 138, 151, 160
propaganda for women, 1, 4–5, 7, 8, 9, 161; Bolshevik, 16–17, 74, 88, 102; Soviet, 17, 73, 79, 83, 94–95, 115, 123; Stalinist, 103, 145, 155, 196*n*36. See also International Women's Day propaganda
propaganda plays, 8, 75, 82, 84, 87, 88–104, 115; characters in, 88–95; and three phases of women's liberation, 95–102
prostitution, 26, 73, 89, 120, 190*n*45
protests, 7, 154
Protopopov, Aleksandr, 56
public identity of Soviet women, 2, 7, 9, 14. See also Soviet heroines
public/private dichotomy, 69, 86
public sphere, 6–7, 9, 11, 16, 97, 131, 138

*Rabotnitsa* (journal), 15, 29–30, 36, 61, 74, 80, 115; suppression of, 31–33, 42, 171*n*72
*rabotnitsa* (woman worker), 53, 60
raids on stores, 44–46
rape, 52, 111, 113
Raskova, Marina, 148
reading huts, 70, 83
Red Army, 38, 142
Red Corners, 117, 150
religion and clergy, 77, 91
*Rendezvous, A* (Shoshin), 155
repression: police, 34, 35–36, 42, 56; state, 28, 33, 141, 158

revolution, 160–61; Bolshevik, 10–11, 17, 23, 49–50; chronology of, 9, 38, 39–43, 69, 145; Stalinist, 139, 145, 153
Ries, Nancy, 6
Rittikh (Minister of Agriculture), 44
rituals, Soviet holiday, 1, 3–4, 71–72, 84
Rodionova (worker), 50
Romanov dynasty, anniversary celebrations of, 20, 25
Rozimirovich (revolutionary), 31–32, 42
rural areas. See *kolkhozes*; peasants
Russian culture, 70–71, 72, 126
Russian Social Democratic Labor Party (RSDRP), 18, 19, 21
Russian women, 3, 5, 14, 17, 27, 111
Rykov, Aleksei, 112

Sabsovich, L. M., 106
St. Petersburg: and International Women's Day, 20–22, 25, 28–29, 29, 31–35
Samara (city), 28, 35
Samoilova, Konkordiia, 18, 20–21, 35, 42, 167–68*n*30, 172*n*6, 178*n*4; and International Women's Day, 21, 23, 25–26, 29; and *Rabotnitsa*, 30–32, 171*n*72
*samokritika* (self-criticism), 97, 187*n*40
Scott, Masha, 155
Second International, 3, 19
Section for Maternity Protection (OMM), 63, 76, 113, 115, 150, 153, 182*n*53
Seifullina, Lydia, 85, 89
Serafimovich, Aleksandr, 85
Serebrennikov, G. N., 124
sexism, 187*nn*41, 48. See also gender hierarchy; misogyny; violence against women
sexual harassment, 26, 111, 113, 127, 148
sexuality, 118–19, 120–21; in plays, 88, 90, 99–104
Shalfeev, Colonel, 56
shaming, 91–92, 99
Shelavin, K., 57
Shliapnikov, Aleksandr, 40–41
shock work, 116, 125, 131, 132–33, 141
shock workers, 125, 132–33, 141, 142, 155, 192*n*83
short stories, 15, 67, 86, 126, 155
Shoshin, M., 155
Shtange, Galina Vladimirovna, 153
Siberia, 74, 117, 156
singing, 27, 32, 33, 34, 50, 55, 83
Sinitskaia (worker), 51

*Sinnaia bluza* (drama group), 84, 184*n*3
sisterhood, 146–47, 197*n*44
skits, 89–90, 91, 93
Smidovich, S., 76, 143
Smirnova, A. F., 144, 148, 149, 196*n*33, 198*n*52
Smith, Jessica, 70
*sniatie* (forcing workers to put down their tools), 47, 49, 58
Social Democrats, 2, 16, 18, 32; and International Women's Day, 25, 28, 35; and women, 2–3, 14, 17, 19–20, 79. *See also* Bolsheviks; Mensheviks
socialism, 2, 19, 74, 79, 106
socialist construction, 102, 105, 108, 117, 121
socialist feminism, 18, 36
socialist parties, 46, 57
socialist patriarchy, 14, 68
socialist realism, 107, 140
socialists, 28–29, 42, 51, 53–54
social roles, 52. *See also* class ties; gender
social services, 103, 105–6, 122, 123, 129–30, 152–54, 160; deficiencies in, 106, 114, 118, 128, 130–31, 139, 152; inspection of, 117–18, 125. *See also* child care, facilities for; domestic work, facilities for
soldiers, 37–38, 45, 52–56
Solin-Alekseeva, Emilia, 32, 171*n*73
Sorokin, Pitirim, 56–57
Soviet heroines, 4, 9, 14, 72, 103, 134–35, 139–49; life histories of, 140–41, 143, 145; in private sphere, 149–55; in public sphere, 143–49, 160; and Stalin, 155–58
Soviet holiday rituals, 1, 70–71. *See also* International Women's Day, rituals for; May Day; October Revolution, anniversary of
Soviet policies, 80, 106, 123, 129
Soviet propaganda, 81, 95, 129, 131, 138, 151, 160; for women, 17, 73, 79, 83, 94–95, 115, 123
Soviet women: achievements of, 5, 141, 142–43; public identity of, 2, 7. *See also* Soviet heroines
Sovnarkom (Council of People's Commissars), 112, 154, 178*n*3
*Squaring the Circle* (Kataev), 90
stakhanovism (team labor efficiency) and stakhanovites, 131, 140–43, 148, 194*n*11, 195–96*n*29, 202*n*92
Stal', Liudmilla, 78, 81
Stalin, Joseph, 40, 74, 85, 144; cult of, 14, 135, 138, 143; and International Women's Day, 116, 142, 165*n*5; and Soviet heroines, 155–58; statements by, 12, 141, 151, 155–56, 157
Stalinism, 7, 14, 107, 130, 139, 160; and "woman question," 139–40
Stalinist discourse, 9, 103, 135
Stalinist policies, 9, 57, 102, 105–6, 135
Stalinist revolution, 139, 145, 153
*Staroe i Novoe* (film), 144
Stasova, Elena, 52, 63, 144
state, 3, 132, 138, 140, 160–61; patriarchal, 13, 27
strike movement (1917), 39, 43, 47–50, 52, 53
strikes, 43; in factories, 36, 38; general, 40, 47–50, 57; women's participation in, 17, 20, 26, 39, 41
suffrage movement, 18–19, 27
Sukhanov, M. N., 42
Sverdlov (Party member), 76
symbols of revolution, 50–53, 81

textile workers, 26, 34–35, 110, 118; and February Revolution, 37, 43, 46–47, 55, 58, 175*n*35
theater, 8, 59–60, 84. *See also* plays, propaganda; skits
Thompson, Edith, 80–81
trade unions, 130, 141–42; and International Women's Day, 21, 33, 66, 117, 118, 132, 141; and women, 29, 72, 110, 116
transformation as motif, 4, 16–17, 31; in plays, 87, 91–92, 94, 100, 104
transport disruption, 49–50, 58, 62
Trenev (playwright), 85
Trotsky, Leon, 37, 54, 88
tsarist government, 5, 22, 36, 50, 53, 91; movement against, 27, 41, 51
tsarist society, 34, 111
*Tseremonia* (skit), 90
Tumarkin, Nina, 75
Tver province, 26, 117, 118

*udarnichestvo*. *See* shock work
*udarnitsy*. *See* shock workers
Ulianova, Anna, 25, 143, 144
Ulianova, M. I., 39
Ulianova, Taisa, 77
unemployment, 8, 72, 81, 105–6, 113, 121, 123

**Index** 221

unions. *See* trade unions
United States, 129. *See also* America
upward mobility, 140, 143, 144, 156–57, 159
Urals, the, 117, 118, 121, 125
utopian socialism, 2, 106
Uzbekistan, 68–69

values, social, 93–94, 126, 135, 140
Vasilieva, Marfa, 48–49
*Vasilisa Malygina* (Kollontai), 13–14
violence, 80–81, 86, 118–19
violence against women, 67–69, 117, 120, 146, 186n39; in plays, 90, 91, 93, 95, 98–99, 101, 102; in workplace, 113, 127
*Vireneya* (Seifullina), 85
voluntarism, 87, 88, 115–16, 152, 189nn26, 27
*Vos'moe marta* (play), 92
voting rights, 33, 58
VSNKH, 122, 123
VTsSPS (Central Council of Trade Unions), 63, 65, 117, 118, 122, 125, 126–28
*vydvizhenie* (promotion of women), 109–11, 190n31

wages, 26, 29, 44, 106, 131, 143, 155
wartime hardships, 42–43
welfare state, 13, 138, 160
Winter, Ella, 70
"woman question," 2, 8, 72, 79, 124, 138; and Bolsheviks, 10–17, 22, 28, 86; and Lenin, V. I., 73–78, 87–88, 165n6; and Stalinism, 139–40
women, 14–15, 16, 27; agency of, 87, 154; armed, 55–56; and Communist Party, 3, 72, 76, 102–3, 114–16, 142, 148–49; conscious, 13, 68, 73, 78, 95, 103–4, 159; empowerment of, 3–4; invisibility of, 37–38, 59–60; needs of, 76, 83, 109, 112–18, 158, 161; proletarian, 17–19, 64; public identity of, 2, 7, 9, 14; and recruitment to industry, 8, 105–7, 122–28, 129, 131, 139; representations of, 30, 35–36; Russian, 3, 5, 14, 17, 27, 111; single, 88, 100–102; and sisterhood, 146–47, 197n44; and Social Democrats, 2–3, 14, 17, 19–20, 79; speeches by, 24–27, 29, 66, 149; status of, 16, 83–84, 90, 91, 97–98; and strikes, 17, 20, 26, 39, 41; and trade unions, 29, 72, 110, 116. *See also* backwardness of women; Bolshevik women; education, for women; family; husband-wife relationships; New Soviet Woman; peasants; Soviet heroines
women, older, 87, 93–95, 100–102, 144, 150, 154, 158. *See also baba*; counter-revolutionary behavior
women, Social Democratic. *See* Kollantai, Aleksandra; Zetkin, Clara
women and February Revolution, 37–58, 172nn1, 6; and chronology, 39–43, 57–58; and food riots, 43–48; and soldiers, 53–55, 175n43; and strikes, 39, 41, 43, 47–50, 52
women prisoners, 42, 51–52, 73, 176n52
Women's Day. *See* International Women's Day
women's history, 2, 7, 15, 35, 37, 145
women's liberation, 69, 87–88, 124; and Bolsheviks, 81–84; from domestic work, 2, 62, 72, 95, 109, 115, 123–24; and International Women's Day, 17, 73, 108–9, 111–12; and Lenin, 74–76; in plays, 89, 92, 95, 97, 102; rhetoric of, 122, 138, 158
women's movements, 46, 78; Bolshevik, 17, 18, 36; Russian, 17, 181n43; socialist, 22, 75; suffrage, 18–19, 27
women's oppression, 2, 11–12, 17, 26, 30, 80–81, 169n42; in plays, 86, 91
women's rights, 29, 69, 73, 90, 158; legal, 14, 67, 71, 80, 129, 197n41; social, 122, 139–40
women's stories, 4, 72, 140, 146, 161. *See also* Soviet heroines, life histories of
women's subordination, 2, 12, 28, 73, 107; in plays, 95, 97
women workers, 114, 127–28, 194n10, 201n89; and Bolshevik Party, 121–23; and Communist Party, 79; discrimination against, 127, 148, 188nn10, 15, 198n48; exploitation of, 30, 45, 76; and International Women's Day (1913), 21, 23, 25, 36; and International Women's Day (1914), 29, 36; and International Women's Day (1917), 36, 39–43, 45–50, 52–53; and Lenin, 77–78; organization of, 19–20, 23–24, 43, 167n29; plight of, 79, 109; promotion of, 109–11, 118, 122, 132, 140, 188n11, 190n31. *See also* factory women; *kolkhozes*; Smirnova, A. F.; *stakhanovism* and *stakhanovites*; textile workers; *udarnitsy*; wages; women, and recruitment to industry
women workers and February Revolution,

222 **Index**

37–58, 176*n*60, 61, 177*n*67; and food riots, 43–48; and strikes, 39, 43, 47–50
workday, 26, 28, 33, 44, 155
workers' clubs, 27–28, 68, 70, 83, 170*n*54, 179–80*n*27
workers' private lives, 119–21
working class, 34, 45–46, 62. *See also* shock workers; women workers
working conditions, 26, 44, 127, 139
work stoppages, 46–49
World War I, 41, 43, 79

Yarovoi, P., 98

*Za industrilizatsiiu* (periodical), 123, 126
Zarkhi, A., 144
Zetkin, Clara, 14–16, 18–19, 75, 78
*Zhena v dvukh vidakh* (skit), 89–90
Zhenotdel (Women's Section of the Communist Party), 4, 8, 61, 109, 118, 153, 186*n*39; dissolution of, 102–3, 105, 116; and International Women's Day, 62–68, 71–72, 78, 80, 83–84, 106, 112–13; and *kul'turno-bytovoi pokhod*, 112, 114–17, 119–20; and Lenin, 75–76; in plays, 89, 96, 100
*Zhenskii vestnik* (periodical), 22, 28
*zhivoi gazety* (living newspapers), 84, 91
Zinoviev, Grigory, 61, 94